The Dissertation Process

The Dissertation Process

**Planning, implementation and effective write-up
of Master's level investigative projects**

Gordon M. Message

(G}

Independently published by Gordon Michael Message with Kindle Direct Publishing

The Dissertation Process:
Planning, implementation and effective write-up of Master's level investigative projects
by Gordon M. Message

© 2020 Gordon Michael Message

gmm01@teammessage.net

All rights reserved. No part of this publication may be reproduced or transmitted in any form or by any means without prior written permission from the publisher.

ISBN: 9798557383295

The examples and all the case studies except one in this book are fictional. They are based on the author's experiences and that of his colleagues, working with hundreds of students. They are provided to illustrate and clarify the points being made. Any resemblance to a specific individual or a particular situation is entirely coincidental.

Dedication

To my wife Jane

and

my children Simon, Emma and Robin.

When it came to doing my MBA and my own dissertation you made sure I kept at it.
Little did I know that this would later be the key that unlocked the door to my academic career.

Thank you for your love and support.

Contents

Preface

A few years ago I marked dissertations from a cohort of international Master's students. I was not enjoying the work. Nearly a third had failed to reach the required standard, their reports were terrible. I had one more to do and was not hopeful, but then my mood lifted. This one was so much better than the rest.

I wanted to give an A grade, but it was not possible as there were a few basic errors. Grade A is outstanding or impressive. It was so nearly there. I wondered if there had been some external help, but no, her supervisor confirmed that the student had been a thorough independent worker. What really stood out was not the amount of research or the complexity of it, but the fact that the student had laid out explicit objectives and had followed through with realistic activity. She developed clear and logical arguments around her chosen topic. The write-up was convincing. Why did they not all do this?

The supervisors for this disappointing cohort told me that all the students had worked hard and should have been able to produce good write-ups. I have second marked at least five hundred dissertations, working with many other supervisors / first markers. Although many advise on report presentation, few see this as a prime responsibility, indicating that the course guidelines give the students what they need. There seems to be an assumption that Master's students should know how to do research and then produce a satisfactory report. I have also been supervisor and first marker for more than a hundred and fifty Master's level projects. I have seen how even the most capable students are sometimes unable to grasp the academic requirements of a dissertation, while some that do still struggle to produce a convincing submission.

The general standard of students is often criticised with particular comments about their lack of English knowledge. Certainly for some, working in another language, it is a challenge. Marking schemes typically only allocate a small percentage for the quality of rhetoric. If the written statements are unambiguous and the work clearly presented, then normally the marker will not worry too much about precise English usage. To get onto a Master's programme is not easy. The student has to have significant ability; even more so when working in another language or culture.

I think the problem stems from the difference between capability and competence. It is assumed that previous course work and exams have enabled the students to develop an appropriate range of investigative skills. These are often supplemented by a research methods class. Hence the student should have the capability, the wherewithal to do the project, but they may not be competent to do it and write it up effectively. The dissertation process typically spans many months and the writing is usually bigger than anything they have done before. They may not know how to go about it and lack relevant experience to build on.

Although my own coaching style was to guide the students on the complete dissertation process of topic selection, investigation, critical assessment and write-up, I came to realise that a focus on the research effort was also part of the problem. Unlike PhDs, a Master's dissertation does not have to be original research. It is about following a process to demonstrate a range of skills in the context of research activity. Usually these are only assessed by considering a final written report. In nearly all cases students have more than enough material to develop a document that is worthy of a higher mark.

Reviewing a number of cohorts and consulting with colleagues identified repeated write-up issues: common errors and omissions, poor or confused structures, assumptive reasoning and spurious digression. It seemed to me that the students were generally doing enough practical work; reading, researching and recording, but then the effort stalled. Poor marks followed despite all their research efforts because their reports were unsatisfactory.

Guidance notes covering specific writing topics are often available on university intranets or as part of dissertation preparation handouts. Likewise commercial books on dissertations provide some comments on write-up but tend to focus on specific language skills. Overall the advice tends to be lost in the discussion of topic choice and its investigation: how to do the research rather than how to use the report to demonstrate the desired learning outcomes. What seemed to be lacking was guidance that integrates write-up with the whole dissertation process. I feel that if the focus is moved from the research itself to consider the report as a vehicle to demonstrate skills associated with researching, then marks would be higher and the students would be more effective in managing their projects. They would learn more from the dissertation process.

I have tried to follow my own advice by presenting material in progressive and differentiated sections using headings, bullet points, check lists and illustrations. Colours and fonts were chosen to aid clarity and to help those with reading issues such as dyslexia. However the work is not succinct. This is deliberate. It tends to be repetitive, but few will read the book right through. I wanted to be sure that some important points were not missed. The work is also based on my opinions, a school of thought if you will, and they are not shared by all. A few academics have reviewed the work, but not all disciplines are represented. I stress the importance of this because in a dissertation choosing reliable sources is critically important. What I suggest should therefore be treated with caution. Throughout I encourage students to work closely with their tutors and supervisor. I hope that the presented ideas can be related to their own specified dissertation requirements and will facilitate an effective project. My intention is to help students do better, not to tell them what to do.

There are no short cuts. A report cannot be created without the basic material that comes from the project activity. The research and its write-up have to go hand in hand. Furthermore I believe that the planning for the write-up will help guide the project, keeping it on track. The result will be a more effective investigation with a report that will get a mark truly reflective of the student's sustained effort. That is my goal for this book.

Tutors get pleasure and learn a lot from reading good submissions. I hope this book helps us all; students and their tutors alike. We like giving out high marks where justified. We want our students to do well. I especially like outstanding or impressive.

Gordon M. Message: November 2020   gmm01@teammessage.net

Acknowledgements

I was a latecomer to teaching and so thanks are due to all my colleagues at various universities who helped me establish my academic career. In particular I am indebted to:

Professor Julie Newlan at the University of Hertfordshire who took a chance and offered me work in the Business School under the watchful eye of the late Mary Deuchar. Mary taught me the importance of academic rigour while maintaining an open and enquiring mind. When it came to evaluating situations she always said, "It all depends".

Gill Stark, as the head of the Fashion School at the American InterContinental University, London, (now part of Regent's University) also took a gamble when she offered me the post of Assistant Dean for Fashion Marketing. Working with Gill and her academic leadership team of Dahren Davey and Vera Urban taught me that creativity is possible through application, commitment and a willingness to consider different perspectives.

Molly Mills and Dr Adam Dunn on Master's programmes covering luxury and fashion marketing and management at the Winchester School of Art, part of Southampton University, showed me that many skills are transferable and can be applied effectively across different disciplines.

I have been significantly supported in my role as a university lecturer and dissertation supervisor by Caroline Large who, as a principal lecturer, programme leader, external examiner and consultant researcher, has provided ongoing guidance and encouragement. Initially this was at the University of Hertfordshire, but Caroline has continued as a mentor as we have followed different career paths. I am grateful for her support. She reviewed my manuscript in detail and made a number of valid suggestions. Her help has been invaluable.

Writing can be a lonely business and so a good support infrastructure is vital. It is not just about giving encouragement. I have had people around me who have listened to my ideas, helping me get them clear. They have shared their knowledge and experiences, making useful contributions with suggestions for content and structure. Friends and family have played a key role in this respect.

I had several false starts with this book and at times came close to giving up. Friends at the Ampthill Writers' Group have been a tremendous source of encouragement that has kept me going.

My children and their partners have helped me shape the book by contributing significant ideas based on their own university and work experiences, likewise several other family members and friends. In describing their own university studies, they added to my knowledge of unfamiliar disciplines so that I could present what I hope is a broader picture.

Two close friends, John Marshall and John O'Leary stand out as long term advisers. They have been excellent sounding boards, always interested in my ideas and activities. Their enthusiasm for my work and family has been a precious gift.

In many ways having the ideas and gathering related data is the easy part. Putting it together as a professional text is more challenging. I am extremely lucky that my wife, Jane, is adept at proof reading. She has checked my work in forensic detail, finding a host of issues, but I must stress that any errors or omissions that remain are entirely my responsibility.

It is said that if you want to learn then you should teach. My students have given me a wealth of knowledge relating to their project themes. Many have also shared detail about their homelands and culture. Through them I have seen a full spectrum of the practical realities involved in Master's dissertations. Without their ups and downs this work would not have been feasible.

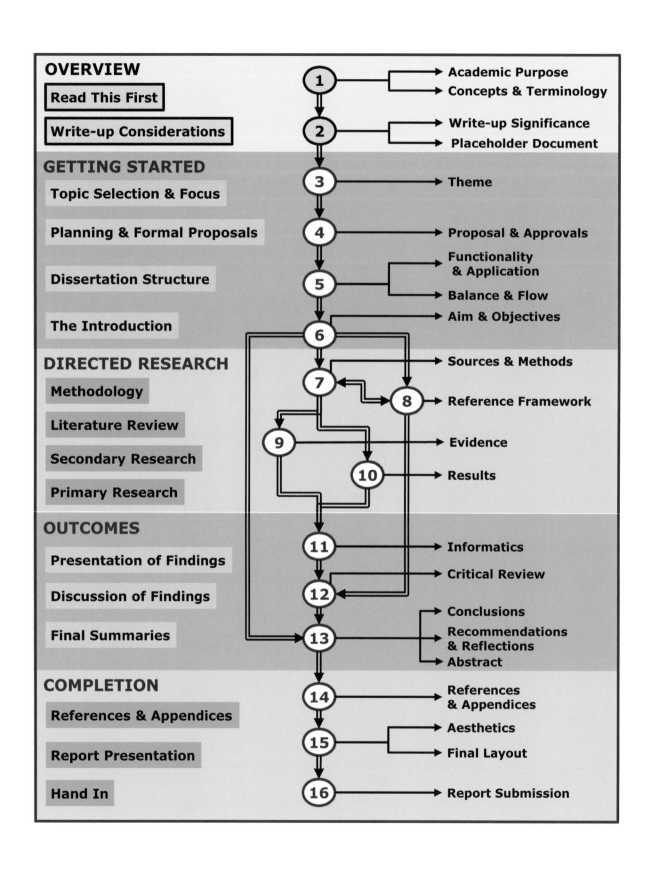

OVERVIEW

Read This First

Write-up Considerations

1 → Academic Purpose
→ Concepts & Terminology

2 → Write-up Significance
→ Placeholder Document

GETTING STARTED

Topic Selection & Focus

3 → Theme

Planning & Formal Proposals

4 → Proposal & Approvals

Dissertation Structure

5 → Functionality & Application
→ Balance & Flow

The Introduction

6 → Aim & Objectives

DIRECTED RESEARCH

Methodology

7 → Sources & Methods

Literature Review

8 → Reference Framework

Secondary Research

9 → Evidence

Primary Research

10 → Results

OUTCOMES

Presentation of Findings

11 → Informatics

Discussion of Findings

12 → Critical Review

Final Summaries

13 → Conclusions
→ Recommendations & Reflections
→ Abstract

COMPLETION

References & Appendices

14 → References & Appendices

Report Presentation

15 → Aesthetics
→ Final Layout

Hand In

16 → Report Submission

OVERVIEW

Master's courses in a wide range of disciplines require students to undertake a sustained project of investigation. In doing this you must demonstrate a level of knowledge, understanding and a range of skills in a research context. The task is far from trivial and will require considerable effort over a significant time. There are no short cuts. However, following a process of planning and organised activity will lead you to a successful outcome.

As shown in the process diagram this is a major project, but it can be broken down into a series of stages. Within each stage there are a number of elements and these form the basis for the chapters of this book. A number of deliverables or outputs relating to the activities of the investigation and its write-up are identified for each part of the process.

This book is intended to support your Master's project by providing appropriate information and practical tools. The book is not a substitute for your university's requirements, guidelines or procedures. You must make yourself aware of the set requirements and adhere to them. You should seek guidance from your tutors and supervisor.

Overview: Section Summary

It is recognised that you may already have a clear plan and could be well into the project, but regardless of which stage you are at you should review this first section as it will explain how you can use this book to support your work:

Dissertation Terminology: This glossary lists and explains common terms and phrases associated with the academic requirements of dissertations.

Chapter 1   Read This First: The academic purpose and overall concept of Master's level dissertations are explained.

Chapter 2   Write-up Considerations: The main, sometimes the only, element of dissertation assessment is a significant written report many thousands of words long. The book will discuss how each activity area and its write-up can be integrated to manage the project to produce a logical and coherent report. This chapter gives general advice about producing a written report, highlighting write-up as activity planning, the use of placeholder documents to capture information as it is acquired and templates for gathering and recording data and research results.

Dissertation Terminology

Aim and Objectives: The aim is the specific overriding purpose for the dissertation. It is a bit like the end point of a journey. The objectives are intermediate goals that serve as markers or way points along the way that help you achieve your aim.

Analysis vs Description: Describing situations does not explain them. Analysis is about going further in an attempt to characterise them by identifying relationships and driving forces.

Argument: The presentation and discussion of evidence in support of an idea, aim or objective. It is not about disagreement with a stated view, but this is a possibility.

Bibliography: A list of sources in a specified format that have served to support the current investigation. As such, a bibliography could contain references as well as other works that have not been cited. To avoid duplication, it is common to use a bibliography only for uncited material that was of general relevance, with a separate reference list being used for cited sources.

Critical: Discussion that weighs up relevant points, for and against; the pros and cons of a presented argument. It does not imply negativity.

Desk Research: Investigation of existing material for a Literature Review or Secondary Research.

Dissertation: A sustained academic project investigating a topic of interest and its associated report. The specific requirements of the activity and write-up are defined by an academic institution and tend to follow a format that may be discipline specific.

Empirical Research: Investigation based on observable situations, interactions or experimental activity rather than non-empirical, which is based only on theoretical or logical argument.

Grading Criteria: This is a template or set of guidelines that indicate how a dissertation is to be marked. It usually follows the outline defined by the institution's learning objectives for the course of study and serves to ensure fair and consistent marking.

Learning Objectives: A Master's dissertation, like any other university course, has a particular purpose. The learning objectives provide specific detail to support this intention.

Literature Review: At face value this could be a consideration of anything written previously about a topic of interest. However, different disciplines tend to ascribe a more focused interpretation. In general it is about the perceived or accepted wisdom within a subject area. This can range from established theory to a range of views where differing ideas prevail in specific circumstances. These can be schools of thought each with their own leading disciples. In some controlled environments it covers the accepted rules and regulations. Overall a literature review generally describes the way things are expected to work within a given environment and discipline.

Methodology: The process by which research is carried out. This includes procedures for identifying written material, the desk research, and primary research methods whereby original information is gathered.

Narrative: The text flow in a dissertation report.

Plagiarism: The presentation of work done by others as your own without acknowledgement. It can include work done previously by you but presented as new. Plagiarism is considered unacceptable academic cheating and may result in severe penalties. It follows that if your work references a source, including any of your own earlier work, then it is not plagiarised. However the over reliance on a limited number of sources may be deemed unduly derivative and still be unacceptable academically.

Primary Research: Original research carried out specifically to address areas of interest in a current investigation.

References: Formal acknowledgement of the cited work of others that has been used to develop the current investigation. They have two parts: the text tags that are the identifying markers within the text body and a full listing that is structured in a specified format to facilitate source identification.

Schools of Thought: Differing ideas or views about the interpretation and explanation of established situations.

Secondary Research: The use of findings from related investigations that were carried out by others for a purpose that was their own and not necessarily the same as the current research focus.

Self-directed: Although you will be bound by dissertation guidelines and may have the support of tutors and a supervisor, the decisions and execution of the dissertation process must be initiated and managed by you.

Succinct: Brief and focused text, to the point without unnecessary elaboration.

Supervisor: A tutor who is assigned to support and guide you through the dissertation process. You should consider your tutor as a mentor and advisor. A supervisor is not your project manager or the editor of your report. You should prepare for and manage the supervision meetings following a process agreed with your supervisor.

Sustained: Work of some depth that is developed over a significant period of time.

Unduly Derivative: The over reliance on or extensive use of only a few sources even if they are referenced. This is not plagiarism, but it is effectively unacceptable academic copying liable to penalties.

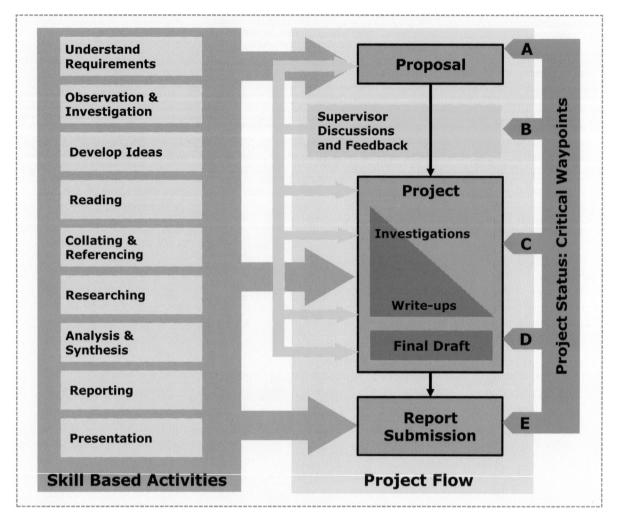

Figure 1.1 Activities and Project Flow in Master's Dissertations

A: *Before you begin the main dissertation activity make sure your plans are in place even if there is no requirement to submit a formal proposal.*

B: *Review with your supervisor before starting and then regularly to get advice and feedback.*

C: *Make sure you are putting time and energy into writing as well as researching.*

D: *Write-up takes time. At this point stop investigating; you have to go with the material that you have.*

E: *You must get something in on time even if you feel that it is incomplete or not to the standard that you would like. Your report cannot be marked if you do not submit it.*

Chapter 1

Read This First

Your project will be a long journey. Before you set out it would be a good idea to have some idea of your destination and possible routes. If you have already started, the status of your project, your progress and ongoing requirements, can be evaluated by identifying waypoints, Figure 1.1, so that you can consider and act on their implications.

It would be reasonable to think that a successful dissertation is about impressive research, but if you examine the grading criteria, it is likely that you will find that it highlights a set of skill based learning outcomes, not just the research results. It is important that you are aware of the academic purpose as well as the activity of your project so that you can understand the prescribed requirements and how you might achieve them.

Typically you will have to write a major report. This can be integrated into your activity to be both a planning tool and a reporting vehicle so that you can effectively manage the overall project to demonstrate the requisite learning outcomes.

Dissertations and Investigative Projects

The focus of this book is Master's level investigative projects involving a range of skills and activities, Figure 1.1. These are often called Dissertations, but other descriptors such as Research Project, Illustrated Review and Major Investigation are used. In this book the term dissertation or report will be used to indicate all types of sustained investigative projects and their write-up.

A topic is normally chosen by the student who may have to initially write a justifying proposal. The follow on work will be detailed, lasting several months, involving considerable reading and some practical research activity. Most of this book considers empirical investigations; projects that involve the gathering of research evidence and its evaluation. Usually this requires some primary research. Where this is not practical, an investigation based only on secondary research may be allowed, but in these cases it can be harder to demonstrate all of the expected learning outcomes.

Some types of investigation are non-empirical; that is they are evaluations of the work of others, where contrasting ideas and schools of thought are considered in relation to your theme. Or they may be experimental, where an idea is investigated and tested. As such these may not require primary research and the overall project and its report will have a different structure. Chapter 5: Dissertation Structure gives an overview of these formats.

Key Activities and Tasks

The dissertation flows through key stages: project preparation, perhaps with a formal proposal, directed research activity, evaluation of outcomes and report submission. It requires a range of activities and skills as shown in Figure 1.1. Even if there is no requirement for a formal proposal you will have to get your topic agreed in terms of subject matter, ethics and activity approvals. You will be expected to have read around your subject beforehand, so that you have some justification for your project in terms of relevance to your course and significance in your field. With such a large project it is important to plan and get organised. Your planning should address the requirements, but also reflect the way that you work best and the limitations of your situation.

Normally you will be allocated a supervisor. Remember it is your project not your supervisor's and so you must take the initiative to make contact and to prepare material for the supervision discussions. Your supervisor will encourage and support you and this can be done best if you both have a clear idea of what you are trying to achieve.

The project itself will require considerable reading and activity planning before any primary research is undertaken. The reading needs to be focused and the information obtained referenced and collated. Your research plans must be realistic and achievable as well as appropriate to the project aims.

You will have to write a significant report, but it is risky to consider this as an "after the event" record. It is better to integrate your writing into the overall activity to help with the planning as well as activity and results presentation. Leaving it to the end will lead to a great deal of stress and is less likely to produce a convincing result.

You must submit your report on time. Deadlines are very strict and meeting these is ultimately a key skill that will be assessed. No submission, no marks!

Who is the book for?

This book is aimed at Master's level students studying in a wide range of programmes where there is a requirement to undertake a significant investigative activity. It will provide information, tools and guidelines to help plan, manage and write-up the project to achieve a professional and academically strong result.

Some undergraduates have the option to do a major final year project instead of taught modules. The basic principles, at an appropriate academic level, are the same and useful material will be found in this book.

It is hoped that dissertation supervisors will also find this book useful. It will give them some tools to help guide their students. Better still; both students and tutors could use the ideas in this book to help prepare for supervisor meetings leading to a more effective supervision process.

The Academic Purpose

You may have many reasons for doing a Master's course, but the academic purpose of a dissertation is to test you in a range of research related skills over an extended period. In fact persistence and tenacity are among the key transferable skills that you will develop.
The key requirement is to demonstrate academic rigour in executing the dissertation process:

- Do you understand what an academic investigation is all about?
- Can you articulate a research question or issue?
- Do you understand the context, theory or prevailing wisdom in your selected field?
- Can you develop an appropriate and feasible research method and carry it out?
- Can you present data and develop meaning through analysis and synthesis?
- Can you draw realistic conclusions and make justified recommendations?

Even if you can do all of this you will get no marks unless you meet the submission requirements:

- Will you follow the set guidelines for layout and referencing?
- Can you present your work professionally, fully referenced and in an appropriate style?
- Can you get it done on time, meeting the submission requirements and deadlines?

The aim is for you to demonstrate a range of academic principles in a research context. It is not just about the effort of getting detailed research results.

Originality and Realism

Dissertations at Master's level involve research-related activity, but there is rarely a requirement for the topic to be new or the research to be fundamentally original. In fact on some courses the area for consideration may be set within narrowly defined boundaries. Originality comes from your own efforts to find, correlate and analyse information with an informed and justified presentation of findings and conclusions. It is not sufficient to just reproduce the work of others.

Through this process of sustained activity you have to demonstrate a range of skills to address set programme learning outcomes. Typically you will need to show knowledge and understanding, cognitive abilities, logic, critical argument, analysis and synthesis, as well as a range of research related transferable skills. These include the organisation and management of the project and communication skills; the ability to present your ideas and results clearly and succinctly.

The project must be realistic and realised. That is you should have a reasonable prospect of achieving your objectives at the outset, saying what you plan to do, followed by a process whereby you actually do it or at least something close to your original intentions.

Specific Requirements and Variations

Inevitably this book will present generalised ideas with examples of specific variations. They may not match your own academic institution's approach. Each programme will have its own detailed requirements. It is important that you understand exactly what you are expected to do. Most courses will provide some detail about your project implementation and the basic format of your final report in terms of layout, word count, fonts and spacing, referencing protocols and use of appendices. These may seem trivial, but the ability to follow guidelines is one of the skills tested. There may also be workshops and handbooks or online guidelines setting out requirements for your topic selection and the process of investigating it.

Some courses will require significantly different approaches. Specific topic selection, extensive contemporary reviews, illustrated reports and prescribed research procedures are examples. Even if you feel that the requirements are crystal clear, you should confirm details with your tutors and supervisor before, and not after, you do your work.

Assessment by a Written Report

Despite all the activities involved, the whole project is often judged only by consideration of a written report. It is vital therefore that the write-up is professionally presented in an appropriate academic style with a convincing narrative.

Each Master's programme will have its own set of norms and requirements that determine the look and structure of the written submission. Examiners will expect you to follow these principles with appropriate content and structure. Beyond this they will be looking for adherence to professional practice in terms that demonstrate the learning outcomes detailed in the grading criteria.

Dissertations are typically marked by two people, your supervisor and an independent person. They have to compare notes and agree a final mark. In addition, the university will have oversight procedures to ensure quality and consistency. It is normal for your supervisor to offer guidance and direction. In some cases, circumstances may dictate that you agree to follow an unusual or non-standard path. When marking, your supervisor may then be able to see that you have followed a suggestion or an agreed route even if you have not made it explicit. The second marker does not have this insight. Hence it is imperative that your report tells the whole story. You should not assume that a reader knows what you were trying to do.

Demonstrating Skills

Working hard on your research project is not enough. Assessment will be based only on presented evidence. This must show your application of skills in executing the project and not just the research findings. You will need to demonstrate knowledge and understanding about your selected topic and the process of investigating it.

Inevitably you will have to make choices; selecting material, identifying appropriate methods and positioning findings. These all require critical assessment; what are the pros and cons, the benefits vs the disadvantages and the implications of choices and trade-offs? Working through these can seem like a mammoth task, but you should recognise them as opportunities. Explaining your selections is one way of showing cognitive skills. Creating logical structures by arranging your material and presenting reasoned argument based on evidence are other ways to demonstrate capability. The process of researching requires many transferable skills from planning to presentation. Some will be obvious from your report, but other aspects need to be explicitly described if your skills are to be recognised.

You are expected to work independently on your project, but it is professional to seek help when needed. Also your work in part will be based on material from other researchers. You should acknowledge all forms of assistance. In particular avoid plagiarism. Using the work of others presented as your own is unacceptable. All source material should be appropriately referenced. Identifying, collating and acknowledging the work of others is a key academic skill.

How To Use This Book

Few people will read this entire book and it is unlikely that you will read it sequentially. After this initial section, the chapters follow a typical dissertation project flow. You should therefore be able to dip in at appropriate places and times so that how you use it will depend on where you are with your project and your own particular working style. A planner at the start of their project will have different needs and approach from a procrastinator nearing the end of the process.

Consider it as a guide book if there is not one for your course or for the area that you are working on. Think of it as a box of tools to help you tackle specific jobs. Use it as a planning guide, an aide memoire, a prompt or check list to ensure you address the set requirements logically and systematically. Use it to facilitate meaningful discussion with your supervisor so that you can get good advice and clear direction.

Priorities: Book Structure vs Course Requirements

Think of this part as a health warning or disclaimer. It is your project and you need to take responsibility for it. The book tries to answer many of the questions that students have when doing a dissertation, but inevitably it is generalised. Any specific course instructions should take precedence over suggestions made in this book.

However, dissertation guidelines and handbooks often provide only basic details about overall project activity, report structure and its format. In the chapters that follow the requirements of the dissertation elements and their write-up are examined in detail with ideas about how they might be managed. In some cases there will be differences between the advice given in this book and that implied in your course guidelines. Do not guess, hope or rely on comments from your friends. Seek advice from your supervisor. This book may not give you the right answers, but it will help you ask the right questions.

Current Status of Your Project

Consider where you are in the process. The process diagram at the start of each major section of this book shows how its chapters are mapped to a typical project flow. There is an indication of outputs for each stage. This repeated diagram along with the index should help you find areas of interest. However it is possible to get bogged down in the detail and so some critical waypoints are identified in the basic overview, Figure 1.1, at the start of this chapter.

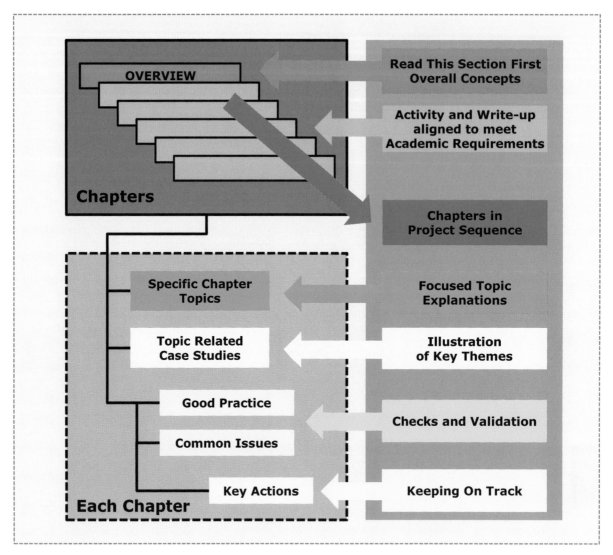

Figure 1.2   Book Structure

Access Points and Strategy

Figure 1.2 shows how the main chapters of the book provide topic specific material in a structured way. Block diagrams are used to illustrate key aspects and are useful for a quick review. Most chapters have a short focused case study to highlight significant points. Good Practice and Common Issue summaries provide easily accessed reminders and will be particularly useful as check lists when time is short. The chapters conclude with a list of Key Actions that should help you keep your activities on track.

Write-up is critical to the whole project. The next chapter will provide focused detail on this aspect providing a reference for all stages of the project.

Consider your own working style and adapt the book's features to your needs:

- **Planner:** As an organised person who likes structure, you should find the detailed chapters and their sequencing useful. However if your course requirements differ significantly from the ideas presented then skim to find specific topics of interest and use the chapter case studies and check lists for ideas and prompts.

- **Pragmatist:** If you live in the moment and just get on with things then everything might seem OK. However dissertations have a nasty habit of getting away from you and time pressures can be overwhelming. Dip in and out to find material that supports your activity, but give the Key Action sections particular attention as these will help keep you focused and stop drift.

- **Procrastinator:** The adrenalin rush of an impending deadline can help some people produce good work. You might be able to do a thousand word essay over a weekend. Multiply this up by a factor of ten or more and you will see that last minute is really last month. Get control by using the Key Action sections to create meaningful intermediate deadlines. One way to force these is to book supervisor appointments in advance with a promised agenda and then deliver.

- **Panicker:** Even the best organised can become overwhelmed by such a big project. Use the section and chapter overviews to understand the overall process and where you are in it. The Good Practice and Common Issue sections will give you reassurance and the Key Action section will help you focus and keep on track.

Resources

Although you may seem to be on your own with very few resources there is a range of things that you can call upon in the course of your dissertation:

- **Manpower:** A dissertation is supposed to be about your own sustained effort but some support is acceptable. Your supervisor and tutors will advise and guide you. They are not your friends, but they are not unfriendly. They have a lot of experience and may well mark your submission. It is worth seeking and following their advice.

  University and external library staff can advise and guide your search for appropriate material. Friends and family can assist with reviews and proof reading as well as presentation and language issues, but the work and content of the dissertation must be your own. In addition they are part of your network that can help you find information and contacts. Your research participants are a major element of your dissertation and critical to your success. Treat them with respect.

- **Money:** There will be expenses associated with your activity and normally you are expected to cover these costs yourself, but you will not be expected to make major financial commitments. For example: if a market report is only available commercially at significant expense then you might indicate that such a thing exists and would be of value to your research, but within the constraints of the dissertation say that it is unavailable. A review of this limitation can become part of your write-up and will enable you to demonstrate knowledge and understanding.

- **Materials:** In most cases a dissertation project does not involve the significant use of materials beyond your own pens and notepaper and the university library resources. In cases where experimentation and display materials are required these may be available through your university department. If you need more than the basics, check with your supervisor to establish if materials or funding for them are available. Do this early in the project, not as an afterthought.

- **Machines:** Your IT devices, PC and phone, as well as the university computer facilities are the basic machines that you will use. In addition you may require the tools of the trade such as surveying equipment in geography projects, gymnasium apparatus in sports science investigations or lab equipment in science disciplines.

  In some projects there may be a need to use specialist facilities such as test rigs, studios, wind tunnels and so on that are part of the established university facilities. There will be set procedures for the access and use of these. Make sure that you make your request well in advance of the actual requirements and follow the protocols for permission and use.

- **Methods:** Get into a way of working with systems in place to keep your project moving. This includes the organisation of your activities and interactions with your supervisor and tutors. Have a process for managing your notes and creating regular back-ups.

  Your university will have a range of student services offering notes, study guides, online and classroom courses that can help you improve your skills. These cover things like English quality, specific research tasks such as referencing and the use of software tools, for example data presentation. Ask your supervisor, the library and student services staff for information to know what is available before you need to use it.

- **Minutes:** You have all the time that is available, no less and no more. Make every minute count. Always have a notebook with you to record ideas that pop into your head or to detail any observations. Always have relevant material with you to read or review. Learn to use those dead times when you are waiting around to do something useful for your project. Be prepared and aware. Track your progress and anticipate deadlines. Minutes are also about recording what is said and done. Keep a record of all your activities and meetings with your supervisor and with others.

Further Reading

This section is deliberately sparse for two reasons: the possibilities are too big and the landscape changes too quickly. However this is not an excuse to avoid further reading about the skills and processes involved in a Master's dissertation.

Each course, department and discipline has its own specialist resources of books, journals and websites. It is just not realistic to list all the relevant possibilities here. Offering a limited selection would be highly presumptive. New research and media interest along with a range of rapidly evolving and updating websites and blogs make it impossible to offer a reasonable cross section of appropriate material that will be current when you see it. Things change too quickly. Not usually the background foundations of a discipline but the commentary available about it.

However these reservations do not mean that you should not read around your subject. Your tutors and library staff will probably be able to point you to a recommended discipline specific reading list and online resources. In addition you will find that there are preferred publications or internal guides for specific aspects of the dissertation process such as research methods and academic writing. In addition example dissertations by previous students may be available. These things can be examined carefully before your project starts and will enable you to get up to speed on the style and normal practice in your field and university department.

There are some areas that might not be covered by recommended reading lists. A significant aspect of your project is to make sense of collected data in a succinct way. There are some excellent books covering data visualisation and infographics. Library listings and Google® searches will find these. You should look for ways to present your material effectively and in a convincing manner.

One of the trickier aspects of your dissertation is to identify in scope ideas for investigation and development and then in the results discussion section to create meaning through the synthesis of your findings. It would be a good idea therefore to develop your skills of lateral thinking, brainstorming and mind mapping. Your university student services may have workshops or handouts covering these skills and library and online searches will tap into a rich seam of suitable material. However this may not find:

Thomson, G. (2008). **Mesmerization**. London: Thames & Hudson

I recommend this book because it uses a particular format to link factors into recognisable themes. It is the concept of the linking process and the visualisation of related ideas rather than the identified themes themselves that is important. Many students have found this useful and have used similar approaches when considering how they will create a coherent flow in their own dissertation write-up.

Good Practice

- **Set requirements:** Understand and follow your specific course requirements.

- **Learning outcomes:** Confirm the assessment requirement details. Use the various project elements to demonstrate knowledge, understanding and the various skills that are part of these.

- **Organisation:** Match activity planning and time allocation to suit your personal working style and circumstances.

- **Practical:** Be realistic about the project scope, resources and time lines.

- **Planning:** Maintain momentum by making plans and carrying them through. Review and revise as the project develops.

- **Work with your supervisor:** Take an active role in liaising with your supervisor. Agree a way of working together. Provide draft material or notes so that you have some substance to discuss. Consider the given advice and if you choose not to follow it explain why.

- **Project management:** Develop systems to record information, manage activities and writing up.

- **Record keeping:** Document everything that you do. Keep a diary to record your activities along with notes so that you could find material again if needed.

- **Back-up:** Make secure back-up copies of your computer files often.

Common Issues

- **Panic and fear:** Yes, it is a big task, but you can do it. The first step is often the hardest. Create a plan of action and get started. Write your report as you go.

- **Misunderstanding requirements:** Do not make assumptions. Do not rely on your friends, social media or this book. Study the set requirements and seek advice from your tutors if you have any doubts.

- **Overconfidence:** It is too easy to underestimate the amount of work required or to think that you have plenty of time.

- **Lack of focus / planning:** Do not be vague about your intentions. Do not drift and hope.

- **Misdirected:** It is too easy to focus on a specific project activity especially research data gathering while losing sight of the broader, often skill based requirements of the course.

- **Taking shortcuts:** It is sensible to use all the resources at your disposal, providing you do not delegate the principal job of doing the dissertation to others. The project should be managed by you and be your own work. It is reasonable to get advice and specialist help but there are academic and ethical boundaries that you should not cross. Taking shortcuts by using the work of others may lead to disqualification. In the end the satisfaction and the sense of achievement that you get by doing this work yourself will stay with you forever.

Key Actions

- **Confirm requirements:** Make your own check list of the specific dissertation requirements (or proposal requirements if you are at this early stage). Consider approvals, project activity, report requirements and deadlines.

- **Assessment:** Review the assessment process to understand how your project will be marked.

- **Project status review:** Understand where you are in the dissertation process:
  - What are the specific requirements and deadlines?
  - What have you done already?
  - What are the major things still to be done?
  - What issues and problems do you have?

- **Supervision:** Make or review your plans for working with your supervisor:
  - What do you need to say and show?
  - What help do you need?
  - Have you done what has been previously suggested?
  - Schedule your next meeting and provide an agenda. Prepare supporting material.

- **Record keeping:** Document and back-up everything that you do. Keep a diary of your activity.

- **Looming deadline:** If you are close to a submission deadline you will have little scope for action. Review the final chapter and the checklists at the ends of earlier chapters for last minute prompts. Do not give up: submit something on time.

- **Personal problems:** Significant issues or personal circumstances such as illness, accidents or family tragedies can impact your ability to work on your dissertation. Do not delay; get professional help for your problems as soon as you can, but also tell your supervisor or personal tutor. It is very difficult to provide help or allowances if a regulation deadline has passed before you highlight something that prevented you from working.

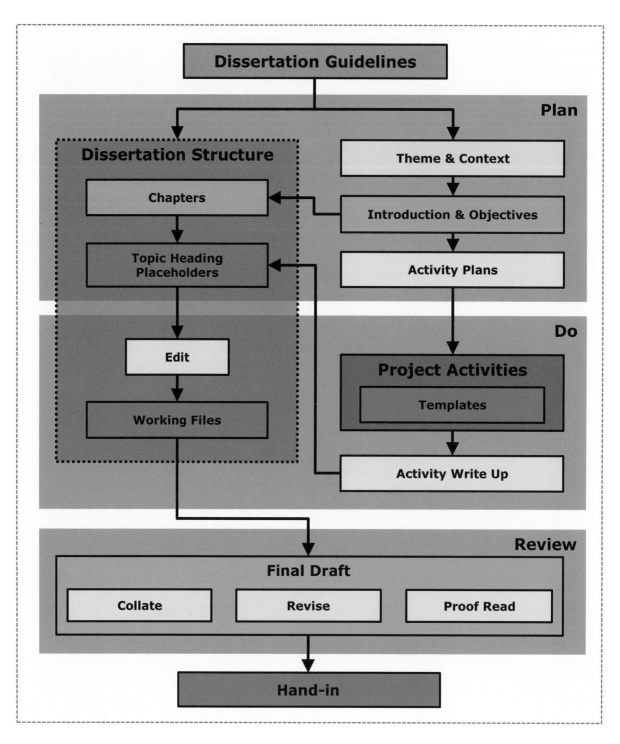

Figure 2.1   The Writing Process

Chapter 2

Write-up Considerations

The prospect of writing a report of many thousands of words can be daunting, but, surprisingly, some students find that they do not have enough word count. They want to make it longer and produce a report with significant overrun and then struggle to cut it down to meet the set requirements. Another common worry concerns English ability. Typically guidelines ask for a succinct, coherent report with arguments based on critically evaluated evidence that is both convincing and academically robust. For many this is not their everyday language and it can leave them uncertain about expectations.

As a report about research activity it might seem sensible to do the write-up at the end when the findings are known, but this can lead to significant stress. Realising that information is missing and that time is running out are typical problems.

This chapter reviews the requirements of write-up and offers some suggestions on how it might be integrated into the project activity to be an effective planning tool that addresses these highlighted issues. As such this chapter is a guide supporting your whole project. The discussion centres on the main project report, but the principles also apply to formal proposal and approval requirements.

The Writing Process

You will find write-up much more manageable if you write and edit as you go along as indicated in Figure 2.1. Inevitably you will be working on a number of areas in parallel and so you should create appropriate files. These will be physical locations for collected material and your own hand written notes as well as a computer-based filing structure for your draft material. You might consider a placeholder document as described below or something similar as a way of developing your main draft. As this will quickly build into a large document, you may find it easier to work with smaller files initially for each section.

Thinking about write-up requirements before undertaking tasks will help you plan the activity and record its outcomes effectively. The resultant file can then be developed and edited in parallel to the activity before copying it into your master draft. An initial review and edit can focus on the immediate material and will help you identify shortfalls of information. After a while you can review larger sections in the master or placeholder document. This time separation will help you get a better perspective to ensure a consistent and logical flow as well as conformance to the overall requirements. Leaving write-up to the end takes away these benefits.

Once all activities are finished you can make a final edit where you revise the material, rearranging sections if necessary to create a clear narrative. You should then write the Abstract before final submission.

Integrated Plans and Activities

A 'plan – do – review' process will help you with both the write-up and the practical aspects of your project. Before you start an activity think about what you will need to say in your report: the task descriptions, option assessments and the presentation of findings. Creating structured topic lists, tables of key themes and templates for result presentation will help you plan the activity and record its outcomes effectively.

Desk work, Literature Review and Secondary Research, should be focused. The overall requirements and your specific project theme will enable you to identify key subjects. Your aim and objectives, typically detailed in your Introduction, will broaden these into a number of search areas. These create the placeholder headings and form a structure that will give direction to your work. As you find material you will have a place to put it. Detailed sort and selection is then part of the later review process.

Primary (and some types of empirical Secondary) Research will generate data that must be presented in ways that will facilitate explanation, evaluation and analysis. Templates in the form of prepared tables and charts can anticipate the findings either as raw or derived information. A clear understanding of how the findings will be presented can improve the framing of the research questions and the process of answer collection. It is very frustrating to realise afterwards that a question was badly articulated or that one was missing, such that the presentation of the findings has gaps that are now obvious. Preparing a template for results presentation and testing with dummy data gives you the benefit of hindsight before actual data collection.

The various parts of the dissertation are not independent. While initially you may not know the outcomes of your research, your objectives will define a framework for the Discussion and Conclusion. Hence you can create a template of headings or bullet points to give structure to these sections based on your initial intentions. This ensures a focus and logical flow to your argument.

Structured Review

The process of integrating write-up with activity helps break the project into manageable parts. The use of placeholders and templates allows parallel working making sure things end up in the right place. Divide and conquer is the plan, but the resultant placeholder document is likely to be unbalanced and topics may be misaligned. Your initial thinking will be modified as the project progresses requiring a structured review to resolve these issues as you create a final draft.

Review and rearrange your sections so that your overall report has a logical flow matching your objectives. Edit and consolidate your material, removing unnecessary description and duplication so that you meet your target word count for each section. You may have to make hard decisions about what to include and what to leave out. At this point you should have a sufficient overview to create the necessary focus and flow.

At each stage of writing you should check for errors and omissions, but a systematic process of proof reading with the final draft will create a polished report ready for submission. You should verify that your references are complete and that the whole report conforms to the set requirements. This level of care requires time and you should plan for it.

Reference As You Go

Keeping track of references can be problematic. An effective approach is to write the full reference listing into your write-up notes immediately after the corresponding text tag every time you use a source. Highlight or put them in a different colour so that they stand out. As you edit and move your material the references will travel with it. It is much easier to adjust the text tag to the appropriate writing style with the full listing next to it.

During the final edit, copy and paste the text tags and the reference listing into the references section. This can then be edited into the correct alphabetic order. You can ensure that the text tag will point correctly to the listing. Duplications will be identified and if there are too many it is a signal that you have over relied on one publication. Multiple publications from the same author and year become obvious and you can easily add differentiating numbers to the tags and listings. The final edit task is to delete the full listing from the body text and the tags from the reference list. This process may seem tedious, but it is simple, all cited references are captured correctly and you end up with a bit of spare word count for your final edit.

Back-up

It is really important that you protect your work by making back-ups. Make copies of all your files on a suitable memory device updating them each time you make additions or alterations. Memory sticks and your own computer can get stolen, lost or damaged so you should also regularly save files on to the university system. This will be a maintained facility with extensive protection. Should the worst happen these measures will enable you to recover your work.

Sadly there are sometimes issues of academic integrity with accusations of copying or buying in work from others. It is not always clear who created the original material. You should protect yourself by keeping a detailed diary of your dissertation activity and retain your physical files of notes in an organised form until grades are awarded. Always date your notes. These precautions and your back-up files will give you the evidence to show that the work is yours.

Unfortunately people can get sick, have accidents or may be diverted by personal circumstances. Universities and their exam boards are not unsympathetic, but they need evidence of work if they are to help you. Regular supervisor contact, a diary of activities, organised files, draft material and back-ups will provide this. Tell your supervisor of issues as soon as you can. It is very hard to resolve problems after delays, especially if they are advised after the submission deadline.

Report Elements and Project Flow

Work flow and the report sequencing, Figure 2.2, do not always correspond. It makes sense to write the Introduction as a detailed draft before starting any other activity. This will provide a sense of direction and a basic plan for the whole project. Logically the Methodology should come next since one of its functions should be to consider how sources are to be found and selected as well as considering the options for original research, but it is common practice to position its write-up after the Literature Review. Other elements follow but not necessarily in order:

- Desk research, Literature Review and Secondary Research, may run in parallel.
- It is not unusual for some Primary Research to start before desk research is finished.
- References should be recorded throughout the project as soon as they are first identified.
- The Abstract which is placed at the start of the report should be written last. It is a summary of the whole project and can only be done when all the main work is complete.

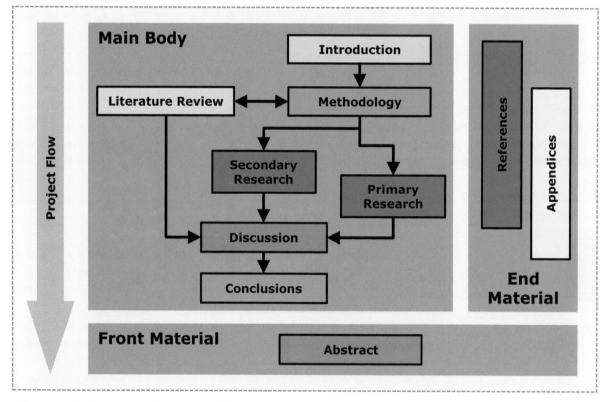

Figure 2.2   Project Flow and Report Sequencing

You will generate material as the project proceeds. Keeping track of notes, results and collected information can be problematic. Writing up as you go along can collate this material. Using a placeholder document and working templates are an effective way of doing this and can also provide guidance for project activity.

Creating a Placeholder Document

Overall your report will be a large document, but it can be broken down into smaller more manageable blocks, each divided into functional sections. You should be able to identify the report chapters and their principal topics from the dissertation requirements, your own planning and any initial proposal material. A detailed draft of the Introduction will give you further indications of content. All of these lead to headings that can be put into a working document to create placeholders for your written material as it is created.

Set the document formatting: margins, text size, fonts and line spacing, to match the dissertation requirements. Add some notes, perhaps in a different colour, under the headings as a reminder of the layout requirements and to capture ideas for content and associated activities. As your work progresses write in or cut and paste material into the appropriate sections maintaining the styling. In this way you will have format control, a planning guide and placeholders to build a master draft document that can be reviewed and later edited into the final submission.

Normally only the main body elements are included in the word count. An early decision is to allocate a proportion of the word count to each chapter to create the right balance. Note the allocations in the placeholder document, but concentrate initially on writing to capture your material. Review and editing to the right length can come later.

Logical and Critical Evaluation

A dissertation report is not an entertainment or a saga of endeavour. It has the particular purpose of describing your investigative work in a logical and critical fashion. Logical means that there is a structure to it so that it flows in a meaningful and justified way. You start with a topic, identify relevant themes, propose objectives or hypotheses and then examine them, seeking evidence to support your description, analysis and conclusions. There should be a clear and obvious flow.

The evidence should be critically assessed leading to an informed discussion and valid conclusions. Critical evaluation does not imply negativity. In an academic context, it is about a careful consideration of a situation's merits, the pros and cons, the good and bad points of a given set of information. It is about reasoned argument when selecting options. While you may have your own strong opinions on a topic they do not count. You should be impartial, presenting evidence that illustrates the situation under consideration showing that meaningful judgements were made and justified.

English Quality vs Clarity

English quality is generally considered as part of the professional presentation assessment. Although only a few marks are typically assigned to this, there is no excuse for poor writing. Make it clear: mean what you say – say what you mean. One way to do this, especially if English is not your strength, is to keep the language simple. Avoid long sentences as these can confuse you as well as your reader. A short punchy style is acceptable for most reports.

It also helps to keep your paragraphs short. The gaps between each idea aid clarity. Common or repeated themes become more obvious when reviewing your work. The paragraph breaks make it simpler to re-sequence the material to remove duplications and improve the flow. Short paragraphs also help your reader. Each point is separated and the overall narrative is easier to follow.

You may be tempted to use the words of others. These should be properly referenced to avoid an accusation of plagiarism. If you use a lot of material from one source, even if it is referenced, your work may also be considered negatively as being unduly derivative. Likewise too many actual quotes will raise questions about your own contribution. Paraphrasing, putting the ideas of a number of different referenced sources into your own words, makes it easier for you to develop your themes convincingly.

Succinct and Focused

Writing has a habit of getting off track. Do not worry about this: just write. Get your ideas down, recording them as they occur even if you ramble or mix things up. Allow yourself time to later edit into a succinct and focused report. Being succinct is about making your points clearly and briefly. Avoid flowery language, long winded phrases and unnecessary repetition. Few have the talent to do this straight off. It is much easier to edit existing material into sharper prose.

Focus by creating a logical flow around your selected themes avoiding digression. A review will recognise that some valid material is in the wrong place. Cut and paste it into the right areas. Other points may be out of scope, not part of your main topic. These should be put in a separate file, do not throw them away. As your work progresses you may need to review your focus and these ideas may then be useful.

These reviews need time: you have to give them attention, but it is also good to have a gap between the initial writing and its edit. The elapsed time will help you get a better perspective. When reviewing a section ask yourself: "So what? Does this section support my objectives?" This will help you test the clarity and significance of your writing.

Optimising Word Count

The apparently large word count of your dissertation may not be so generous once you break it down into sections. Letting one part overrun squeezes the others creating an imbalance. Repetition and digression can be resolved by careful editing. Long-winded writing undermines everything.

In all but a few disciplines your report does not need to be an essay of free flowing prose. It is acceptable, even desirable to adopt a terse business like style. It is easy to lose one or two hundred words with waffle. Avoid:

- **Filler words and phrases:** *However, moreover, furthermore, as previously mentioned, to name but a few, all things considered …* They soften your presentation but add no value. Leave them out.

- **Verbose doubting:** *This might be …. perhaps…. because…. maybe… sometimes …* Do not waste words hedging or apologising. Be confident, state your point.

- **And / but / or:** There is no need to arbitrarily join up short sentences to make a long one. Use these words only when you need to explicitly link or contrast ideas.

- **List Words:** *Firstly, secondly, thirdly …. eleventhly, twelthly … nineteenthly ! …*Numerical notation with chapter and main section headings is normal. Using words to delineate individual points is wasteful, inelegant and can make editing difficult. Use new paragraphs for each sub-section or a bullet list if the themes are short.

The use of tables, bullet point lists, charts and diagrams are ways of optimising word count by conveying a lot of information in a compact way. In the report they break up long sections of text making it easier to read, but avoid wasting word count by then over describing them.

Appendices are not normally included in the word count, but should not be used as a dump for items that should be in the main body.

Helping Hands

You should never get others to do your work for you. No matter how you look at it, this is cheating. The work must be your own, but there are areas where it is both sensible and allowable to get help. Your tutors and supervisor will be able to give you some specific advice and can point you to other services in your university that might be useful. It is also possible to use friends or professional services in some limited ways.

Working with Your Supervisor

Most supervisors will be pleased to review some draft material. This gives them a basis from which they can guide you on themes, content, methods, progress and presentation. They may make some comments about write-up style and quality, but it is not reasonable to ask them to be your editor or to proof read your work. If things need attention they may refer you to other services offered within your university.

You should first get your supervisor's agreement that you can send draft sections for review. Present material in good time prior to a scheduled meeting to create the best opportunity for detailed feedback on content and write-up.

Support Services

Many universities have support services offering tutorials and online courses that will give general advice about English quality, academic writing requirements and how to present results in charts. They may be able to give you feedback on some of your draft material with coaching to help you improve, but the ultimate writing and edits must be your own. Most universities have support and provision for students with specific difficulties such as dyslexia or physical disabilities. Do not be shy or too proud to seek the help that you need and deserve.

There are many private organisations offering help from complete dissertations to assistance in specific areas such as referencing and rewriting to improve English quality. Clearly some are going beyond the area of acceptable help. A simple test is to consider asking your supervisor about these. If you do not feel comfortable doing this then it is likely that you already know that the service would compromise your academic integrity.

By all means discuss your ideas, approach and progress with your colleagues. Your peers are an important support network, but they may be as confused as you. Do not rely on them for advice. Instead check with your tutors except perhaps in one significant area. If English is not your first language it can be very difficult to make your intentions clear. All languages have their subtleties and expressions. It would be reasonable to ask a native English speaker, a friend perhaps, to read through your text to give you advice on any misused words, inappropriate phrases or awkward constructions. It is important that they do not assist you with the content. You must do your own work crafting the language of your report in the light of their advice.

Write-up In Perspective

Initially, many students find the whole dissertation process overwhelming. There is so much information to take in and the pressures to get on with it can cause a premature rush of activity. The importance of write-up can be forgotten or considered something that can be left till later. The significant information overload at the start makes it difficult to understand the actual purpose of the write-up in the overall scheme of things. In fact understanding the overall scheme can itself be a major difficulty.

Requirement guidelines will indicate various dissertation activities and if you are not careful the write-up can become a saga of your journey through the project without fully addressing the academic requirements. Detailing your actions and the outcomes can demonstrate knowledge and understanding, while describing the various tasks undertaken can demonstrate transferrable skills, but it requires more to demonstrate cognitive capability. This is about your ability to evaluate evidence and present reasoned argument. One way to think about this is to consider how your knowledge develops as the work progresses.

Figure 2.3 shows a knowledge cascade from data to insight with the various dissertation elements aligned to the sequence. At the beginning you identify your theme explaining its importance and relevance in the context of current theory, prevailing opinion or prescribed regulations. You identify what you need to find out. The Introduction and Literature Review set the scene. The Methodology then explains how data will be collected and where it might be found. This leads to a collection of information that will be detailed in the research findings.

Up to this point the exercise has been one of identifying and gathering information. You now need to make sense of it. The Discussion of Findings extracts knowledge from the results and indicates how it might be applied within the context that you initially defined. This will require analytical skills and the synthesis of ideas. Realistically there will be gaps and it is unlikely with the resources that you have that the investigation will be extensive or complete. The Discussion must also critically evaluate these limitations.

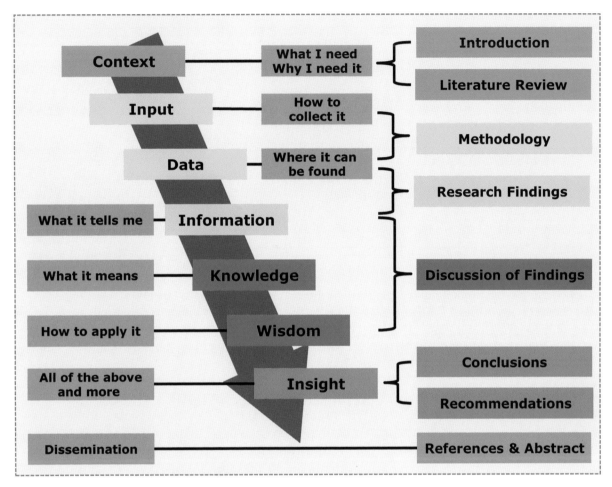

Figure 2.3   The Knowledge Cascade

The Conclusion summarises the key aspects of your dissertation. You may make some recommendations relating to your project theme if you have gained sufficient insight. With the benefit of hindsight you might also consider some comment about the approach followed, recommending improvements or future developments. Finally you should give an overview of the whole project in an Abstract. This along with your source references enables other to make use of your work.

Thinking of the dissertation write-up as a knowledge cascade as described above will help you create the right focus and emphasis to meet all the academic requirements for your report.

Write-up Considerations: Good Practice

- **Write from the start:** Get into the habit of writing as you go along, integrating it with other activities to build your report.

- **Manage the word count:** Allocating word count to the different sections makes the task more manageable and leads to a balanced report. Adjust the scope of your project if your count is too low or too high.

- **Plan-do-review:** Understand the write-up requirements at each stage and use them to plan and record activities. Review and edit periodically.

- **Placeholders and templates:** A master document with chapter and section headings will serve as a placeholder for your write-up material. Prepared templates help with activity planning and serve as data collection tools.

- **Format guide:** Follow the dissertation writing guidelines. This is more easily done if your notes, placeholder document and templates are correctly formatted from the outset.

- **Back-up protection:** Save copies of your writing in your own media and on a university system. Keeping a diary and organising files of your collected materials and notes are an insurance against lost data or personal misfortune as well as evidence of your activities.

- **Use appropriate help:** Be responsible for your work, seeking help only from legitimate and academically acceptable sources. If in doubt ask your supervisor.

- **Referencing:** Being thorough with referencing from the outset saves a lot of work later.

Write-up Considerations: Common Issues

- **Too little, too late:** Write-up is a much bigger task than most realise, but the effort can be spread across the whole project to make it manageable.

- **Writer's block:** It is a good idea to create the headings with indicators of content even if you do not yet have the material. This is what getting started means. This placeholder approach helps you identify required material. Write in what you know as soon as it is available. Do not worry about English quality at this stage. Get something down. Give yourself the perspective of time and then come back and edit into a working document. Regular writing and revision helps build confidence and skill.

- **Ignoring format guidelines:** Your report may be rejected or lose marks if you do not follow the set requirements.

- **Word count issues:** You need to keep to the set limit, typically +/- 10%, to avoid penalties. Check for balance first by allocating amounts to the different sections. Sharpen your writing style to avoid wasting words. Then review your project scope and focus to add or remove material to meet the requirements.

- **Plagiarism or unduly derivative:** Your work must be fully referenced. Relying on a single source or too many literal quotes is considered unduly derivative. Find several sources for a theme and paraphrase into your own words.

- **Flowery language:** You will get no credit for an inappropriate writing style. You work should be succinct: clear and to the point.

- **Third person:** Most institutions advise you to avoid a personal writing style. Write in a detached way using third person format. Say "The investigation found that ..." instead of "I found that ..."

- **Mishaps:** Advise your tutors or supervisor as soon as you can if you have a major problem such as losing your computer or adverse personal circumstance such as illness. Do not delay; ask for help and advice straightaway.

Write-up Considerations: Key Actions

- **Get organised:** Set up systems and files for your work at the outset. Back-up frequently. In particular make sure you capture source reference details as you find them.

- **Plan:** Create a placeholder document or something similar that indicates your main chapters and headings. Make sure it matches the format requirements. Create individual tables and templates for data recording. Use these as guides when planning activities.

- **Do:** Get to it, start writing. Anticipate write-up requirements for each stage using them to guide actions. Initially focus on capturing material rather than worrying about writing style.

- **Review:** Periodically edit your material into a working draft such as a placeholder document. As larger sections are completed undertake a detailed review to ultimately create a final draft. Check this for conformance to set requirements and proof read carefully.

- **Help:** Identify approved sources of help before you need them.

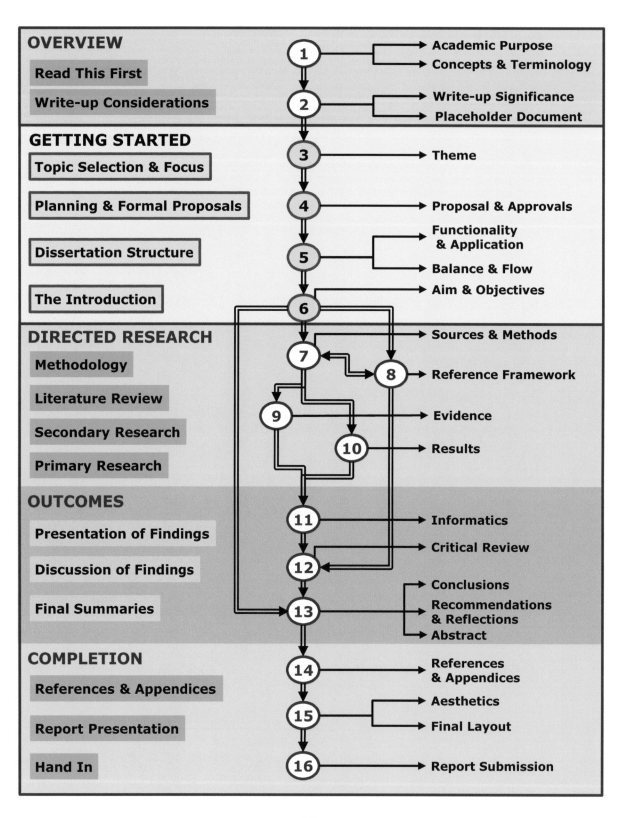

OVERVIEW

Read This First — 1 → Academic Purpose / Concepts & Terminology

Write-up Considerations — 2 → Write-up Significance / Placeholder Document

GETTING STARTED

Topic Selection & Focus — 3 → Theme

Planning & Formal Proposals — 4 → Proposal & Approvals

Dissertation Structure — 5 → Functionality & Application / Balance & Flow

The Introduction — 6 → Aim & Objectives

DIRECTED RESEARCH

Methodology

Literature Review

Secondary Research

Primary Research

7 → Sources & Methods

8 → Reference Framework

9 → Evidence

10 → Results

OUTCOMES

Presentation of Findings

Discussion of Findings

Final Summaries

11 → Informatics

12 → Critical Review

13 → Conclusions / Recommendations & Reflections / Abstract

COMPLETION

References & Appendices — 14 → References & Appendices

Report Presentation — 15 → Aesthetics / Final Layout

Hand In — 16 → Report Submission

GETTING STARTED

You will be aware from the outset of your Master's programme that a dissertation is a requirement. Do not assume that the teaching sessions prior to this will provide detailed preparation. Most of your sessions will be focused on specific aspects of your discipline, but it is common to have a course on research methods. This can leave you thinking that a dissertation is all about the quality of your research data. This would be a presumption. The dissertation tests a whole range of skills in a research context. The quality of results is only part of it.

There will be a number of preparation activities leading up to the dissertation period. You can use this time to get ready by understanding the norms of your discipline by doing background reading. You will also have to decide on your topic and get the necessary approvals. It is a good idea to review the dissertation requirements and the detail of how it will be assessed. This early activity will prepare you for the task ahead.

Getting Started: Section Summary

Getting off to the right start will ensure that your project proceeds smoothly and effectively:

Chapter 3   Topic Selection and Focus: Your research topic must be relevant, focused and approved. Your institute may specify the subject or principal theme for investigation. If not, you will need to identify an area appropriate to your course with sufficient focus to enable an in depth study that will hold your interest and keep you motivated throughout.

Chapter 4   Planning and Formal Proposals: Typically you will be asked to submit an outline of your ideas along with information about your planned contacts and the research activities that will involve them, so that formal approval can be given. This will require a consideration of ethics, health and safety and other areas of concern to the university. In some cases a formal proposal is required and this may be marked as part of your dissertation assessment.

Chapter 5   Dissertation Structure: A number of alternative dissertation formats are possible. It is important to understand these and the way they are reported so that you can make appropriate choices to meet the requirements of your course. Dissertation activities and their sequencing as well as the structure of the written submission in terms of content and presentation format are discussed.

Chapter 6   The Introduction: Writing a detailed draft of the dissertation Introduction chapter before you start the investigative work will provide a guide that explains your project rationale. It should use material from your Proposal and other planning initiatives. By writing it first you will create a clear sense of purpose and direction for your project that will help keep your activities focused and on track.

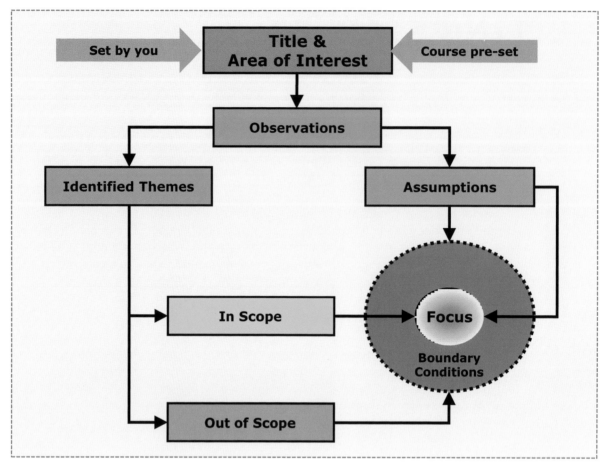

Figure 3.1   Creating a Focus

Create a focus by asking yourself a set of key questions:

- *What is the dissertation about?*

- *Is there a particular angle or requirement of interest?*

- *What are the prevailing general assumptions about the topic?*

- *Why is the theme important or relevant?*

- *What are the main sub-topics?*

- *How will sub-topics be selected or rejected?*

- *What are the implied boundaries from this process?*

Chapter 3

Topic Selection and Focus

Most dissertation topics are open to wide interpretation. They can be viewed across a broad front or narrowly considered by drilling down into fine detail. Setting a focus and context is an important start to your planning and essential for a formal Proposal. You should identify a particular area of interest and associated topics. Your theme may be based on your own observations and interests, but could be pre-set by the course guidelines. It should be relevant to your programme of study.

Create a focus by following the process and asking a set of questions as shown in Figure 3.1.

It is hard at an early stage to know how much work there will be in the dissertation. A mind mapping technique is a good way to identify the principal theme and key topics as well as setting some boundaries. The in and out of scope limits can be revised as your work progresses.

Choosing a Meaningful and Manageable Topic

Your topic must meet the requirements of your course as well as being meaningful and manageable. Be realistic. Will you be able to do what you are proposing? Will it hold your interest over the life of the project?

Relevance and Interest

You must show that your overall theme is relevant, important and that it will enable you to meet the set requirements for your programme. This requires evidence beyond your initial observations and some argument to justify your ideas.

Topics identified from a mind mapping technique or from similar brainstorming activity should be investigated to give more detail. This serves two purposes: it provides initial evidence to support your project and will establish that you know how to conduct basic desk research. You should make this evidence explicit by showing how the topics were identified and how the additional information was found. This material will be useful if a formal Proposal is needed, in discussions with your supervisor and later can be used in the Introduction to your dissertation report.

This initial investigation will also allow you to reflect on your topic. You will have to live with it for a long time. It is important that it will hold your interest so that you can maintain enthusiasm and motivation to complete the project. Also think about the bigger picture. Will this topic, when you have completed your dissertation, be useful in your future career? Your dissertation report is powerful evidence of a broad range of capabilities and will be especially useful if it is directed at an area you wish to pursue after your Master's course such as further studies or work activities.

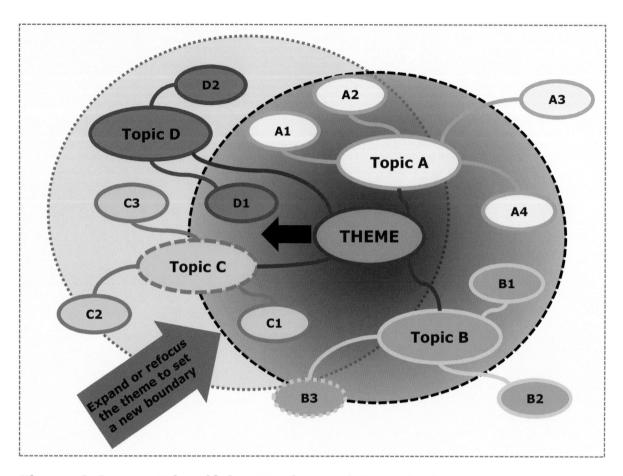

Figure 3.2   Identifying Topics and Boundaries

Project Scope and Boundaries

It is important that your main theme is not vague. Clarifying it by preparing a statement of interest will enable you to define your key topics and sub-topics that will support your investigation. Figure 3.2 shows how an initial theme can be expanded to a number of topics, A, B, C and D and their associated sub-topics. Setting a boundary and adjusting the topic positioning shows what could be included and what might be left out. Obviously things can be drawn in a number of ways and so the real benefit is the time spent thinking about the topic relationships in the context of your theme. Do they really support it or are they peripheral? In this case it can be seen that topic C is marginal and may be included if time and word count allow it. Topic D is out of scope, but has one relevant sub topic. This might be included, but the rest could be left undeveloped and only indicated as a potential avenue for further work.

This approach is a good way to create a project focus around a particular area of interest and provides a tool for reviewing the dissertation scope as it evolves. A difficulty arises when your area of interest is restricted by a course requirement. Supposing there is a direction that your project should be related to ideas associated with topic D. Moving the boundary will accommodate this and will also bring topic C in scope while eliminating ideas around area B. The theme will then need to be redefined so that it is central to the new set area of interest. This is not a particular problem unless there was a strong desire to cover the original ideas, but with a bit of creativity it is often possible to align areas of interest to an aspect of the set focus.

For example: a Business Studies student wished to investigate the use of social media as a tool for commerce. His preparation was thrown off balance when a requirement to consider ideas around Corporate Social Responsibility, CSR, was announced. This is equivalent making topic D in Figure 3.2 central to the project. The student realised that the business need for communication: gathering stakeholder inputs and presenting CSR policies, has elements associated with social media. He was able to reframe his ideas to consider the use of social media as a tool related to stakeholder/business communications about CSR. A discussion with his tutor confirmed that this was acceptable and a suitable dissertation title was agreed.

Title and Subtitle

The dissertation theme is best developed around a set of ideas initially articulated in a statement of interest. This might need one or two sentences and would be ineffective as a title; something shorter is needed. For the example above:

> CSR and Social Media

is a valid working title derived from the overall theme but not very explicit. As the dissertation evolves something more appropriate may emerge. A longer statement provides initial clarification for your ideas and can later be used as an opening for a Proposal and in the Introduction of the main report.

 A short title is easier to use in discussion such as communication with your supervisor. Adding a sub-title enables you to clarify the overall intent of the dissertation. For the CSR example:

> An investigation into how online activity influences corporate policies

or

> How organisations use online communication to improve their reputations

are two very different subtitles indicating a focus that is not clear from the basic title.

Initial Preparation

Make haste slowly. Rushing into your project without adequate preparation can lead to a great deal of wasted effort and frustration. Think about the implications of your title. Is it feasible? Will you know when you have completed the work? That is, do you have a clear idea of what you are trying to find out and what it might involve?

You will need to do quite a bit of work before starting to be sure that the project is manageable and aligned to the set guidelines. You need to prepare yourself, your university and your supervisor for the project ahead. Thinking about all the elements of doing the dissertation will help you get your own systems in place. Your institution will require some details for ethical approval and risk assessment. You need to make contact with your supervisor to establish a working relationship.

Project Approval

Increasingly academic institutions are asking for more and more detail about intended projects before they start, perhaps a term ahead. Typically the first stage is to define a basic outline of your subject with some initial ideas about the areas of investigation. This will give enough information for a suitable supervisor to be allocated. Many universities will ask you to submit a formal Proposal and in some cases this will be marked, as well as being used for project approval. The Proposal and the detailed planning associated with it are discussed in the next chapter.

You should consider the research requirements implied by your theme. Will you be able to get access to suitable groups and individuals who can throw light on to your investigation? What sort of methods might you use? Surveys, online questionnaires, group sessions or individual interviews are some of the choices. Is there an obvious approach and is it open to you; will you be able to get access? This information will be needed by the university for ethical approval and risk assessment. They have a duty of care to you and to anyone that is involved in your research. In addition universities are aware of the significance of their reputation and will want to ensure that your activity does not put this at risk.

It is very important that you understand the approvals process and that you follow it precisely. Do not do any active research such as approaching organisations and individuals asking if they might be willing to help you; making public statements about your intentions such as posting ideas relating to your project on public forums and social media or engaging in any form of primary research, until formal approval has been given.

Planning and Organisation

Get organised: use the period between initial idea presentation and formal approval to get ready for all activities that will follow. You will gather a lot of information; newspaper and magazine cuttings, notes from your reading of books and websites as well as extracts from online sources. These will be in hard copy, paper format, and computer files. You can start gathering these any time as they are passive, not active, research, but you will need some way of cataloguing them all. Anything you use in your write-up will have to be referenced. You need a system to record and correlate these. Later when you start active research you will generate more material: questionnaires, observations, interview responses. These too must be catalogued. Prepare your systems first. Create working placeholder documents, templates and check lists as described in Chapter 2: Write-up Considerations to provide working frameworks for the activity and its write up.

Although you should not approach anyone yet you can start to identify contacts or target groups for your research. Think about how you will engage with them. Consider your timelines and the order in which you will do things. In short make a plan.

Back-up

Even at this early stage you will be generating significantly important material that you will be relying on for your report. Protect it; you do not want the pressure of having to repeat this work if the information is lost. Set up systems to back-up your computer files; not just a memory stick but also on to university systems that are more secure.

Paperwork is more problematic. A good filing system should be sufficient, but notebooks are easily lost. Get into the habit of writing up notes and references to a computer system that can be backed up often. You might consider scanning critical documents so that they too can be managed as an electronic resource.

Advice from your Supervisor

It is normal to meet with your allocated supervisor at an early stage, but it may be down to you to make the initial contact. Your supervisor will have access to your submitted dissertation details about topic selection and approvals. Unless there are queries about these, students often assume that it is reasonable to press on with their project without the benefit of a consultation. Your supervisor will have significant experience, with detailed knowledge about what is realistic and practical. An early discussion about your plans will enable you to benefit from this experience and may save a lot of heartache later.

Preparing for and having a discussion about your project ideas and your plans for the investigation is a very good way to get things clear in your mind. If you have any doubts about the process your supervisor and tutors will put you straight. An early discussion with your supervisor should also make expectations explicit and resolve any issues or misunderstandings, clarifying any queries that you have.

Your supervisor is a valuable source of guidance and help, but this only works if you take responsibility to prepare for meetings. Make notes of any queries or issues beforehand so that these are not forgotten. It is also a good idea to provide sample or briefing material to your supervisor in advance so that it can be considered. However it is not reasonable to send large amounts of material for review unless your supervisor asks for it. It is important that you agree a way of working that is acceptable to your supervisor so that the supervision process can be effective.

Topic Selection: Case Studies

Pushing the Boundaries

Ling was studying for an MBA in the UK prior to joining the London office of her family's company as a marketing manager. Her dissertation would consider brand recognition. Her family in China had a thriving business exporting Asian foods. They saw Ling's studies as an opportunity for market research and were giving her a lot of encouragement to get started.

Ling approached a number of UK based importers and arranged interviews during which she asked about supplier and customer relationships. One contact was concerned that the questions went beyond the scope of Ling's dissertation, amounting to a detailed market investigation. He contacted the university for clarification about how his information was going to be used.

Ling had not yet been given approval for her project and was asked to attend an academic review panel where she met her supervisor for the first time. It was made clear that she faced disqualification from her course if she continued with her unapproved investigation. She was also criticised for not being honest with the contact about the requested data and its use.

In a follow-up meeting, her supervisor helped Ling differentiate between the academic purpose of the MBA and her outside business interests so that she could deflect the commercial pressure from her family until after she had completed her studies. She was then able to focus on her selected theme and obtained the required approvals.

Plain Sailing

Gino had worked on cruise liners before starting his Master's in Tourism Management. He noted that cruising was focused on an older generation, but he thought there were opportunities to appeal to a younger audience. He decided to use his dissertation to investigate this. He was not required to generate a formal proposal, but he did have to complete a questionnaire for his university approval process. In this he outlined his theme: understanding the needs and wants of a teenage audience and their families for a floating fun palace. For research he said that he intended to do online surveys to gather information from youngsters about their holiday interests.

Gino's idea was rejected by the university's ethics committee. University policy only allowed research involving minors, people under the age of 18, in exceptional circumstances and only then with considerable safeguards. Gino's supervisor was sympathetic and advised that the ethical issue could be avoided if he addressed his questions to parents rather than directly at their children.

However Gino's supervisor pointed out that this was not the only issue. The research theme was framed in an assumptive way. Gino had jumped to the conclusion that his ideas did not currently exist. He had only limited experience to justify this. With his supervisor's guidance Gino reframed his investigation to identify and critically assess cruising offers to a younger audience and to consider how they might be enhanced or developed.

Purple Mist

Olga arrived just in time but flustered for her Research Methods class; she was not prepared. The class always started with a review of things seen during the week. Observation was a key research skill for the Fashion Management Master's students. Someone commented on her vibrant jacket. "I can't think why I bought it," she said, "I hate purple." This saved her as she was able to then talk about current trends and how purple was everywhere.

Later, reflecting on the discussion she realised that at last she had found a topic for her dissertation. She sent a note to her tutor with the suggested title:

> Why am I wearing purple?
> Fashion trends – what they are, how they happen and why we follow them.

She was sure she could meet the ten thousand word requirement with this. Her tutor had other ideas. "Which one of your three suggestions are you going to do:

> What constitutes a trend?
> How do trends happen?
> Why do we follow trends?

You only have enough word count for one!"

Observations

- If you ignore university regulations and guidelines, especially ethical considerations, you run the risk of being expelled.

- External pressures can divert you from your project and may cause you to stray into unacceptable areas. Having a clear and approved focus will ensure academic integrity.

- The students had not thought about the implications of their stated ideas with sufficient consideration for academic purpose, topic focus, ethical requirements or their capacity to do all that would be required by their title.

- It is very difficult to get approval to work with children and vulnerable groups, but you can often demonstrate the principle of your research ideas by speaking with associated adults.

- Supervisors are there to help. Seek guidance about your ideas early on to ensure you start on the right track.

Topic Selection: Good Practice

- **Focus:** Being explicit about the theme and the particular aspects to be considered will give a clear focus to your project. It easier to expand a narrowly defined area later if you need to, rather than trying to narrow down vague or more general ideas.

- **Identify related sub-topics:** Developing the theme into closely related topics and sub-topics grouped as threads around your main idea enables you to demonstrate knowledge and understanding even if the all the topics are not fully developed.

- **Define boundaries:** Consider the limits and context of your theme by defining in and out of scope boundaries for the identified topics and sub-topics. This will keep you on track.

- **Consider implications:** Reflect on your theme and its focus to ensure that it is relevant, feasible and of sufficient interest to keep you motivated.

- **Statement of interest and title:** A short statement that defines your intentions can be tested for clarity by showing it to friends and your supervisor. This can then be used to develop your title and project focus. It will be useful as a project description in the approval processes and as part of your main report Introduction.

- **Approval process:** Make sure that you understand the requirements to get your project accepted and your intended activity approved.

- **Get ready:** Think about how you will manage your project. Set up systems to record your activities, findings and references. Protect your efforts by establishing back-up procedures.

- **Involve your supervisor:** Make contact and review your ideas with your supervisor. In particular check that your project is suitable and that you are following the necessary guidelines and approval processes.

Topic Selection: Common Issues

- **Vague or diffused ideas:** If your project has more than one theme it is like a journey with more than one destination. You will not know where you are going.

- **Word count concerns:** The project may seem very big at this early stage and as a safeguard you may be tempted to expand or combine themes to give you enough material. Instead maintain an explicit focus, but be ready to adjust the boundaries of what is in or out of scope. You can then develop more of the related topics if you feel that you do not have enough material. In practice most students find that they have the opposite problem. It is easier to leave some areas undeveloped but identified than to try and reduce the word count across a wide front.

- **Over ambitious:** It is good to challenge yourself, but be realistic about the suitability of your theme and its implications. Will you really be able to get the data or access that you need?

- **Long winded titles:** If your title is more than one sentence, then it is a statement of interest or intent. If it spans across more than one line consider breaking it into a short working title with a qualifying sub-title.

- **Starting before you are ready:** Get your systems organised first. This will save you time and stress in the end. On no account should you start any primary research before you have the necessary ethics and other project approvals. The excitement about a project or external influences can lead to impatience or pressure to get started. Desk research is an appropriate way to deal with this and has the benefit of helping develop a greater understanding of the project implications.

- **Ignoring your supervisor:** Your supervisor is a valuable resource. Make contact and seek advice and confirm details. Remember it is your project so you must give him or her something to work with. Do not expect your supervisor to manage your activities.

Topic Selection: Key Actions

- **Statement of interest:** Write two (or three maximum) sentences that describe your area of interest and investigative intentions. This is your project theme. Test this for clarity and viability by getting feedback from others especially your supervisor and tutors.

- **Working title:** From your statement of interest develop a short working title; use a sub-title if this needs clarification.

- **Identify related topics:** Make a list or brainstorm your theme to identify associated ideas. Group these into related areas.

- **Define a working boundary:** Decide which topics are in and out of scope for the focus of your theme. This can be reviewed and adjusted later.

- **Consider implications:** Verify that your project is possible and practical. Start your planning. In particular create an outline of what you will need to do.

- **Organise your systems:** Get ready for your sustained activity by setting up physical and computer filing systems. Think about how you will safeguard your work with back-up arrangements.

- **Seek approval:** You are now in a position to seek project approval. This will normally involve ethical and sometimes other considerations. You may also have to submit a formal proposal.

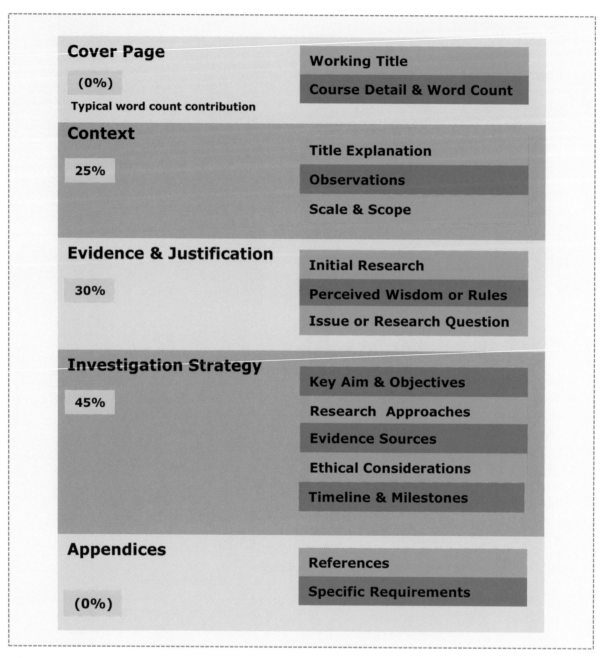

Figure 4.1   Typical Proposal Structure

The percentages indicate a typical word count allocation as a proportion of the word limit for a dissertation proposal document.

Chapter 4

Planning and Formal Proposals

You do not have enough time or word count to wander aimlessly through your dissertation. Some planning will be necessary. The preparation associated with a Proposal provides this. Think of it as a set of navigation tools to help you find your way. A Proposal maps out the dissertation territory, sets a course and considers how the project will be completed in the available time.

Even if you have no requirement to submit a formal Proposal you will have to get approval for your project. Hence preparing equivalent material will be of significant help.

Project Planning

After identifying and justifying your area of interest, your planning should indicate a strategy for investigation based on potential information sources and available research methods. Timelines and other constraints such as ethical dimensions need to be considered. Initial preparation will help you understand the detailed requirements of the overall dissertation project: the academic purpose, the direction and dimensions of your investigation, the ethical obligations and the write-up specifics. It will show that you appreciate the magnitude of the task and have a realistic plan to realise your intentions. A Proposal, formally submitted or your own detailed notes, ensures that you are setting out on a considered path and verifies that you are addressing the set requirements.

It is said that the plan is nothing, but planning is everything. At this early stage your plans will be somewhat generalised, but should provide enough information to show a clear aim and sense of direction to achieve it. As your project unfolds, the detail of implementation may need adjustment in response to your findings and circumstances. Your plan should set out an overall aim around a selected theme and this should not change significantly, as this would be equivalent to starting again on a new project. You only have time to do one effectively. However situations can change requiring a modification to your approach. Your initial planning prepares you for this by giving you a background against which you can assess alternative paths.

It is not uncommon for students to think that a Proposal is a mini dissertation with an identical format and associated activities. They are obviously related, but there are significant differences. The Proposal is a planning document outlining intentions with just enough evidence and supporting material for justification. These may be appropriate for inclusion in the main dissertation report, but there is no requirement for extensive investigation. Primary research is not normally required. The dissertation itself is the delivery of your plan; the implementation of the approved Proposal detail.

Conformance Check Lists

To differentiate the planning from its delivery consider creating two check lists to identify what needs to be in a Proposal or planning document vs what needs to be in the dissertation. The university guidelines are a good starting point to identify the main points. Where there is no requirement for a Proposal, use the structure discussion below to identify appropriate elements.

Go beyond the basic section headings to identify the key aspects of each list. Some things will seem to be the same. For example both may require an Introduction to explain and justify your theme. However they have different functions. In a Proposal you are seeking approval for your intended approach. The dissertation report builds on this, giving much greater depth, showing how the project will proceed. The dissertation then goes on to explain what was actually done and why as well as drawing conclusions. It can be seen that some of the Proposal material is a subset of the dissertation write-up. A section at the end of this chapter shows how this material can be reused and mapped into the main report.

Supervisor Considerations

Your conformance check lists are a useful aid in discussions with your tutors and supervisor. They will be able to see if you have understood the requirements and are planning to follow them. Your intentions will be clear and can be tested for practicality and relevance. In particular they will be able to guide you with regard to approvals; for your overall project theme, for your intended approach and with respect to any ethical limitations. It is good to get this advice early on so that you can tune your project submissions to maximise the prospect of a quick approval.

This preparation will also give you details for discussion. Your supervisor will have significant experience of dissertation projects; the nuts and bolts of what makes an effective process and ideas about sources and investigation approaches. You should not rely on your supervisor to tell you what to do, but having a clear outline will create opportunity for positive debate that you will find useful. Detailed attention to this planning will make your task easier and improves your prospects of a successful outcome.

Marked Proposals

Some institutions require the submission of a formal Proposal that is then assessed as part of your course. It is important that you conform to the set requirements for content and presentation, and hand in on time. Remember that your Proposal is a plan indicating how you will do the dissertation. They are linked, one leads to the other. It is no good trying to maximise your Proposal marks by describing what you think is a *"good"* submission and to then follow a different path for the dissertation. The best approach is to demonstrate effective planning. State your intentions ensuring they conform to the requirements and then, when approved, try to follow through on them.

Formal Proposals

A Proposal can be an effective planning document even if you have no formal requirement to submit one. When they are required, individual courses may set out specific formats and section titles. You must follow these. Some will include an ethics review part, but it is common for this to be a separate document or questionnaire that is designed to established alignment with university standards and practices.

Figure 4.1 shows a typical structure with suggested word count allowances in percentage terms. This split will lead to a balanced proposal, but course guidelines may vary and should be followed. The cover page, front and final sections are not usually included in the word count allocation, but these should not be unduly long. Formats and section titles may be specified. In general you will need to address the following areas:

Cover Page

The title should be the same or at least similar to your dissertation title. A short title is better than a long rambling one. This makes it easier for everyone when referring to the report. A subtitle may be used to improve the clarity of intentions. At this stage you may choose to use a working title that covers your area of interest. You may find a better one once your project is under way, but the basic theme should not be changed.

The cover page should also have the course details as specified by your university along with identifier information. This may be a reference number rather than your name to ensure anonymity. It is also a good idea to indicate the word count even if this is not explicitly requested as this helps the reviewers and is also a reminder for you to check this requirement.

Context

In this section you explain your title and develop your theme to create an overview of the dissertation project. The area for investigation may be specified by your course in precise terms, but even if it is not your ideas should be relevant to your programme. It is reasonable to use your own observations to identify an area of interest. Something you have seen, heard or read may be the trigger for your theme or it may arise out of your own particular interests or experiences. Put your ideas into a context that meets the course requirements by explaining where they come from and why you feel they are important and relevant.

Nearly all topics can be considered from multiple points of view. Identify your selected angle and set some boundaries. These may be pragmatic: time and word count may limit your field of investigation, or practical: access to some sources and research participants may be difficult. Acknowledge limitations by identifying areas of your plan that are in and out of scope.

Evidence and Justification

It is understood that you will not yet have had the opportunity to investigate your topic in any detail, but it is necessary to provide some evidence that your ideas are valid. Your theme will be fully developed in the dissertation, but you will need to do some initial desk research to support your ideas, showing that your subject is significant and worthy of further study. You should not embark on primary research at this stage. You must wait for project and ethical approvals.

The initial secondary research does not need to be extensive, but it must be sufficient to show that there is something of interest with avenues that are worth exploring. Only investigate one or two rather than trying to visit them all. At this stage you are not trying to find all the answers, but should show that there are questions to explore. Look for reliable secondary sources that shed some light on your initial thoughts and observations giving support for your project. Support in this case does not always mean agreement. Conflicting evidence can be a justification for further study so that the confusion can be resolved for your particular area of interest.

To provide a framework for discussion and to set your ideas in a wider context your dissertation will require a detailed review of the literature; the perceived wisdom for your subject. This typically means that you will have to identify the prevailing academic views and theory related to your theme as well as any policies or directives that apply if your field is in a regulated environment. It is usually a large part of the dissertation and you should show that you understand its importance by identifying a few key sources that identify relevant theory, schools of thought or regulations.

The evidence and justification discussion can be summarised with an explicitly articulated issue statement or research question. Finding an explanation or answer is then the overall aim of your dissertation. The more detailed questions implied by this should be presented logically in a progressive list to form the basis for your investigation strategy.

Investigation Strategy

You now need to explain how you will actually investigate your research issue or question. Divide and conquer is an appropriate approach. The overall aim can be broken down into a set of objectives that together will achieve it. These will be the building blocks of your investigation. Some will be straightforward, identifying and explaining the background detail for example, while others will need to be more involved and challenging to get to the heart of your subject.

At the proposal stage you should indicate possible research approaches. To a certain extent these will be dependent on your field of study. Each discipline has its own norms and common practice for the style and format for dissertations and the investigative methods within them. Different types of dissertation are discussed in Chapter 5: Dissertation Structure.

You will need to take into account practical realities; you may have to make compromises. These need to be explained. The actual methodology employed will depend on findings from your initial dissertation investigations and circumstances that might dictate a particular route. At this stage you need to indicate the most likely options to achieve success. It therefore follows that any approval requests must cover all of the potential research methods that you might employ. Avoid being uniquely prescriptive. You do not have to use all your proposed methods, but you should not use one that has not been approved. Getting approval later as an afterthought may not be easy.

If your research requires contact with specific groups you should indicate how these people will be identified and selected. You should also explain how you will find and choose sources for the Secondary Research and Literature Review. You need to be realistic about what you will be able to do. Identify possible limitations and difficulties that your methods might encounter and discuss how you will compensate for any issues these create.

You need to be aware of the ethical implications of your research and should indicate how you will safeguard all parties involved. You may have to present these details as a separate submission, but some comment in your Proposal is appropriate. If your dissertation relates to children or vulnerable groups it is unlikely that you will get approval for direct engagement. You will need to indicate how this can be overcome by working through acceptable contacts.

A dissertation is a large project and it is normal to indicate how you plan to sequence your activities. Often there is a requirement to present a Gantt or project flow chart showing start times and duration for each of the major sections and their components. A simple list is not sufficient. Considering this level of detail is one of your most significant planning exercises.

Appendices

You will be expected to demonstrate a wide ranging review of available material in your dissertation. At the proposal stage you may only be looking at a small subset. This should be fully referenced as an appendix with identifying tags in the main body text. You should follow the referencing format defined by your course. The references should cover academic theory and research methods in addition to your collected data. The objective is to show that you are following reliable sources for theory and methods and to show where your own research material has come from so that others could find the originals.

Other appendices should only be used if they are specified in the course guidelines. For example the Gantt timeline chart may be an appendix requirement. You should avoid dumping material into appendices in an attempt to save word count or to provide background information when a reference would have been sufficient.

Ethics and Integrity Considerations

Fundamentally the Proposal, or dissertation approval submission, is about protecting the university's reputation. They want you to succeed with a project that is academically sound and that all parties involved are protected. The planning indicated by a Proposal is a good indicator of your capability and should show that you intend to follow a realistic and academically robust approach that has a high probability of success.

The university will also be looking to safeguard a number of other interests. It will want to avoid any adverse social, political or ethical situations. Sensitive subjects are usually acceptable if explained and justified but controversial methods are not. It is important that you are open about your intentions and seek guidance from your tutors before submission if you think that your ideas might be considered marginal.

The university has a duty of care to you and to your research participants. It will need to ensure that your intended activities are safe and not likely to cause stress or discomfort. The data that you seek may be sensitive with legal as well as social considerations about how it is collected and used. From a liability point of view, you as the researcher will be seen as part of the university that is bound by regulations and conditions relating to public liability. By monitoring research proposals and limiting activities that might be considered risky, the university can protect all parties while managing its insurance costs and legal liabilities. They may choose to reduce their risks by restricting your research activities giving only a limited approval. This may narrow the scope of your proposed dissertation, but it is not a disaster. Managing and explaining the implications of this limitation is one way that you will be able to demonstrate academic research skills.

Research Methods Approval

You need to recognise that you are the university's representative when conducting your research. As well as acting responsibly by following socially acceptable procedures, you must abide by any restrictions set by the project approval process. If later, you find that you need to use an alternative method, one that was not originally specified in your Proposal or project request, you will need to seek additional approval. This is very time consuming and is often impractical.

To prevent this difficulty it is a good idea to ask for more than you might need. Specifying every possible method is not likely to be approved, but indicating a few different approaches is a good idea. For example you may intend to rely on a questionnaire, but these can throw up unexpected responses. Indicating that a focus discussion group might be used to review findings would give you alternative options.

In some cases you may be expected to provide explicit detail of your selected method; actual interview or survey questions for example. Asking you to supply this information before you have started the dissertation secondary research can be problematic. One way to deal with this is to present the detail in a generic but structured way. Start by indicating the intention of each method element by referencing back to your objectives. For example, you could indicate that an online survey will be used to address specific objectives b and c in your list. For clarity it is a good idea to repeat the objectives in full instead of just relying on a numbering sequence. Then provide typical survey questions that will be used in each section indicating that precise wording will depend on initial desk research and approval by your supervisor. You need to make sure that the example details do actually align with the selected objective. In this way you give a clear indication of your intentions without locking yourself into pre-set wording.

Minimising Method Limitations

Pragmatic selection of non-optimum methods and restrictions that might be imposed by university regulations and guidelines can lead to research limitations. To a certain extent these can be anticipated and countered. You may be able to get at the information you need by asking associated groups: parents instead of children or young adults looking back a few years to consider a teenage viewpoint for example. Practical difficulties within your time scale may also be a problem. Ideally you might feel that a survey of a hundred participants is needed, but you only have time for twenty. Inevitably the findings will be limited.

The important thing to realise is that your approach will be credible as long as you do not try to over extrapolate from limited data. Instead recognise the implied restrictions and indicate that these will be discussed and their significance to your overall findings considered. In this way you will be demonstrating the principles of good research even if the findings are not definitive.

Using a variety of methods to cross-correlate findings is another way of overcoming barriers providing you anticipate the need for additional approaches. In your Proposal you could identify a potential requirement for a focus group to review the findings from other areas. You may not need to do this but can if the approval is in place. Managing limitations in your research methods in these ways demonstrates a greater understanding of the overall investigative process.

Timeline Projections

Even if there is no requirement to provide a Gantt chart or timeline presentation it is a good idea to prepare something that will help you keep on track by identifying key tasks, intermediate milestones and critical deadlines. It is difficult to do this at the outset of your dissertation as you will find it hard to identify some aspects that will later become important. Also estimating realistic durations for many of the activities is not easy. Your university's dissertation handbook and project guidelines are a good starting point. These typically identify the main elements of the work and will certainly draw your attention to specific deadlines and restrictions.

University Timeline Guides

The official dissertation handbook and course guidelines will provide timeline information on the main project elements and critical dates. Sometimes these are presented as a chart or flow diagram or they may just be listed. Extract timing information to create a Gantt chart similar to Figure 4.2. The timeline is shown as calendar week numbers at the top of the diagram. (Note: The charts below this are aligned to the same timescale for easy comparison.) This exercise will identify critical deadlines for submitting a project request, formal proposal, ethics and other approvals and the final hand in date. It will also indicate project activities and may give some indication of their likely duration. Sometimes specific supervisor meetings are highlighted as checkpoints to ensure that you are on track. Arranging these meetings at the right times will be your responsibility.

This review will then give you a framework for your detailed planning. Deadlines and restrictions will be clear. For example: Primary Research must not start before ethics and other approvals have been given, but you can do preparation so that you are ready to act as soon as this happens.

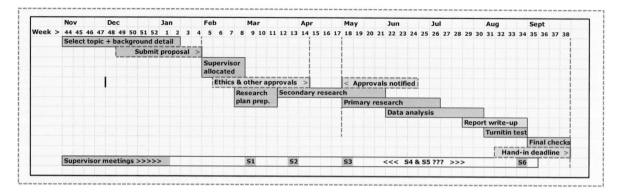

Figure 4.2   Gantt Chart based on University Guidelines

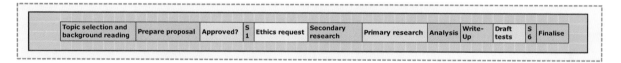

Figure 4.3   Typical Linear Interpretation

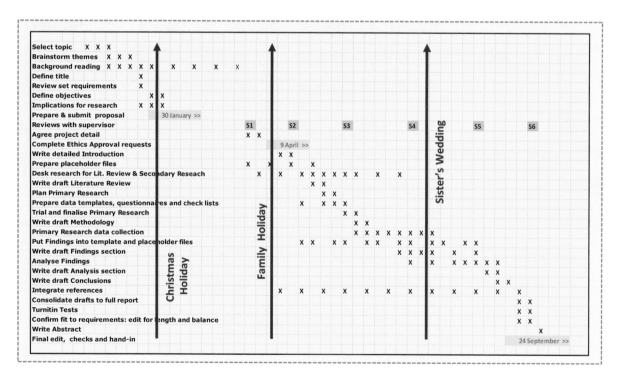

Figure 4.4   Timeline Derived From Action List

Some students make the mistake of trying to create a linear activity timeline as shown in Figure 4.3 but this is not realistic. This describes the basic sequence priorities, but does not allow sufficient time for most of the activities. It would not be suitable for a formal Proposal. You will not have enough time to do everything in a linear fashion. Everything will take longer than you think, but you will also have periods when you are waiting for information to come in. It is therefore appropriate and very necessary to consider some parallel working.

Personal Considerations

Something similar to Figure 4.2 is needed as a working planner, but it requires more detail and should consider your own working style and personal commitments. Figure 4.4 shows a Gantt chart created by a student from an action list. A spreadsheet, with a line of Xs where each cell corresponds to a week, has been annotated with some personal events, but the timelines have not yet been adjusted. To be realistic these should be modified to allow for the impact of the events.

This approach has the benefit that it is easily reviewed and modified. Main tasks can be expanded to show specific detail that will tie action lists to timelines and related activities. The impact of holidays and personal events can be accounted for. One thing is certain you will soon realise that your time is a precious and scarce resource. If used well the timeline planning tool will help you get ready to start each activity as early as possible giving you the maximum time for each element. This will help avoid pressures and the panic of a squeeze at the end of the project.

Reusing Proposal Material in the Main Report

Preparing a formal Proposal or the equivalent planning material for an approval submission is time consuming. This can be frustrating and the temptation is to minimise effort so that the real work can be started. Resist this temptation. Your planning effort will pay dividends later. Furthermore your initial material is useful and can be exported into the dissertation report, but this is not just a quick cut and paste job. Things change. It is not uncommon, following tutor feedback and further reflection, for a new thread or specific focus to emerge. Remember that the Proposal was only an indicator, but you should not divert too much or you will be operating without an effective plan.

As shown in Figure 4.5 proposal materials can then be incorporated into various dissertation sections after revision to reflect the actual aim, objectives and activities of the full project.

Cover Page

These sections tend to be similar for both documents. The initial working title should be updated to reflect the selected final dissertation theme.

Context

Most of the context or background description can be moved into the dissertation Introduction providing that the main theme and intentions are the same. If things are changed then you will need to decide which parts of the material are still valid and usable.

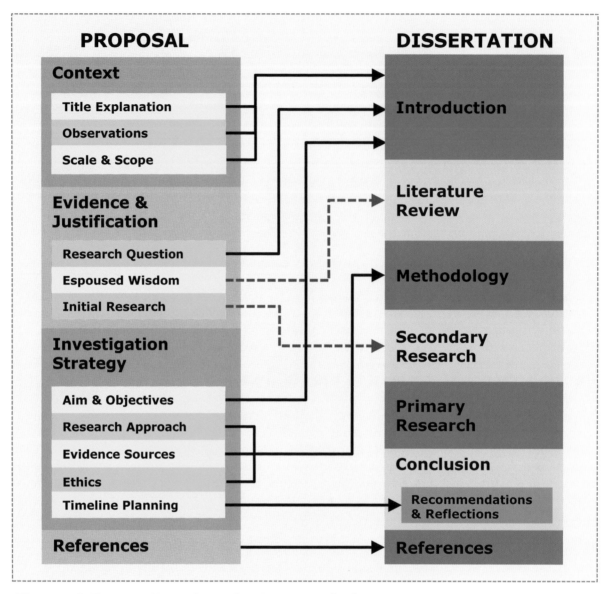

Figure 4.5   Reusing the Proposal Elements

Evidence and Justification

A dissertation report needs greater detail than a Proposal in terms of evidence and justification. The Proposal material can therefore be a contribution to various sections. A research question or issue is an appropriate element for the dissertation Introduction. Espoused wisdom covers theory, schools of thought and applicable regulations. These become part of the Literature Review. Initial research can be integrated into Secondary Research findings.

Investigation Strategy

Most of the investigation strategy discussion will contribute to the Methodology section, but the aim and objectives section is usually placed in the Introduction. A dissertation report should be considerably more developed than a Proposal and so this section may also provide some material or direction for other dissertation areas.

Some courses require a separate reflections section. Timelines and milestones provide a reference for this and for any recommendations on project improvement as part of the summing up.

Appendices

Be careful to only incorporate source references and appendix information if they are actually used in the dissertation.

Planning and Proposals: Case Study

High Street vs Online

Elaine had a pre-set requirement for her MBA dissertation to consider a strategic issue facing senior management. The following is based on her planning activity.

Observations: Internet shopping is growing.
The high street is experiencing reduced footfall and shop closures.

Issue: Structural change in fashion retailing is putting high street stores under pressure.

Initial Title: An investigation into the impact on high street retailers due to the changing attitudes of consumers to online purchasing by considering how young women buy fashion items.

This long statement was almost an introduction rather than a title, but it identified the key theme of High Street vs Online with a focus on young women in the fashion segment. Elaine drew a mind map to identify related topics and discussed this with her tutors. They advised that she was trying to do too much, possibly covering three or four different themes, but the focus on young women was perhaps unnecessarily narrow. She rearranged her mind map, Figure 4.6, to separate various themes and decided to concentrate only on the left hand side based on a new title and subtitle.

Revised Title: Bye-Buy High Street

This intriguing play on words was typical of Elaine's sense of humour. It is much shorter, practical for communication and signals the main issue. This was clarified with a subtitle:

Subtitle: An investigation into changing consumer profiles associated with the shift to online fashion buying.

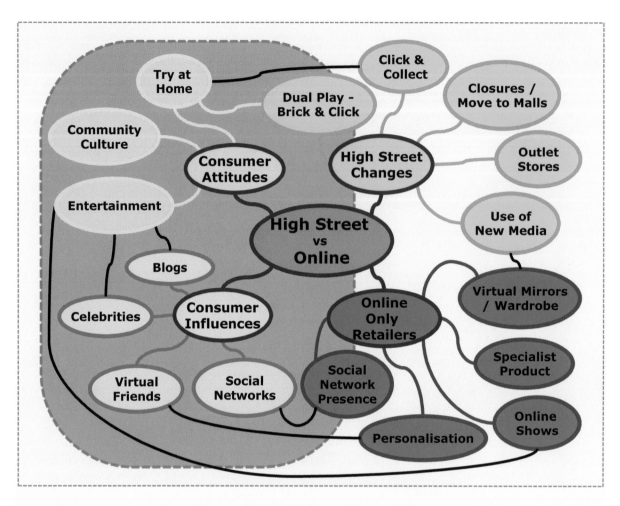

Figure 4.6   High Street vs Online Mind Map

In her Proposal Elaine suggested that identifying factors that influenced customers to shop online would have strategic benefit for retail management. The focus was on consumer behaviour seen through the lens of new media and online activity. She acknowledged that the more general aspects of consumer attitude and influence were of interest but out of scope.

To develop her aim and objectives Elaine brainstormed some key questions. At first these were somewhat mixed up and not all were relevant, but with some review she finished with a working set and was able to consider their implications:

1. Which group makes the most use of online fashion purchasing?
    - Identify online purchasing groups by age, gender, income …

2. What sort of fashion goods do they buy online?
    - Identify product categories favoured by the main group(s)

3. What online and new media activities do the main group(s) use?
   - Investigate use of online and new media facilities such as web sites, blogs, social media and smart phone apps by the main group(s)

4. What influences these group(s) to buy online?
   - Categorise influences for different groups

5. How are high street retailers contributing to their own problems?
   - Consider factors caused by the retailers themselves

6. What can high street retailers do?
   - Identify response strategies; what has been tried and other potential ideas

Elaine decided that questions 1 to 4 could be addressed by an online survey. She recognised that this particular medium was not appropriate for all types of consumer. Since her focus was related to online activity this seemed reasonable. The limitation that she would not get a view from traditional only shoppers would have to be discussed, but she identified a small reference group – friends of her family, whom she could interview for some perspectives.

Questions 5 and 6 would be partially addressed by the survey and also by contemporary secondary research reported in marketing journals and trade publications. A couple of examples were presented. Elaine acknowledged that her fashion focus was a subset of the wider picture. Ideally she would have liked to include retail managers, but recognised that her access was limited. As a substitute Elaine identified a group of student colleagues who all worked in part time retail jobs who could at least provide some commercial perspectives.

The questions were developed into specific objectives and the associated research approaches were presented in her Proposal. Approval was given and Elaine was able to use the initial planning to guide her dissertation project effectively.

Observations

- Tutors were asked for advice.

- Mind mapping was used effectively to identify key aspects and to select a focus.

- Elaine chose an area that had practical research opportunities with realistic access for appropriate primary research.

- A logical set of questions were developed and their implications for research methods were critically reviewed.

- Limitations were considered and some additional research methods were proposed. It is possible that not all would be used, but they were identified as a safeguard.

Planning and Proposals: Good Practice

- **Understand requirements:** Make sure you check and follow the set requirements for the Proposal and approval submissions.

- **Effective planning:** An articulated plan using structured notes, brain storm listings and diagrams such as mind maps, are useful for tutor discussion and serve to guide effort even if there is no requirement for a formal submission.

- **Time spent preparing a proposal is not wasted:** It may seem like a chore, but a good Proposal will provide a detailed plan that will help guide your dissertation. Much of the material can be reused if allocated to appropriate dissertation sections.

- **Clear articulation:** Your title, subtitle and first paragraph of the proposal should leave no doubts about your intentions.

- **Keep it simple and structured:** Be direct and to the point with a structured flow. Define your principal aim, objectives and implied research methods clearly.

- **Research flexibility:** Indicate possible and probable research methods, avoid a single prescriptive approach. Explain that the initial dissertation work will be needed before finalising the detailed methodology.

- **Ethical considerations:** Follow ethical guidelines set by the university and the normal practice for the country in which you are working. These may vary from expectations back home. Formal ethical approval requests, if required, should cover all possible methodology elements.

- **Time planning:** Create a detailed time plan to show a realistic sequence of dissertation activities. It should reflect how you like to work – steady or bursts to intermediate deadlines. Say how you will manage the project, especially if you are a last minute person.

Planning and Proposals: Common Issues

- **Over ambitious:** It is tempting to have a very broad topic because you have to write a lot of words, but a narrower focus will support the academic capability that you need to demonstrate.

- **Unrealistic:** Do you have the necessary resources: time, money, contacts and so on? There is no shame in scaling back to something achievable and you will avoid a great deal of stress.

- **Vague vs prescriptive, broad vs narrow:** Avoid extremes. Have clear intentions, but avoid being too prescriptive. Give yourself room to adapt if things do not work out as you hope.

- **Assumptive:** It is too easy to assume that others see the world the way you do. Use your observations and researched evidence to support your ideas.

- **Preconceived ideas:** Avoid jumping to one approach without justification, especially for research methods. Consider alternatives, develop and test all ideas.

- **No theory:** Even if your topic is new there will be some established ideas about how things are supposed to work. Identify a reference framework (theory, schools of thought or regulations) against which your ideas can be tested even if it is not completely aligned to your current observations.

- **Lack of balance:** Including too much research evidence is a common mistake. You need enough to justify your ideas, but the rest should be in the dissertation.

- **Weak aim and objectives:** Create a sense of purpose by having a main aim that is supported by a logically structured set of objectives.

- **Unrealistic timelines:** Give consideration to a detailed time plan identifying key and sub-tasks, parallel working, milestones and check points. Your plans must match your way of working and any personal commitments. It is your plan not theirs.

- **Lack of confidence:** Yes, it is hard but so was getting this far. You are capable and if you apply a bit of organisation, time and energy you can do it.

Planning and Proposals: Key Actions

Explain your project plan to a close friend. Make notes so that you can present the following as briefly and as clearly as you can. Use only one or two sentences for each point:

- Your title / subtitle
- What your dissertation will be about
- Why it is important / relevant
- Some background observations
- The most appropriate theory and principal schools of thought
- Outline of laws and regulations if these apply to your project
- The sort of research needed
- The target group(s) for the research
- How you might do the research
- Key project milestones and timelines
- Limitations and likely difficulties including how you will deal with personal time commitments

This will give you a framework plan for your Proposal write-up, but verify that this template aligns to the specific requirements of your course and adapt if necessary.

Now you have a guide to do what is necessary to complete your Proposal. If a Proposal is not needed do this exercise anyway as it will be an invaluable guide for the journey ahead.

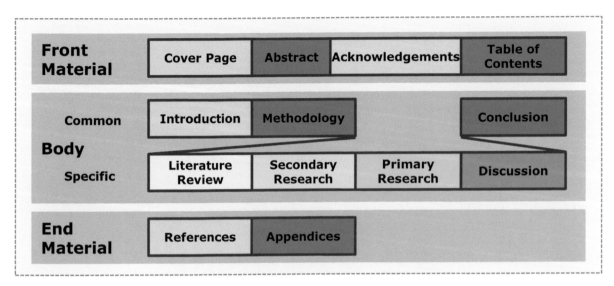

Figure 5.1   Basic Dissertation Structure

	Lit. Review	Secondary Res.	Primary Res.	Discussion
Enquiry	Theory or accepted rules	Existing Evidence	Verify Old & Find New Evidence	Insights & Answers
Schools of Thought	Differentiate & Characterise		Opinion Leaders	Compare Contrast & Develop
Non – Contact	Context	Existing Evidence	Accessible Opinion	Implications
Experimental	Context & History		Practical Trials	Review of Outcomes
New Field	Paradigm Positioning	Indicators	Verification	Future Implications
Critical Review	Extensive consideration of Literature	>>> to find >>>	Validate Ideas	New Perspectives

Figure 5.2   Specific Elements for Different Dissertation Types

Chapter 5

Dissertation Structure

The dissertation report must show a logical and progressive flow that links initial ideas through actioned objectives to reach realistic conclusions and recommendations. Understanding the relationships between the various dissertation elements will enable the presentation of a complete and convincing story. The basic plan will have been outlined in a Proposal or a similar preparation that will provide some material for several sections, but more detailed work will be needed.

It is important to remember that the report should reflect the project activities. A consideration of the required dissertation structure will determine not only the format of the written submission, but will also influence the nature and emphasis given to the different practical aspects of the investigation.

Basic Dissertation Structure

Although the focus of this book is on investigative projects it would be wrong to assume that all dissertations require the same structure. The key elements and basic layout of a dissertation are shown in Figure 5.1. The front and end materials are common to all types, but their specific format may be determined by the requirements of your course. The main body is the heart of the project and will contain elements similar to those shown. The format and names of these may vary depending on your discipline and the type of investigation. It is important to follow all the specific requirements of your course for format and content. This is something you should review with your supervisor if the guidelines are not sufficiently explicit.

Normally, only the main body of your report is considered for the word count allocation, but this does not give you licence to over deliver on the front and end sections. Excess material, especially in appendices, could lead to penalties.

Front Material

The cover page should give the title and required course related information. It is a good idea to also show your main body word count here even if this is not explicitly requested. This is helpful for the examiners. Otherwise they will have to estimate it, whereas you can give them a precise figure. This is important if your work is close to the limit where penalties might apply. However, do not add any other unrequested information. For example, it is common for submissions to be anonymous and so adding your name as well as your ID number is not appropriate.

A short Abstract is normally the next item. This should give a complete overview of your work: the aim, a summary of activities and the key findings. This is an academic convention to help others who might be considering your work as a source to inform their own research. Dissertations are typically many thousands of words long. A one or two page summary is helpful to position the whole project so that the big picture is not lost as the fine detail is considered.

Many students like to thank those who have supported them. Any Acknowledgement should be placed next before the table of contents. Typically the table of contents needs to list the chapters and first level subheadings. Some courses will also require additional tables placed after the contents list detailing illustrations and images.

Main Body

The main body is all the material from Introduction to Conclusion that details your dissertation intention, methods of investigation, research activity, results and analysis. The body section shown in Figure 5.1 lists a typical range of topics in a logical order. Different types of dissertation may give them other titles and there can be some overlap and variation in the function of each. The type of dissertation employed will determine the specific nature of these elements.

Although the elements are shown running sequentially, the practical reality is that some sections will be interdependent and may operate in parallel. Hence the chapter order may be different. Also there are various conventions and submission requirements that determine the layout of the report. For example, it is common for the Literature Review to appear before the Methodology, but logically somewhere you will need to show your method for selecting the source material. This has implications for the report in terms of format and chapter sequencing as well as influencing the project activity implementation.

End Materials

Generally the end materials should be limited to the source referencing and appropriate appendices that provide evidence of your research activity, such as blank questionnaires and examples of completed ones. Use other appendices only if this is a set requirement or if they are essential to your report. Do not dump material here.

Main Body Functional Elements

The dissertation body elements shown in Figure 5.1 serve a variety of functions:

The Introduction

The Introduction provides an explanation of your title and should outline the key theme with some justification for considering the selected topic. From these an overall aim or description of the intention is developed. It is normal to break this down into smaller parts either as a set of intermediate objectives or a group of targeted outcomes. The nature of these will depend on the styling and specific requirements for the chosen type of dissertation.

Methodology

The Methodology explains how the dissertation's aim and objectives might be achieved with a justification for the actual methods selected. Alternatives and trade-offs should be explained. It is important to indicate how the Literature Review and Secondary Research sources are to be chosen as well as how any Primary Research will be carried out. Hence the Methodology ought to come immediately after the Introduction to give a logical flow. However, it is common practice to place it after the Literature Review.

Literature Review

In many cases the Literature Review is a particular form of secondary research that identifies the rules associated with your theme. These can come in a variety of flavours. Many fields have established theory that shows how things are supposed to work. In some areas, even if there is no formal theory, there can be a well-defined espoused wisdom that describes accepted practice. Sometimes these cover a range of valid opinions or schools of thought. In other types of investigation there really is a set of rules as defined by laws, policies or regulations. In this case the Literature Review should identify and explain these. Your topic does not have to conform to these accepted parameters as long as their relevance and positioning is understood. The Literature Review will then provide a backdrop for a contrasting view.

Some types of dissertation need a different approach. In these the Literature Review is a summary of selected topics that have been developed by others. It is then not about identifying the prevailing wisdom, a single idea or set of regulations, but about considering a spectrum of established thoughts aligned to your areas of interest.

Secondary Research

Research work and information relating to the dissertation theme that has been reported by others comes under the general heading of secondary or desk research. As discussed above, specific aspects that represent accepted and established ideas will fall into the Literature Review category. Otherwise it is Secondary Research. This is material that can be used as evidence to support your particular investigation.

Work reported in professional journals is generally peer reviewed: it is considered and validated by experts in the field. This ensures that the associated research methods are robust and reliable. Beyond this there is a wide range of sources from official reports to contemporary comment in newsprint or blogs where the material may not be as academically robust. However all are valid sources, providing the implications of provenance and reliability are considered. Secondary sources should be formally acknowledged by appropriate referencing.

Primary Research

This is original material that you obtain through observation, experimentation or by engagement with targeted participants. There is a wide variety of ways to do this ranging from a one to one interview with an identified individual to anonymous surveys of a widespread cohort. The Methodology should detail the approach used. You should always have formal approval from your institution before gathering any of this material. The original or raw data should be placed in this section before any detailed synthesis or discussion.

Discussion

Separating the discussion from the actual data presentation allows you to look across the results, selected themes, sources and key ideas that flow from the Literature Review and research activity in a structured way to address your stated objectives. This holistic approach allows you to synthesise meaning by combining results and ideas, as well as interpreting a range of outcomes that are within your project scope and to highlight any other topics of relevant interest.

Conclusions

The Conclusions summarise the key findings. These should be referred back to the original objectives detailed in the Introduction. This is called closing the loop. If appropriate, recommendations may be made, but these must be derived from the research data and discussion. Avoid personal opinions about the findings. However, it may be appropriate to reflect on the dissertation process and highlight or recommend aspects of your project that, with the benefit of hindsight, could be improved or that you would do differently.

Different Dissertation Approaches

The basic format of your dissertation may be predetermined by your course to match the norms appropriate to your discipline. Typically these will be outlined in your dissertation guidelines and you should follow these pre-set requirements. As discussed above there are common aspects to most dissertation structures, but certain elements have a form and function that depend on the type of investigation.

To a limited extent you will have some flexibility in your overall approach providing it meets your course requirements. A basic understanding of the choices and their different structures will help you choose an appropriate route. Figure 5.2 shows the focus given to various body elements by some of the different types of investigation.

Enquiry

A common investigative approach is to present a research issue or question in your selected area. The aim is then to explain the issues or answer the question by addressing a set of associated objectives. Typically the Literature Review provides a theoretical framework or accepted position against which evidence from secondary and primary research can be assessed. This is considered in the Discussion that normally presents insights and answers to specific aspects of the issues.

In some cases your initial ideas might point to a set condition that can be presented as a hypothesis. The investigation then follows similar lines of enquiry to verify or discount this.

Schools of Thought

In some disciplines there are several, even many, established opinions with no overriding consensus or explicit theory. In this type of investigation the Literature Review typically incorporates the Secondary Research to identify and characterise specific versions of opinion: the schools of thought. Primary Research is often aimed at opinion leaders in the dissertation research area as a way of confirming the identified segmentation. The Discussion is then used to compare and contrast all or selected schools of thought with each other or to address their alignment with a particular aspect of your area of interest.

Non-Contact

Research involving children, infirm or incarcerated adults and politically sensitive topics is significantly controlled by involved ethical considerations that usually make it impractical to consider direct primary research in a student dissertation. Getting approval is too involved. In these cases the Literature Review is used to set the context by identifying relevant theory, prevailing standards, laws, regulations, policies and generally accepted opinions and rules.

Secondary research is used to gather evidence related to the theme, building on the work of others. Your own grouping of topics and ideas may in fact throw up other contrasting views. Primary Research is limited to associated and approved contacts such as professionals and adults, for example parents when considering children. The discussion may follow the lines outlined in the approaches already described, but in addition it should consider the limitations caused by the restricted access to the main group of interest.

Experimental

Your dissertation aim may be to create or to consider a particular process or procedure. This could range from a developing a piece of software in an IT project to an interview technique in sociology. The Literature Review and Secondary research are typically combined to provide the background context detail such as the history of activity in this area and any previous experiments. It should include a review of assumed barriers and any enablers that may now have emerged.

Primary Research is replaced by a summary of trials, your experiments that are used to develop or examine the critical area. The Discussion is a review of the trial outcomes related to the set context and defined objectives.

New Field

Some students, especially where technology is involved, feel that their subject is so new that there is no relevant accepted theory or espoused wisdom. While theory for their specific area may still be evolving, it is unlikely that the topic has no precedents. For example: market influence through social media was an overnight phenomenon and considered unique, but if you stand back it is clear that it is no more than market communications. For this there is a lot of established theory, but certain parameters are significantly changed. The process of contact is different and more immediate. The old theory may not fit exactly, but it does provide a frame of reference for a compare and contrast review. The Literature Review should identify the old paradigm so that the new one can be positioned.

Secondary Research is likely to be based on contemporary materials as these are good indicators of new trends, but they need to be assessed carefully. Primary Research can then be used to verify the new status quo and to identify implications that are then reviewed in the Discussion.

Critical Review

A significantly different form of dissertation is the critical review. This is essentially an extended essay that looks at a topic as currently portrayed in the literature. The Literature Review in this case is a wide ranging Secondary Research consideration of the selected area, usually from a particular viewpoint. Primary Research, if used, may take the form of interviews or focus groups as a way to validate particular ideas. The Discussion and Literature Review are typically integrated and lead to a new or revised perspective / school of thought in the area of interest.

Exercising Choice – Selecting Your Approach

The types of dissertation outlined above are not mutually exclusive. It would not be unreasonable to investigate a new field with an enquiry style of dissertation, for example, or to combine aspects from other formats. This implies that you have some choice. Your starting point should always be your course guidelines followed by discussions with your tutors. Whatever format you adopt you need to justify it in terms of your overall project aim. A critical and analytical assessment of your choices and your selected approach is part of demonstrating the skills associated with a Master's dissertation project.

A Secondary Research only approach is sometimes chosen by students even when there is a suggestion that Primary Research should be undertaken. It may be that ethical and other approvals are difficult to obtain or research participants hard to reach. A critical review with no Primary Research is a choice but it is then hard to demonstrate a full range of skills that will meet the expected learning outcomes. Avoiding the difficulties of Primary Research is not an easy option.

Flow and Balance

Word count is often a major concern for dissertation students. It can seem large and unmanageable but is in fact a scarce resource. To develop a convincing story effectively requires a clear flow and balance in your report structure. The word count needs to be carefully allocated to a set of chapters arranged in an appropriate sequence.

Logical Flow vs Chapter Sequence

Figure 5.3 shows how the key elements of a report might be presented in a structured way for certain types of investigation. It is clear that there is a flow that involves some parallel activities.

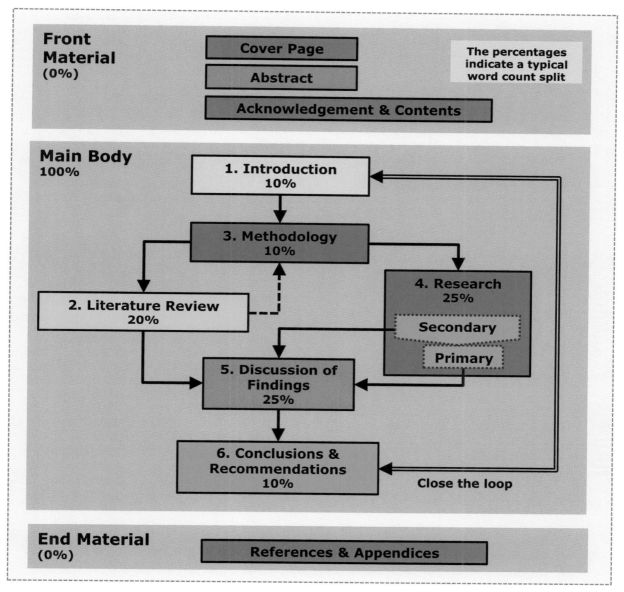

Figure 5.3 Dissertation Flow and Balance

A typical word count for each major section is shown as a percentage of the overall dissertation word count limit.

The numbering indicates the chapter sequencing in a typical dissertation report. Note this is not the same as the logical flow shown in the diagram.

The Introduction leads the main body by setting out the aim and objectives. Logically the Methodology chapter should then indicate how these might be achieved with some detail about the selection of written sources. This is followed by a split to parallel working on the Literature Review and Secondary Research sections.

However the Literature Review sets a context that provides information to guide the Methodology, raising questions about the most appropriate sequencing. Conventionally the Literature Review comes before the Methodology as indicated by the element/chapter numbering, but there needs to be some explanation of how its material was found. One solution is to open the Literature Review chapter with a comment that the Methodology chapter has a section describing how all written sources are identified and selected. This removes the conflict and optimises word count by avoiding repeated explanations.

The Discussion uses the evidence from the research sections combined with the Literature Review framework to draw specific observations and explanations. These are summarised in the final Conclusions and Recommendations chapter. This last section should refer back to the Introduction indicating the degree of completeness of the original intentions with explanations for any unfinished business.

Other dissertation formats can be similarly considered using this approach to create a logical flow.

Word Count Allocation

Allocating word count to the various elements of the dissertation is a way of managing the seemingly high number in the process of creating a balanced report. Typical percentages for word count are shown in the Figure 5.3 example with the assumption that only the body elements contribute. This is a suggested distribution; recommendations for your course may vary. Some courses will indicate that a percentage of marks will be allocated for the research elements, 35% is not unusual. This does not mean that Chapter 4 in Figure 5.3 should be increased to match this figure. After all, research includes aspects of the Methodology and Literature Review that will contribute.

A larger proportion in the Introduction implies over delivery. Some material should be moved to more appropriate sections that follow. Excess material in the Conclusions implies repetition of earlier material, a waste of resources. Only summarise the key findings. In general be efficient: say things succinctly, only once and in the most appropriate section.

Dissertation Element Relationships

The dissertation chapters are interdependent beyond basic flow considerations. An understanding of their relationships will enable the development of a well-structured report and the demonstration of the learning aims for your course.

Purpose and Findings

The Introduction, Conclusions and Abstract are closely related as shown in Figure 5.4.

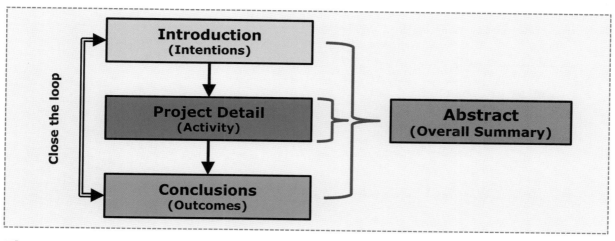

Figure 5.4   Purpose and Findings

The Introduction explains what the dissertation is about and what you intend to do. It makes sense to write this part in the future tense:

> *"the dissertation will investigate x by considering y ..."*

The Conclusion summarises the key outcomes by looking back at the work done and is normally written in the past tense:

> *"the investigation looked at x and found z ..."*

It should also refer back to the Introduction, closing the loop by identifying achieved objectives and giving explanations for those not completed.

The Abstract provides a brief but complete overview of the whole project. It should summarise the intentions, the principal activities and the key findings by combining elements from the Introduction and the Conclusions as well as some basic information about the project implementation. This information is only available at the end of the project and so the Abstract should be written last even though it should be placed at the front of the report.

Research Framework

The close relationship between the Literature Review, Methodology, research activity and the subsequent Discussion is shown in Figure 5.5.

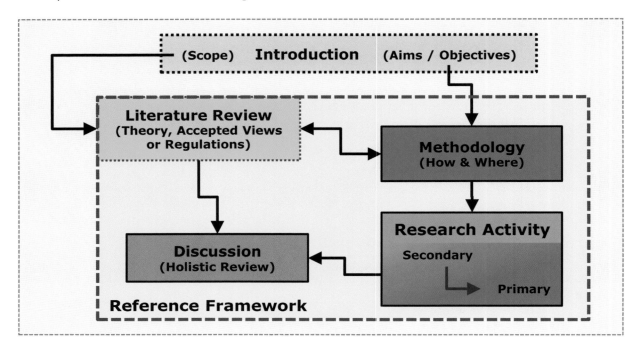

Figure 5.5   Research Framework

The scope of the investigation, defined in your Introduction. guides the Literature Review to create a reference framework based on relevant theories, schools of thought and applicable regulations.

The Methodology should show how the aim and objectives detailed in the Introduction can be achieved through a process of secondary and primary research. This includes an explanation of how Literature Review and Secondary Research sources are to be found and topics selected.

The Discussion should be an holistic review where all aspects of the research are considered in terms of the reference framework derived from the Literature Review. This enables the effectiveness of the Methodology to be assessed and your particular findings can be compared and contrasted with conventional thinking.

Discussion & Implications

In practice you may find that the outcomes are only in partial agreement with the expectations implied by the Literature Review reference framework. Figure 5.6 shows some possibilities:

- **Aligned:** These results fit within the reference framework
- **Complementary:** The findings are perhaps unexpected. They sit outside the framework
- **Non-aligned:** Some aspects of the framework do not apply to the investigation

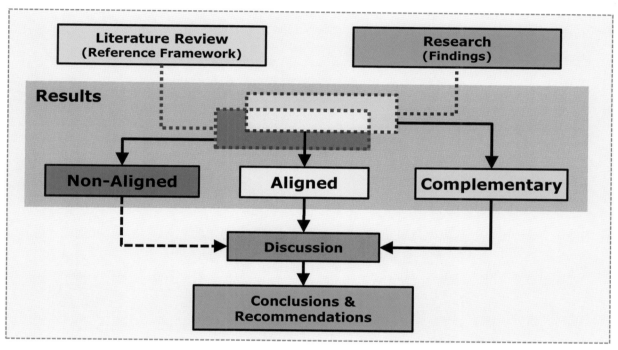

Figure 5.6   Discussion and Implications

Your particular area of investigation may not fit well with established theory; the field may be new or you may be looking at a special case situation. This will lead to aligned and complementary findings that are valid for discussion. Non-aligned aspects may be outside the scope of your investigation. The selected theory or consensus may be too broad or include partially related themes. Show a wide understanding by acknowledging this, perhaps by recognising opportunities for further work. Take care not to give too much space to these out of scope areas.

The Discussion should analyse the results and synthesise meaning by combining and building on the original data. Highlight and explain any unexpected findings. Use the Conclusion chapter to summarise the key points that adequately address your original intentions. Where information is limited you should explain why and offer suggestions to address the issues, possibly as a recommendation for further investigation.

References and Appendices

Figure 5.7 shows how references and appendices are identified and linked. References have two parts: a tag within the body text and an appendix list. The reference text tag is an abbreviation pointing to the full listing. There are a number of referencing conventions and you should follow the one specified for your course. The reference tag should correspond exactly to the alphabetical listing so that it is easy for the reader to find the details of the original work.

Appendices should be explicitly identified in the body text or they may be overlooked and ignored.

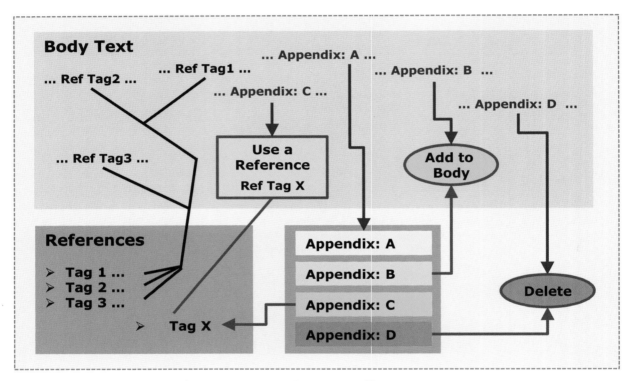

Figure 5.7   References and Appendices

You should only include appendices if there is a specified requirement or if they add particular value. Figure 5.7 shows how to deal with appendices that do not meet these criteria:

A: Valid appendices might include blank research questionnaires and examples of completed ones to show how your research data was actually collected. They are evidence of your activity and not fundamental to your narrative, but they should be clearly signalled in the text body.
B: Material should not be placed in an appendix to manage word count issues. Incorporate the key elements in the main report.
C: There is no need to reproduce established material such as theory. Use a reference instead.
D: You should not use appendices for material that is not directly related to your project aim and objectives no matter how hard you worked to collect it. These appendices should be deleted.

Dissertation Structure: Case Study   Supervisors to the Rescue

Master's students, Amy and Zoe shared a flat. Both were avid readers and found it easy to gather research material for their dissertations. Amy wrote up notes from her reading into her computer as she went along shuffling them into prepared sections that she had previously brainstormed for her supervisor. Her dissertation was taking shape nicely, her tutor was impressed.

Zoe also made extensive notes. She intended to write up from these piles of paper once she had enough material, but was unsure how she would know when this would be. She asked Amy for advice about the differences between Literature Review and Secondary Research. Her friend was pleased to help, explaining the Literature Review was an overview of all the different writings in the topic area; a sort of summary of all the prevailing opinions. Research was then about putting forward evidence to select the best fit to your particular research theme. "What about Primary Research?" asked Zoe. "Not necessary", was Amy's reply, "it's all in the Literature Review."

They returned to their flat after a night out to find it in a terrible state. They had been burgled. Amy's computer was missing as was her back-up USB stick. Zoe's notes were scattered all over the place. She was unable to piece together her reference lists from the torn pages. They both went tearfully to see their respective supervisors the next day.

Amy was lucky. Her supervisor had kept all their correspondence and review material. This was a good starting point for recovery. He was able to arrange a few days of deadline extension. Her final submission fell way short of the earlier promise as she did not have time to repeat all of the lost work, but she managed a reasonable pass.

Zoe had not made any previous effort to see her supervisor. When he saw her screwed up notes he realised she was on the wrong track. Her dissertation was not about assessing different schools of thought but about investigating an issue using desk and primary research. An extension was not justified; the burglary brought these problems to light, it did not cause them. By working long hours Zoe just passed, but her work was criticised for disjointed evidence and poor referencing.

Observations

- The students were on different courses with requirements that needed different approaches. It is folly to rely on the opinions of your inexperienced friends.

- Amy had provided her supervisor with review material that helped her restart and provided evidence of significant work. Her tutor considered the burglary to be an extreme personal circumstance. Zoe was in trouble without the burglary and so the supervisor could not argue for an extension, but was able to help her get on the right track.

- Amy nearly lost everything. Zoe did not have material that she could back-up. Take steps to protect your investment before it is too late. Back-up your work frequently.

- Zoe's extensive notes were too disjointed and vague. Gather information and make notes, but spend time organising and recording key themes, ideas and references. These can then be backed up to a secure system. Get organised.

Dissertation Structure: Good Practice

- **Understand requirements:** Follow the specified requirements. This demonstrates some of the learning aims and objectives set for the course.

- **Logical structure:** An explicit and logical structure based on a clear aim helps you present your arguments convincingly. Word count should be appropriately allocated so that you demonstrate the academic principles of a balanced report with a clear flow.

- **Use evidence:** Do not speculate or state unsupported opinions. Use evidence to support all arguments, conclusions and recommendations.

- **Succinct abstract:** One page is usually sufficient to outline the original intention, the key activities undertaken and the principal findings. Provide sufficient information for others in your field to decide if your work might be of use to them.

- **Dissertation type:** Use an appropriate dissertation format for your investigation that is in line with the requirements of your course.

- **Literature Review vs Secondary Research:** Make sure that the Literature Review is appropriate for the type of dissertation. It should cover the prevailing wisdom in your field: theory, accepted practice, regulations or schools of thought, to provide a clear framework to guide your investigation and to set a context for the discussion. Secondary Research is evidence derived from the work of others to support the investigation of your theme.

- **Methodology for written sources:** Explain how you found and selected material for both the Literature Review and Secondary Research. Identify any limitations in your approach.

- **References and Appendices:** Acknowledge all sources. Follow the set referencing protocol precisely. Use appendices for specific evidence of activity and not as a replacement for body text. Make sure they are clearly identified in the main report with their title or numbering.

- **Close the loop:** Your conclusions should address the stated aim and objectives with an explanation for any that are incomplete or missing.

Dissertation Structure: Common Issues

- **Poor focus:** It is common to have too much material rather than too little. Focus on the in scope areas. Appropriate out of scope topics should be identified, but only developed if the additional ideas fit with your objectives and you have enough space and time.

- **Appendix word dump:** It is hard to let go of material that you have worked on even if it does not fit in the main body. Do not dump this in an appendix or you may still incur word count penalties. Do not cover topics such as established theory, where a reference will suffice.

- **Repetition:** Do not over use material. Avoid squeezing the word count by making sure you say things only once in the most appropriate section.

- **Poor structure:** Abstracts that read like Introductions; Introductions with too much Secondary Research; Literature Review undeveloped and mixed up with Secondary Research and Discussion in the Conclusion are common issues. Plan your structure to guide you before you start your investigation and its write-up.

- **Missing evidence:** Often when writing the Results Discussion or Conclusion sections it is realised that evidence is missing. Find this if you can, but edit the material into the appropriate areas. Including new research in the latter chapters as an afterthought shows poor understanding of the required dissertation structure and weak organisational skills. If you do not have time to locate the missing material acknowledge this and discuss the implications.

- **Inaccurate referencing:** Students often fail to check that each reference tag has a unique entry in the reference listing, but many examiners will use this as a test of quality and research integrity. Appendices should also have pointers in the main body text.

- **Researcher bias:** Avoid the implication of researcher bias due to selectivity by explaining how information, Literature Review and Secondary Research material, as well as Primary Research data were found and evaluated. Identify any limitations implied by your methods.

- **Attention to detail:** Set requirements can be very prescriptive and detail is often overlooked. Are you using the required layout format, fonts and spacing? Are you following the right referencing protocol? Meeting set requirements is one of the skills tested.

Dissertation Structure: Key Actions

Decide on the most appropriate structure to meet the dissertation requirements. Then consider the implications of this for activity and write-up by preparing two working guidelines:

- **A detailed activity time line list:** Verify that this fits with your personal working style and commitments. Include some spare capacity and parallel working to meet the set deadline.

- **A template of write-up headings:** Expand the main headings that form the table of contents down to sub-sections and paragraphs. This is a topic list. Consider the required dissertation structure to arrange this list into an appropriately formatted placeholder document.

The first list gives you a work schedule for the investigation and should include elements of writing activity. The second provides placeholders for each piece of writing that can then be reviewed and edited into the final structured report. [Chapter 2: Write-up Considerations explains the use of templates and placeholder files.]

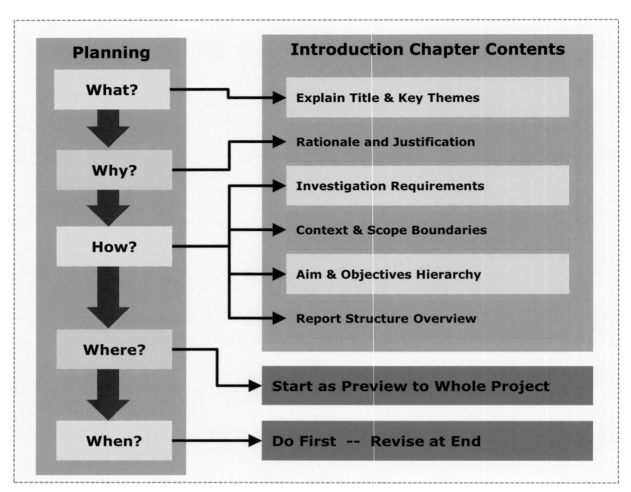

Figure 6.1   The Introduction – Purpose and Structure

The introduction defines and explains your whole project.

If a detailed draft is written at the outset it will provide a planning tool to keep your work focused and on track.

Chapter 6

The Introduction

The Introduction outlines your intentions, Figure 6.1, by stating what your project is about, why it is important and what you are trying to achieve. It is a development of your title to explain and justify your project theme followed by a statement of the research aim and objectives. It should also give a brief summary of the overall report structure. It should be written in the future tense to indicate how the work will proceed, letting the reader know what to expect.

If written at the outset as a detailed draft, your Introduction will provide a clear direction for your project. However dissertations evolve. The Introduction should be revised as the work concludes.

The Dissertation Theme

It is normal to drill deeply into your subject and so it is important to have a clear idea where the dissertation is going in terms of what is to be covered and what is to be left out. This will let you focus on your selected theme with sufficient depth to demonstrate the course learning outcomes.

It is important that your topic is relevant to your study area. You may be given indications of a particular direction as part of the programme requirements. Even so you will normally have a great deal of latitude to choose the specifics for consideration and your selected approach. An explanation of your theme and where it comes from is necessary as a prelude to any investigation. From an academic perspective you need to go further; not only to show relevance to your discipline but also to justify why your topic is appropriate for study. Explaining why it should be investigated and indicating possible uses for the findings will validate your dissertation project.

Explain the Title

Your title indicates the basic dissertation area. A short one has some merit, making discussion and communications with others, such as your supervisor, easier but it may not define your project precisely. Adding a subtitle will clarify the areas of interest, but it is likely that there will still be a number of possible interpretations or directions. A full explanation is needed.

The opening paragraph of the Introduction should expand your title into a detailed description of what your dissertation is about. It should explain the main idea and associated themes. Your earlier work on topic selection, such as brainstorming and mind mapping, with detail perhaps from your Proposal, will provide the necessary material. If you are required to fit your subject into a specific area set by your course you should indicate how your topic flows from this.

Starting with your title and sub-title to build up to a detailed overview will help you identify areas for investigation. When you are expressing interest in a particular aspect of a broad field it is sometimes helpful to clarify your intent at this stage by indicating areas that are definitely not part of your research. Setting the precise boundary between in and out of scope material can be reviewed as your project proceeds. It will be appropriate to reflect on these decisions towards the end of your project either in the Discussion or as a separate Reflections chapter if this is specified.

Rationale and Justification

Having explained what your dissertation is about it is usual to say where the idea came from and why it is important. You may have a personal interest or strong views about certain aspects and while this is reasonable it is not sufficient. Support your basic description of the subject with an indication of what has created the interest and some evidence of why it is important and relevant. The trigger for your theme can come from almost anywhere. It could be an observation or a reflection related to your studies, a report in the media or something someone said to you. Explain why this demanded attention and then provide some further evidence to show how the theme is significant in your study area. This will begin to set your ideas in a context so that its importance can then be understood.

At this stage avoid launching into extensive secondary research. It is sufficient to give a few indicative sources that provide an overview. Ideally these should cover more than one angle. From these you can develop your rationale, your reasons, for studying the subject in detail.

Be careful not to make assumptions about your reader's understanding of the topic. Your theme may have validity in many parts of the world and in a range of circumstances. You should be explicit in detailing the areas of interest in terms of sub-topics, geography, demographics or any other appropriate variables. It may seem like you are stating the obvious, but outlining these specifics will enable you to explain your research intentions clearly.

Before you proceed to the aim and objectives it is worth spending a little time reflecting on the implied investigation requirements and the in and out of scope boundaries that you are setting. These are useful checks to verify that your topic is relevant and that you have considered it sufficiently to create a justified and focused project. It is also a good moment to think about the practicality of what you are trying to achieve and whether it will hold your interest as you proceed.

Investigation Requirements

In your Introduction you are opening up a topic for investigation by justifying its relevance and importance. Detailed research can follow later once you have established just what it is that you want to know. At this stage it is likely that you will have more questions than answers. Considering these questions will help you clarify your investigation requirements.

Breaking your theme into its component parts in this way will identify a number of areas appropriate for consideration. Effectively you are identifying sub-topics that could be examined to give a full view of your subject. Most research themes are multidimensional and within the confines of your project you will have to define some limits to your detailed investigation. Identifying what you need to know is not the same as specifying how the information is to be found. This is research methodology and comes later. Here you are preparing for the investigation, introducing its requirements in broad terms so that a number of explicit research objectives can be established.

In and Out of Scope

Setting boundaries and defining a detailed context will help keep your dissertation sharp and on track. This can be done by considering in and out of scope aspects. Some things will be out due to restrictions of project approval and practical considerations. Interviewing a board of directors might be desirable in a business investigation, but impractical as they are unlikely to grant access.

You need to be realistic in what you will be able to do. You may feel that you are creating too many limitations for yourself, but later you can expand a narrow focus. It is extremely difficult to manage activity and cut down word count to produce a coherent report if your initial aim is too wide.

Identifying areas that are definitely in or out of scope is a good start. This will define the detailed context of your project, but do not be timid. The nuances of your investigation will come as you push the boundaries. Your effort should be in the focused area and not off at a tangent.

Explicit Intentions

Developing your understanding of the investigation requirements along with a consideration of the scope boundaries for your project will enable you to articulate an explicit aim. This is a statement of the overall dissertation intention. Making it explicit will give you a clear focus. A set of derived objectives organised in a logical sequence can then be used as guides for the whole project.

Aim or Principal Objective

A clear aim is like defining a destination. If it is vague you may be trying to follow more than one path. Once you have achieved your aim you know that the journey is finished. In practical terms there are degrees of completion. If you have not addressed the aim sufficiently this is a sure sign that more work is needed. Once past this point you will be in a position to wrap up the project, only doing more research if you have time to improve what you already have.

Say exactly what you are trying to do in unambiguous terms. You should not express a desire for an unrealistic outcome, but you should go beyond the simplistic and trivial. For example: a business student might be interested in why companies fail based on the following aim:

• Understanding how to avoid corporate catastrophes

This is a worthy aim but just too wide, too ambitious. Refocusing to look at the history:

• How companies responded to strategic disasters

runs the risk of being a descriptive saga and might not be sufficient to meet the dissertation learning objectives. In between, the research question:

- How can companies plan for strategic disasters?

is also wide ranging but has a lot of potential to address the requirements when scope boundaries are defined.

Typically your aim or research question will not be simple to answer. It will have a range of possibilities. Your consideration of in and out of scope areas will give focus. You can then develop a set of objectives that will lead to your goal.

Research Objectives

The research objectives are a set of steps that support your overall aim. They provide direction for your investigation. Addressing them enables you to demonstrate a wide range of skills.

Make sure each objective is valid. The acronym **SMART** provides a working checklist:

Specific: Each objective should focus on a single clearly stated topic
Measurable: Will you be able to gauge when it is complete?
Achievable: Is it really possible to do what you are proposing?
Realistic: Do you have the resources and contacts to do it?
Timely: Can you do it in the time you have available?

These will help you avoid vague or impossible intentions, but do not be shy about having stretching objectives in your list. You may not fully achieve all of them but in trying you will be able to demonstrate a range of skills and the learning intentions of the dissertation.

Progressive Objectives Hierarchy

Arranging your objectives in a progressive order will help you build your argument. Think of them as places you wish to visit on your research journey with a sequence that moves you efficiently towards your ultimate destination. The objectives are your way points; valid intermediate steps. They should be in a logical order so that each underpins the next in the sequence. It is not about doing the easy stuff first and the hard later, but it can work out like this. Any journey has a starting point and a reasonable first objective is to clarify this. Do not worry about stating what to you might seem obvious. You need to take your reader on the journey with you.

The next few objectives should then allow you to explore and develop your subject so that the basics of your aim might be achieved. Adding a last objective that goes a bit further is about challenging yourself. You will only know if it is possible once you are into your project.

The corporate catastrophe example above might have the following objectives:

- Understand and characterise corporate catastrophe scenarios
  - This is about knowledge and understanding and will guide the Literature Review.
- Identify contemporary examples of strategic disasters

- Examine company response to the identified malfunctions
  - These two are related but separated. They drive Secondary Research and doing them will show knowledge, understanding as well as critical and analytical skills.
- Investigate companies' awareness of the need for disaster planning
  - This has elements of Literature Review, Secondary and Primary Research that will demonstrate a wide range of skills.
- Review the process and management of disaster planning
  - This is research based and might be limited to a single company or industry as a case study to keep things manageable but will enable you to demonstrate the principles.
- Propose a strategic checklist and process for disaster planning
  - This is synthesis appropriate to the Discussion section and will show critical skills.

These objectives would need to be set in the context of stated boundaries: the detailed research might be restricted to a case study of a particular company or industry for instance. They flow from each other and are each single topics. The research elements are challenging objectives and it may be sensible to limit the focus depending on project circumstances and available contacts. A **SMART** review would help define the scope.

Clarity of Purpose

Having a clear aim, often expressed as a research question, and a set of supporting objectives in a structured order will give your project focus and direction. Writing a detailed draft of the Introduction at the outset will provide you with a high level overview that will have enough detail to guide project activity. Typically things will evolve and change and some revision may be required along the way, but the initial draft will give you a clear sense of purpose. Adding some detail about the main report sections will enhance the overview giving clarity to your project. Overall the Introduction will provide you with a set of topics and headings that will guide your activities and the write-up.

Introduce the Report Structure

Finish your Introduction with a summary of the dissertation structure giving a little detail outlining the purpose of each chapter. Note "*a little detail*". Keep this part brief. You can save word count by using a diagram or table. This overview removes the need to introduce each section individually. You will have flagged them so that they are then expected and positioned in the context of the whole report. This will save word count, makes it easier for the reader to follow your intentions and is a significant guide for you to keep your dissertation project and its report on track.

Word Count Allocation

In Chapter 5: Dissertation Structure it was suggested that 10% of the word count be allocated to the Introduction. Splitting this between the parts shown in Figure 6.1 leads to 170 words per section for a 10,000 word dissertation. A consideration of word count allocation in this way that also takes into account any set guidelines will help you keep your report balanced and succinct.

The Introduction: Case Study

Objective Led

Business study students following an HR specialisation were asked to focus their dissertations on changes in working practices. Prior to preparing a formal Proposal they were required to submit a title with a basic outline of their ideas along with their research objectives. These were then reviewed with their tutors before a Proposal was prepared and submitted for ethics and other approvals.

Joe wanted to investigate aspects of home working:

Initial Title: Benefits of Home Working
Initial Aim: Propose guidelines for good home working practice
Initial Objectives:

1. Describe types of work done at home
2. Identify benefits and issues of home working
3. Get employers' perspectives on home working
4. Get employees' perspectives on home working

Joe's supervisor advised that the all-encompassing nature of the project, looking at all types of home working, made it too big, too general. Also she pointed out that a more logical sequence to the objectives would be 1, 3, 4 followed by 2. The initial objectives would then naturally lead the review of benefits and issues. She suggested that redefining objective one to focus in a particular business area had the potential to make the dissertation more manageable.

A consideration of the investigation requirements identified further issues. Joe realised that finding reliable contacts for primary data would be difficult. However his parents and a number of their neighbours regularly worked from home. A chance remark by one indicating that home working was a lonely business gave Joe a new idea. He agreed a revised approach with his supervisor:

Title: Home Alone
Sub-Title: A consideration of the benefits and issues of home working

The sub-title was selected as the project aim.

The objectives were adapted and sequenced as a logical progression:

1. Describe types of work done at home
2. Characterise a cohort of home workers and use them as a case study group
3. Investigate the group's perceptions on the benefits and disadvantages of home working
4. Get their employers' perspectives on home working
5. Identify the general benefits and issues cited for home working
6. Propose guidelines for good practice for home working

Joe's activity was then objective led. He used his family and neighbours as an accessible research cohort. The group were all professional workers and so aspects of home working that centred on manufacturing were not developed beyond identification in the secondary research. He was able to create a framework with defined in and out of scope topics that focused on professional staff.

Getting access for employer perspectives proved to be difficult, but one neighbour was able to put Joe in touch with his HR director who responded to an emailed questionnaire. The last objective was too ambitious, but some areas of good practice were identified.

As a piece of research the topic was not fully explored or developed. However, it did follow a logical progression led by structured objectives that addressed the stated aim. Overall it allowed Joe to demonstrate the required skills and reflect on how, with better access to resources, the study could be enhanced.

The dissertation was received positively, getting a good mark.

Observations

- A very broad topic was reviewed in general terms and then narrowed to a particular area.

- The context and boundary conditions were based on practical research limitations.

- The objectives were positioned in a logical and progressive order to support the main aim.

- Stretching objectives were included and partially developed.

- The success of the project did not rely on the completion of the stretch objectives.

- The aim and objectives provided clear guidance for the project.

- Although some objectives were only partially completed, there was sufficient progress to demonstrate the required learning outcomes convincingly.

The Introduction: Good Practice

- **Set the scene:** A good Introduction will make it clear what the dissertation and its report are about, what the intentions are and the outline plan to achieve them. It explains the title indicating what is and what is not covered by the dissertation.

- **Justification:** It may be that the area is of particular interest to the student or mandated by the course requirements, but evidence should be used to validate the importance of the subject.

- **Relevance:** The fit and relevance to the course discipline area and the overall dissertation learning aims should be identified and explained.

- **Clear sense of direction:** A single major aim provides a clear and unambiguous sense of direction. Supporting this with a number of intermediate objectives gives structure to the work.

- **Logical hierarchy of objectives:** Simply stated objectives in a developing sequence leads to a coherent flow and shows good organisation. The objectives should be practical, but it is not unreasonable to have some that are ambitious. They may not be completely achieved, but will allow the principles of progressive research to be demonstrated.

- **Stretch objectives:** Objectives in a logical hierarchy allow you to develop your theme progressively. Stretch objectives at the end of the list facilitate extension work if circumstances are favourable. When squeezed by time or word count these will at least provide pointers to further work, letting you demonstrate a wider understanding.

- **Dissertation structure overview:** Introducing and positioning each report section briefly provides a framework for the whole dissertation. Each section is then anticipated and needs no further introduction. This saves word count.

The Introduction: Common Issues

- **Not following set requirements:** Make sure that your Introduction clearly indicates how you intend to follow the explicit requirements of your course.

- **Too much detail:** The Introduction should provide an indication of intent with only a little information to support this. Avoid launching into too much detail; this comes later.

- **Being assumptive:** Your reader may have no knowledge of your topic, help them along by providing explanations. Your initial objective might be to identify or explain the basics.

- **Confused aim and objectives:** Your aim is like a destination. If you have more than one then you have more than one dissertation. The objectives are intermediate points that should lead in a logical sequence to your end point. Make sure they are clear and realistic. The SMART framework is a useful tool for this.

- **Too simplistic:** The aim and objectives structure may be simple, but make sure you try to do something significant and worthwhile to demonstrate your capability.

- **Lacking relevance:** Provide some supporting observations and research to justify and explain why a detailed study would be worthwhile.

- **Over description of structure:** Chapter headings with a short explanation and identification of the relationships between the sections are all that are needed. A diagram or table makes the explanations easier and saves word count.

The Introduction: Key Actions

- **Review requirements:** Study the set guidelines for your dissertation to identify what needs to be in your Introduction. Adapt the following suggested actions to conform to these requirements.

- **Prepare for write-up:** Create paragraph headings with allocated word count for each part of the Introduction to guide your writing.

- **Clear intent:** Review your title, sub-title and aim or research question to be sure that they are clear and focused.

- **Objective progression:** Create a set of objectives that will address your aim or research question. Arrange them in a logical order. Confirm that they will enable you to achieve your goal and demonstrate the learning outcomes.

- **Write a full draft:** Prepare a full draft of your Introduction, not just a set of notes, before you do any other work. This will give you several benefits:

  - You will have a clear overview that will act as a guide to keep you on track.
  - You will be able to share this with your supervisor to get good early feedback.
  - It will get you into the habit of writing.
  - You will be aware of the required activity and its supporting report structure. You can then set up placeholders for all your written material in an appropriate sequence.
  - You will need to establish a process for recording references. This will serve the rest of your project.

- **Confirm Your Approach:** Review with your supervisor to confirm that you are heading in the right direction and that your approach will meet the university requirements.

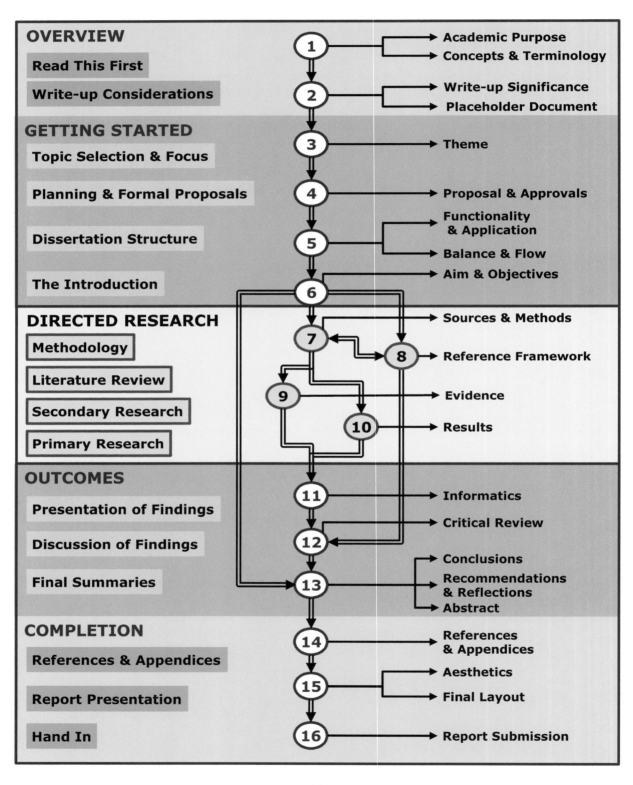

OVERVIEW

Read This First

Write-up Considerations

1 → Academic Purpose
→ Concepts & Terminology

2 → Write-up Significance
→ Placeholder Document

GETTING STARTED

Topic Selection & Focus

3 → Theme

Planning & Formal Proposals

4 → Proposal & Approvals

Dissertation Structure

5 → Functionality & Application
→ Balance & Flow

The Introduction

6 → Aim & Objectives

DIRECTED RESEARCH

Methodology

7 → Sources & Methods

Literature Review

8 → Reference Framework

Secondary Research

9 → Evidence

Primary Research

10 → Results

OUTCOMES

Presentation of Findings

11 → Informatics

Discussion of Findings

12 → Critical Review

Final Summaries

13 → Conclusions
→ Recommendations & Reflections
→ Abstract

COMPLETION

References & Appendices

14 → References & Appendices

Report Presentation

15 → Aesthetics
→ Final Layout

Hand In

16 → Report Submission

DIRECTED RESEARCH

The early planning, a Proposal, if one was required, and your submissions for project approval will all have required some basic research to justify your theme and to set a context for the investigation. These will have been developed in your Introduction. Once the dissertation has been defined and formally approved then the gathering of evidence can begin in earnest.

The process of research is defined by the Methodology and supported by an academic or reference framework detailed in the Literature Review. Secondary and Primary Research are then the implementation of the investigation plan. As shown in the flow diagram some parallel working will be appropriate and often necessary within the timescale allowed for the project.

Directed Research: Section Summary

Chapter 7   Methodology: Normally you have to outline possible research activities in the process of getting university project approval. When approved these methods must be fully developed into a practical operational plan. This is the Methodology. Logically this comes before the Literature Review and the research sections as it will include elements about finding written sources as well as the ways of engaging with research targets. However it is a common convention to place it after the Literature Review in the report write-up.

Chapter 8   Literature Review: As discussed in Chapter 5: Dissertation Structure, the Literature Review can have a variety of formats. These and its role to provide an academic or reference framework for the consideration of research evidence and findings are reviewed.

Chapter 9   Secondary Research: The reuse of material, originally gathered by others, is considered to show how evidence for your intended aim and objectives can be found.

Chapter 10   Primary Research: The process of carrying out original research to implement your stated Methodology is discussed.

In principle, desk research for the Literature Review and Secondary Research can start as soon as you are ready, but you should not do any Primary Research until formal approval is granted.

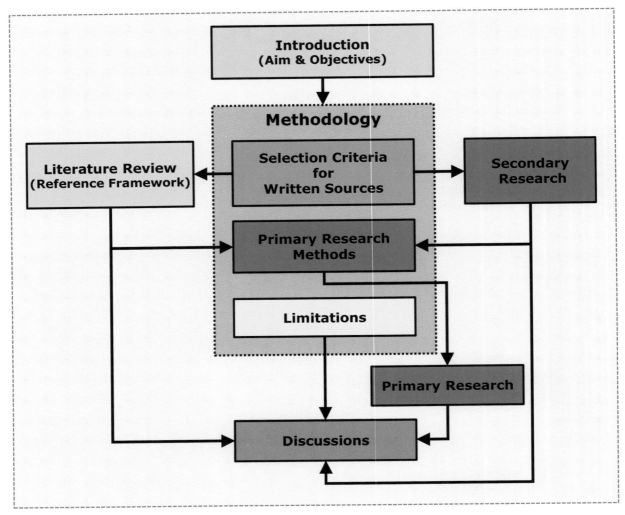

Figure 7.1   **Methodology Functions**

The principal elements to be covered in your Methodology chapter are:

- *The process for identifying and selecting written sources for desk research.*

- *The selection process, testing and implementation of primary research methods.*

- *A review of limitations with a consideration of their implications for the selected research methods.*

Chapter 7

Methodology

The aim and objectives detailed in your Introduction supported by the reference framework of the Literature Review define the research requirements for your investigation. The Methodology should be a critically assessed plan indicating how these are to be managed. It should cover all aspects of research including the selection of sources for the Literature Review and Secondary Research data as well as the processes to be used for Primary Research. Choices should be justified and any restrictions considered.

The Research Process

The Methodology, Figure 7.1, must support all elements of the research process. Desk research, the identification of sources written by others, will provide material for the Literature Review and Secondary Research. The nature of these and the relationship between them will depend in part on the type of investigation. Generally the Literature Review should set a context defining academic theory, accepted wisdom or regulations that relate to your topic area to create a framework against which the research findings can be discussed. Secondary Research is typically gathered evidence to support or clarify the ideas and topics implied in your Introduction.

The choice of material for this desk research should not be left to chance. Having a process for searching, identification and selection of these items will show academic skills and avoid any criticism of researcher bias. This is particularly significant for investigations based only on desk research. A well-defined process of identifying and selecting material might be the only way that you can demonstrate the requirements of a robust and academic Methodology. However, you might be able to augment this by discussing potential Primary Research ideas even if these are not an option for you.

Both types of desk research have an influence on the Primary Research. The Literature Review framework will suggest certain research processes as being more appropriate to address specific objectives. Secondary Research will cover a lot of what you want to know, but its reliability might be questioned. It could be out of date or a poor fit to your particular circumstances. It is also likely that there will be gaps. To avoid unnecessary repetition of work and a waste of word count Primary Research could be limited to the verification of key aspects and the collection of missing detail.

For Primary Research you should identify the specific information needed and a target person or group who can supply this. Use an appropriate method to find and question your targets so that they can be asked specific questions or engaged in discussion. Appropriate in this situation means a method that has been approved as well as being suitable for the task. Some objectives will imply different techniques and so it is likely that more than one process will be required. It is important that your earlier planning and approval requests anticipate these requirements.

Once gathered the research data will feed into the Discussion for consideration. To maintain the focus of your dissertation and to give it structure, arrange the research findings into common threads. Criteria identified in the Methodology along with the in and out of scope aspects from the Introduction can facilitate this.

Perfect or Pragmatic

The best research methods may not be the most practical for your project. Inevitably there will be choices. You have to be realistic in terms of your abilities, resources and time frame. Compromises will be necessary and need to be explained. You may have to be pragmatic using only sources and approaches that are readily accessible. You may also be restricted by a limited number of approved options. These methods may not be perfect but the best available to you.

Demonstrating the principle of good researching rather than having perfect findings is typically embodied in dissertation learning outcomes. Hence you must critically assess your choices and explain the trade-offs between the methods open to you. This is not the same as a detailed review of all research methods. Make sure you describe how and why you selected a particular approach. Where possible you should indicate how limitations can be overcome or their effect minimised. In your Conclusion you might also make recommendations to indicate how the research methodology might be improved if you had a wider choice of methods or more resources to implement them.

What, Where, How Approach

The Methodology needs to cover all aspects of your investigation from the selection of sources to processes for Primary Research. To get good answers it is necessary to ask appropriate questions:

- What is it that I wish to know?
  - Translate your aim and objectives into specific research requirements.

- Where can this information be found?
  - Consider all the sources available to you.

- Who can answer my questions?
  - Identify individuals and groups that can provide relevant information.

- How will I get to them?
  - Find ways to establish contact and to engage with your targets.

Questions like these are very broad and open ended, but they encourage you to stand back and consider the requirements carefully. Usually there will be a variety avenues open to you. This review will help you optimise your efforts.

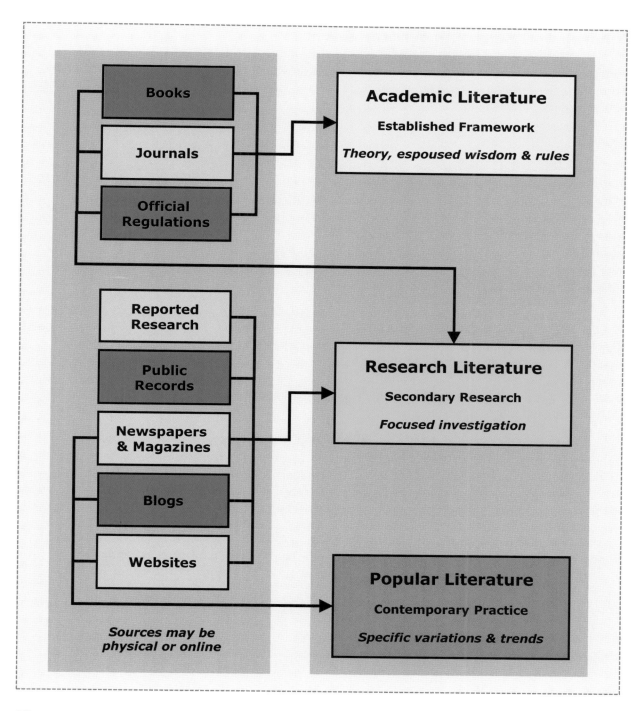

Figure 7.2   Written Source Categories

Finding and Selecting Written Sources

In the context of your dissertation, literature can be anything relevant to your theme written by others in any media form, be it book, journal or online. However not all source material carries the same weight or application.

Types of Written Source (Literature)

Figure 7.2 shows how different written source types might be used within a dissertation.

Academic literature is material with a high level of academic integrity in that it has been professionally checked. Text books and professional subject journals are the main sources. These are typically reviewed by a panel of experts; peer reviewed before publication to confirm their academic status. Theory tends to be well established. Research findings are typically based on well-defined and reliable methods. For rule based environments this area also includes official regulations: laws, policies and directives.

Research literature encompasses all forms of secondary material that might be used as evidence. Investigations by others, official statistics and public records usually have a well-defined method of acquisition and data presentation so that their suitability can be assessed. Aspects of popular media are also potential sources, but the reliability, accuracy and bias of this writing can vary considerably. At best, research material should be quite recent but much of it might be old and potentially out of date. You should consider the implications of provenance and age as part of your Methodology for source selection.

Popular literature covers just about anything else that is written. Its reliability and general applicability must always be suspect as the writer may be expressing a completely unsupported opinion. Its principal value is its timeliness. Popular sources provide a view of contemporary practice and thinking that can identify change and trend indicators and they are especially useful in identifying new paradigms, that is new or changed scenarios.

All three types of writing can contribute to a Literature Review, but academic literature will be the principal element providing the established theory, schools of thought or the governing regulations. The other two indicate potential variance or new situations that might be appropriate to your theme. Their academic limitation should be recognised. The expanded detail from research and popular literature will typically be used as evidence in the Secondary Research section. A small sample of this may also be used in the Introduction to highlight and justify the dissertation theme.

Identification and Selection of Written Sources

The index and table of contents and sometimes chapter summaries can be used to locate items of interest in books, magazines and journals. Online resources can typically be scanned by entering a search word or phrase. Finding things is straightforward if you know what you are looking for. To identify these search vectors use a process shown in Figure 7.3. From the dissertation theme brainstorm to create a list of topics, but focus your selection on areas that you have defined as being in scope. From these identify key words and phrases: single words and combinations, that can then be used to search for information.

This process will find material once the written source is located. Make use of libraries (not just the university facilities), archives, data bases and other stores of information, many of which are on line. Things are not always categorised the way you expect. If you are stuck ask your university library staff for help.

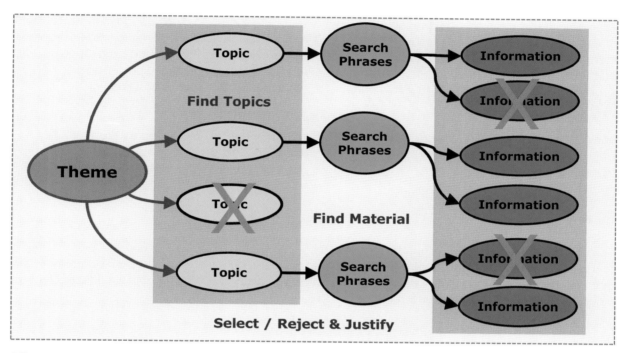

Figure 7.3   Finding and Selecting Written Sources

Each discipline has its own text books and professional journals which will provide you with information in appropriate categories. The process works for Literature Review and Secondary Research with sources actively selected and searched. You topic brainstorming will also sensitise you to spot relevant articles elsewhere but only if you are a regular reader of general publications, the trade press for your area and appropriate blogs. You need to be constantly on the lookout for source material.

Source Reliability

The outcome of your findings, the Discussion and Conclusions, will depend on the quality of your source data. Is it valid and can you rely on it? Aspects of relevance and fit to your specific investigation are discussed in more detail in the Literature Review and Secondary Research chapters that follow this one. In your Methodology you should outline a basic process for identification and selection as discussed above. In addition, demonstrate a critical assessment of reliability by considering the provenance and age of the any identified material.

Academic literature is the most reliable in terms of its original context, the situations in which the material was developed or collected. Theory tends to be accepted and well established. Research methods are considered robust. Regulations are definitive. However these do not make the material right in the context of your investigation. You may be considering a special case or new situation. What you can say is that this material is professional and able to provide a clear reference framework.

Various research sources, especially the popular press, may not be considered as thorough, but they may be the most valid indicators for your situation. You can deal with this lack of credibility by indicating that you will not rely on a single source. Instead, cross checks with several sources will provide supporting evidence.

Current vs History

The age of source material should be considered carefully. Ideas that have stood the test of time represent reliable theory or schools of thought that may still be valid. Your investigation may question this or at least identify a new or emerging trend away from the established ideas. The older material provides a good frame of reference.

Research reports, statistics and historical data can have a very limited shelf life. Some fields are very seasonal and cyclical. Fashion and popular culture are good examples. Evidence more than a few years old may no longer be relevant, things will have moved on. However some things seem to repeat once in every generation or business cycle so that aspects of the past inform the present. Hence old is not necessarily bad, new may not always be good. When discussing the selection of sources in your Methodology you should critically review the significance of timelines to your research area indicating how this aspect will be managed if data age is a significant factor.

The Importance of Record Keeping

Your methods of investigation should include aspects of documenting what you do. This has two dimensions: what was planned and what actually happened. Most of this will eventually come out in the description of the research activities and the findings, but a separate diary of your activities is an important record. It is useful evidence to show to your supervisor and will be of value if you experience any problems that need university intervention. On a more positive note the summary of activities helps put your work into perspective. It can provide guidance if you need to go back to redo or reconsider work in the light of other findings. It will provide a tool to help you with the results Discussion and any review of the overall dissertation process. Some institutions require a reflective element as part of the submitted work and your diary will be a source for this.

Another aspect of record keeping is source referencing. Do not wait until you have decided to include a particular piece from your literature searches before establishing its reference. As part of your Methodology set up systems to collate your notes and to record references as the material is gathered. This will save time and potential heartache later as you finalise your report.

Practical Primary Research Methods

There are only a few categories of Primary Research, but the nuances of how they are applied are vast giving you considerable opportunity for investigation. Resource and time restrictions will inevitably narrow the possibilities available for your dissertation. This is a practical reality, but it need not stop you demonstrating wide ranging research related skills. The important thing is to make effective use of your research evidence with each part playing its role in producing a convincing story.

Desk work will typically provide the bulk of your evidence. Primary Research is far more time consuming and difficult with the limited resources available to you. To make it effective in your overall project consider its application carefully. It is not realistic or sensible to repeat the work of others except to confirm secondary data that might be in doubt due to age or its collection in different circumstances. Where possible use Primary Research to cover the gaps so that you get a more complete picture.

Using more than one method will give you the opportunity to demonstrate a wider skill range. It is unlikely that all your objectives can be completely covered by a single approach and so planning to use several techniques will have benefits in terms of results and learning objectives.

Figure 7.4 provides an overview of some Primary Research categories. This is not an exhaustive list and the descriptions below are not extensive. The objective is to provide some insights into their usefulness, practicality and limitations. You should reflect on these practical considerations as you make your choices and justify them in your Methodology and also reflect on them in later Discussion or Conclusions sections.

Category	Type	Description
Non-Contact	Observation	Record of observed activity using tally sheets or check lists
	Image Analysis	Assessment of display, image or video content set against pre-set criteria
Indirect Contact	Mystery Shopping	Behaving as a customer or client to gain information
	Role Play	Insertion in a group for active participation by assuming a genuine role
Direct Contact	Self Selected Survey	A broadcast request for people with certain characteristics to participate in a survey
	Targeted and Guided Survey	Questionnaire sent to a specific group or individuals propositioned to answer questions
	Focus Group	A group invited to take part in a prompted and observed discussion
	Interview	One to one discussion with an individual
Experiments	Tests	Checking performance of people or processes
	Intervention	Changing a situation to observe outcomes

Figure 7.4   **Primary Research Categories**

Non-Contact

Any original research work that you undertake is Primary Research. It does not always involve contact with others although people may be involved. Non-contact research includes observations and the analysis of media forms, typically images, but other senses may be relevant in some fields.

Observations

A number of situations can be investigated by observing how they play out. For this to be effective you need to be close to the action, located where you can see clearly without interfering in any way. A video recording of the situation will allow you to play back the scene. Special permissions may be required and the approach must have university ethical approval.

Things can happen quickly and it is easy to miss detail. Overcome this problem by anticipating the critical aspects that you wish to observe. Tally sheets enable you to record the number of times a specific thing occurs: different types of vehicle passing in a given time for an urban transport study, for example. If things are more involved then detailed check lists can make the job easier. This may involve ticking off things as they happen or having a space to record detail under pre-prepared headings. Always be on the lookout for the unexpected and have a notebook where you can record additional observations. Do this as soon as possible while things are fresh in your mind.

Image Analysis

Image analysis involves looking at photographs, printed pages, paintings or other visuals to identify particular characteristics. These may include dynamic images, such as television, cinema or video streams. Here the process of research follows similar lines to real life observations. For static images including video stills, playback images that can be frozen, you have more time to capture the key points. Nevertheless it is good practice to anticipate requirements and prepare check lists or tally sheets as a way of systematic recording.

Some types of research will require aesthetic or subjective analysis that require interpretation by the viewer/researcher. For these the check list needs to describe how the image is to be considered. There needs to be a justified protocol to guide the assessment.

Indirect Contact

Indirect contact is an observation of situations where there may be interaction with others, but they are not being questioned explicitly for their knowledge or experiences. Their involvement may be necessary but almost incidental to the process being investigated. Types of engagement typified as mystery shopping and role plays fall into this category.

Mystery Shopping

In this form of investigation the researcher acts as a customer or client of an organisation following a particular scenario. The objective is to observe how the organisation handles particular situations. The word shopping should not be taken literally. The investigation could look at complaints handling, enquiry management, problem diagnosis and a host of other service interactions. Inevitably it will depend on the people involved and the limitations and issues related to this factor must be considered.

Mystery shopping is a common review process in many industries and staff are often advised to act normally if they suspect this is happening. This does not release you from social and ethical responsibility. You may need approval from the target organisation as well as from your university for this type of research and you should always respect the rights of the individuals involved.

Role Play Observation

In this methodology the researcher shadows participants or takes an active role in a situation. This enables close observation of activities and events. In a team scenario the researcher fits into a group which is likely to be aware that its activities are being watched. The first hand observations are generally realistic representations of practice, but you must consider that the regular players may modify their behaviour or processes to show you what they think you are looking for.

The active involvement may mean that there is little opportunity to note observations at the time. Recording your observations on an electronic device may be a solution if talking into it or filming does not distract you or the other participants. Delay can create memory issues, so always review the recordings and reflect on the activities as soon as possible after the events.

Direct Contact

In direct contact research methods the participants know that they are actively involved. The level of engagement can vary from anonymous surveys to being identified in one to one interviews.

Self-Selected Surveys

There are various ways to ask people to participate in a survey. Handing out forms to passers-by at particular locations and events, mail shots or leaflet drops and online questionnaires are examples. Ideally the survey should ask participants to qualify themselves as valid players and it is good practice to include some questions that will confirm this. The survey delivery route is fundamental to engaging with an appropriate cohort. The methodology should consider carefully how the targets are contacted to ensure effective connection and credible responses.

Targeted and Guided Surveys

Approaching people directly to ask them to participate is one way to ensure an appropriate sample group. The danger is researcher bias. Individuals may seem to fit a particular profile but without some early qualifying questions this cannot be guaranteed. Even then, leaving a survey form with one person for return later does not mean that they are the one who actually fills it in. To overcome this potential weakness, targeted participants could be guided through a series of questions with the researcher doing the writing. This has a disadvantage in that few people are willing to stand and respond to more than a few quick questions and so the survey depth may have to be limited.

Focus Groups

Surveys are useful vehicles for getting the answers to closed questions, but the richness of the data can be limited. Answers to open questions in a survey are very hard to interpret without some discussion. The use of focus groups is a way to address this. A selected group is assembled and a facilitator asks specific questions and guides the subsequent debate. They group is observed and comments noted.

The effectiveness of this approach is significantly dependant on the skills of the facilitator who can only keep the group focused if they know what is required. They must have a set of clear guidelines to steer the activity. They should not be active participants in the discussion and should not seek to influence the others beyond getting them to talk about the set questions and topics. They must have sufficient status to command authority and respect if they are to keep the discussions under control, but they must not be too authoritarian or managers of the participants. These aspects can be intimidating and may lead to forced or false discussions.

Capturing the consensus views and minority opinions is challenging, data can come thick and fast. Having several observers to each monitor a section of the group works well, especially if there is an established agenda. It is easier to then collate the separate logs after the meeting.

Interviews

Interviews can provide a rich seam of information that can easily get off track if not managed effectively. One way to do this is to have a structured interview where prepared questions are presented in turn. In fact sending some of these in advance as a briefing helps get the interviewee thinking in the right context. Make sure your contact knows that you will want to expand on the list in a face to face arrangement or you may find that you get a survey-like response and no meeting.

Overly structured interviews can be too formal and stilted. Always make room for side questions and digression from your list. A less structured approach is to start a discussion going with a few open questions. You then try to steer the conversation along your chosen lines. A way to do this and to verify what you have heard correctly is playback and review. At various points stop the conversation, explain what you have heard so far and get confirmation that this is correct. Then ask another question to move off again in your set direction. Always summarise at the end using a check list so that you do not misunderstand key points or miss out important topics.

In some cases the person interviewed is used to being in charge, a senior manager for example. The use of an agenda with check list questions helps keep you in control and the discussion on track.

Experimentation

Understanding the performance of devices, systems and processes typically involves a degree of experimentation. This approach is common practice in engineering and science but can also be applied in other disciplines. Cause and effect as well as other dependencies can be examined under different circumstances by varying input parameters. Experimentation is a valid methodology to investigate why things work the way they do or if they work at all in various circumstances.

Tests

Tests are about checking the performance of people, machines and processes under controlled circumstances. This can range from validating a software algorithm in an IT project to the measuring of the impact of a training regime in sports science. With test methodologies there is often an element of: "Did the idea work?" confirming that a performance metric has been achieved or changed significantly. However, many tests may fail to show a positive outcome, but they should not be rejected. The analysis of these "failures" is an important part of the investigation process. It is not just about finding the winning formula.

One challenge is to create sufficient separation between inputs, outputs and other related factors so that cause and effect can be reliably measured. Without this you are just measuring system variability in an arbitrary way. In some fields the range of responses to an input can be very large or spread across a long time period. These situations require extensive testing to capture a complete spectrum of possibilities and may not be feasible for a dissertation study.

Interventions

Interventions are similar to tests, but the focus is more on why or how something works. Variables are altered and outcomes observed so that the particular situation can be understood. This method is useful when the relationship between variables is less clear. It is not about achieving a specific goal, but about characterising the scenario under investigation.

Sometimes simple observations are insufficient to explain why things happen the way they do. Change and disruption are needed to show up what drives a particular situation. In business and urban planning fields, for example, changing the signage, the position of furniture, the lighting, even odours are interventions that may lead to a better understanding of flow as people move around a shopping mall, store or commercial buildings.

Interventions relate to behaviours and when people are involved your Methodology requires careful consideration of social, safety and ethical factors. It would not be feasible to conduct experiments like the ones suggested above without permission, even active sponsorship, of shopping centre, store or office management.

Research Method Feasibility

The limited dissertation timeline, university approval conditions and practical realities mean that you need to consider the feasibility of your chosen methodology. You must try to get it right first time. There will be little opportunity to repeat or replace a flawed element of your investigation.

Primary vs Secondary Research

Secondary research is a lot easier than primary. For a given amount of information it takes less organisation, the process is much easier to control and data can be acquired more quickly. However the information may not be sufficiently focused to your particular needs. In contrast

Primary Research is very involved and can take a lot of time, but it can be very specific, addressing exactly your target areas. The temptation is therefore to start primary investigations quickly, but you should make haste slowly.

Your Methodology should consider the timelines and interactions of the various research elements so that they are integrated to address your requirements. Information from Secondary Research can inform the requirements for Primary Research. The investigation of secondary sources is multidimensional. It can provide information for a wide range of topics.

Primary Research tends to be narrower in scope and so needs to be more carefully aimed. It is therefore a good idea to gather as much secondary information as quickly as possible. If this is done across a broad front, albeit at a shallow depth, the preparation for Primary Research can be enhanced but timely. Additional Secondary Research can then be gathered while the primary methods are under way.

Ethical Considerations and Formal Approval

There is a degree of corporate social responsibility in dissertation activities. You need to abide by the formal project approvals from your university and should not commence Primary Research until these are given. It is a good idea to critically review the ethical and approval dimensions of your research as part of your Methodology to consider implications and limitations.

Obtaining approval does not mean that you have no further responsibilities. Typically your investigations will involve people and organisations. You must be aware of individual sensitivities. Protect the rights, identities and confidences of those whom you observe or engage with unless they have given you explicit permission to do otherwise. Wherever possible thank people and organisations for their help.

You may also observe or obtain commercially sensitive information about organisations. While it may seem that you obtained data that is in the public domain, your university may have provided you with privileged access through their library and other systems. As a representative of the university you need to consider how such information should be used so that embarrassment or even legal jeopardy are to be avoided for all the parties involved.

Justify Choice vs Alternatives

Be careful not to describe an arbitrary range of general research methods. A dissertation is not an essay about the relative merits of different approaches. The Methodology section is about how you intend to find what you want to know. You should indicate the various ways that individually and together they will enable you do this.

Review the merits of the alternatives, considering their fit, effectiveness and feasibility for your situation. Reject unfeasible methods and explain why. Be explicit in identifying the routes you actually used with a justification for your selection. This requires planning and review. You may try one approach only to find that it needs to be modified or replaced. Your write-up should reflect on what you wanted to do and what you actually did. The plan goes in the Methodology section and the explanation and review should be in the Discussion.

Explain Limitations

All research methods have some drawbacks. In your dissertation you will have additional restraints imposed by project approvals and the difficulties of implementation. Ideally you want to achieve your research goals completely, but you should keep in mind that satisfying of the learning aims and grading criteria are more significant. Typically you will be judged on your academic approach to the investigation not just on the quality of your results.

Critically assessing the various methods available to you, identifying their limitations, not generally but with respect to your project, and reviewing how these issues were mitigated gives you ample opportunity to demonstrate the required skills. You need to be prepared to trade the certainty and completeness of research data for the demonstration of competence in a research context.

It is not unreasonable to have some stretch objectives. You might not achieve them, but your explanation of the plan to try and the outcomes of the attempt will help you present a broader picture.

Trial Runs

Once a Primary Research method has been chosen you need to consider how it will play out in practice. The preparation of questionnaires and guiding templates for observations and interviews is discussed in Chapter 2: Write-up Considerations. In the Methodology your process for developing these research tools and verifying their effectiveness should be discussed.

A typical test approach is to have a trial run or role play session where friendly assistants attempt to fill in your forms or answer your questions as if they were real participants. It is helpful if they have some knowledge of your subject area but only enough to understand what you are asking. It can be particularly illuminating if you ask them to be as awkward as possible. You want your method to be robust with no confusion about your questions or procedures. If your friends are unable to make a hash of it then the real contributors will probably manage fine giving you reliable responses.

When you are confident in your forms and templates it is a good idea to review them with your supervisor. In fact some universities insist that all questionnaires are vetted prior to public use.

Write-up of Research Methods

Your dissertation write-up should clearly differentiate between intentions, choices and actual methods used. It is reasonable that the planning part is an overview, but the implementation and outcomes need to be detailed. Some of this tends to happen naturally. The collation of secondary material into themes and its referencing provides evidence of activity, but you need to explain the process of getting to this point. Likewise for primary methods: questionnaires, checklists and the structured presentation of findings illustrate your methods, but you should also describe the detail of your research process preparation. Using appendices with examples of the prepared templates provides appropriate evidence especially if completed examples are also presented.

Record Keeping and Record Creation

A lot of the Methodology write-up can be done before the results come in. Anticipating findings and how they might be presented is an effective planning tool that can help avoid problems of missing data. For desk research your initial search topics provide a framework, but new and revised threads will emerge. Creating placeholder documents in which this material is recorded can give an effective overview to consider scale and scope. It is easier to see the relationships of the headings in terms of fit and flow before they are lost in the volume of added data.

For Primary Research the process of data acquisition and presentation can both be tested. Reviews of templates, check lists and questionnaires with trial runs provide the collection preparation. Using dummy data enables you to consider how it should then be presented.

Write-up forces you to articulate detail, moving from vague ideas to concrete expression. This is particularly good for the considerations of feasibility and method limitations. Understanding barriers and potential problems clearly before events will help you identify solutions before the harsh realities of the situation become pressured.

Alongside the recording of material and results you should also keep a diary of your activities with observations about the project implementation, especially its flow and issues. This will be a useful tool as your write-up progresses to other dissertation sections where you will need to review outcomes in the light of the method selection and the research intentions.

Methodology: Case Studies

Disconnected

Ting was on a Business Master's course in the UK. For her dissertation she was required to review a company that was a UK household name and to investigate a strategic option for it. She was from China but had visited London several times with her family. Shopping trips with her mother had given her some familiarity with western brands and she selected a major high street clothing retailer for her study.

Information from her mother, comments from her UK friends and the business sections in the general press implied that the company was falling behind on what was once a dominant presence. Ting's proposal indicated that she would review the company's market position, identify strategic forces and then outline a strategy to give it a new sense of direction. Her plan for the Literature Review was to search the business press. She did not indicate any need to consider theory or conventional thinking related to retail business management. For Primary Research she intended to survey the company's senior management although what she would ask them and how this related to her aim was not clear.

Her supervisor pointed out that the project plan was very broad and weak on specific detail as well as being unrealistic in terms of senior management access. Despite this Ting was confident and indicated that she already had some contacts.

In the end her report relied heavily on a published business review of the company that was over eight years old. She used its strategy suggestions, paraphrasing recommendations that had long ago been implemented by the company. Her Primary Research was based on a questionnaire. This was completed by a store supervisor who was her mother's friend and by several student colleagues who had weekend jobs with the company. Although she met with her supervisor she did not prepare for the meetings or share her plans beyond the original brief outline.

Her dissertation received a very low, fail, mark. Feedback indicated that it was naïve in concept with an unrealistic and inappropriate Methodology. Her research was considered unduly derivative without any theoretical underpinning. Overall it lacked critical review.

Breathless Ambition

Nadia was in a cohort of physiology students who were asked to undertake practical investigations related to exercise and health. For her project she asked volunteers to ride on an exercise machine while their heart rate and blood pressure were monitored. Her dissertation plan was to link heart performance under stress to information about the participant's lifestyle and exercise history. She intended to use a questionnaire to gather this information as part of her pre-screening of the volunteers. It was soon clear to her that the aim was too ambitious. For one thing getting enough volunteers and conducting the tests in the time available was not realistic. She asked her supervisor for advice.

Nadia's supervisor suggested she continue since the test activity met the course requirements but to revise her aim with regard to the results. She decided to reframe the project as if it were part of a much larger trial where she would not be expected to reach any overall conclusions about her own test data. Her focus then was to ensure that her part produced reliable evidence suitable for a larger study. Nadia changed her aim to the investigation of the issues surrounding clinical trials related to exercise stress testing. The difficulties associated with this type of experimental research actually created a subject for her study. She reviewed the specifics of medical testing protocols and associated ethics, health and safety, patient understanding and permissions as well as the practical issues of finding and selecting participants.

She was able to demonstrate a wide range of skills including knowledge and understanding of medical testing using exercise experiments. Before doing any of the tests or issuing questionnaires she worked with a group of student colleagues to trial the procedures and questions. Her dissertation was praised for its critical review of the issues associated with this type of Methodology based on clear desk research and the evidence from practical experience.

Observations

- Both students underestimated the magnitude of their proposed projects. In particular their initial ideas were unrealistic. Ting's Methodology required access to senior management that was not likely to happen. Nadia needed many more participants than she was likely to find with the resources at her disposal.

- Nadia made good use of her supervisor to develop a workable idea based on his comments and turned her difficulties into an opportunity to demonstrate research principles.

- Ting had not really understood some of the academic requirements. Perhaps the terminology was unfamiliar to her or it might have been a cultural thing where reporting "expert" opinion was more important than independent thinking. For some reason she had not identified with the expert who was her supervisor.

- In both cases it was not about the quantity of evidence, or even its quality, but the critical evaluation of the processes involved to get it.

Methodology: Good Practice

- **Identify alternatives:** Review different approaches to achieving your objectives.

- **Justification:** Critically assess your choices and give reasons for your selected methods. Be explicit with the details and show that the approach is derived from the implications of your aim and objectives.

- **Limitations and trade-offs:** Identify the compromises in your methods and explain any steps that might be taken to minimise these.

- **Reality:** Describe your proposed methods in detail but when presenting findings and results state what was actually done. Differences can then be reviewed in your Discussion section.

- **A scalable approach:** Your methods must be realistic. They do not have to be perfect. Demonstrate valid principles that could be expanded if you had the time and/or the resources. You might only interview five people, but you could indicate that ideally you could talk to fifty using the same approach.

- **Literature selection criteria:** A good Methodology covers all research aspects. It is not just about the Primary Research. Explain how your Literature Review and Secondary Research sources were found, how some material was selected and the criteria used for rejecting others.

- **Selecting participants:** Access to research participants can be difficult. Demonstrate your understanding of this aspect by explaining how targets were identified and approached. Critically review any compromises or pragmatic choices that you had to make.

Methodology: Common Issues

- **Describing research theory:** Your Methodology should not be an essay about research theory. Avoid broad descriptions of alternative approaches. Focus on what you actually did by identifying the relevant choices open to you and how your specific method was chosen.

- **Assumptive approach:** Do not jump to a single research approach without justification. Show that a selected method is appropriate to your aim and each of the objectives.

- **Ignoring alternatives:** Make sure you identify alternatives and trade-offs. Critically assess your choices giving weight to both practical and academic considerations.

- **Proposal lock-in:** Your initial proposal or plans may have indicated a particular approach. You may find that an alternative method is more appropriate. Be prepared to change from the original ideas, but explain and justify your selection. Make sure you have the necessary approval for the revised method. (This is much easier if your original Proposal and approval requests included a number of options.)

- **Approval issues:** Failure to follow approval guidelines may disqualify your dissertation. Typically approvals are requested at the start of the dissertation process and may be part of your initial Proposal. Make sure you follow the set guidelines. If your plans change you may need to get additional approval. If in doubt discuss the implications with your supervisor.

- **Poor sample choices:** Do not assume that the available secondary material and primary targets are completely appropriate to your stated aim and objectives. Sometimes you have to adopt a pragmatic approach and use what information and sources that you can get. Critically assess your selection criteria, identify limitations and where possible minimise their impact.

- **Wishful thinking:** You may write a detailed methodology to support an intended plan, but then find that circumstances force a different approach. Submissions have been made with extensive information about primary research when the work was actually based only on secondary material. Make sure you say what you intended and what you actually did.

Methodology: Key Actions

- **Preparation:** Will your proposed methods address your aim and objectives? Ask yourself:
  - What do I want to know?
  - Who has or where is this information?
  - How can I get it?

- **Desk research:**
  - Prepare a method for finding and selecting material based on a structured list of in scope topics related to your aim and objectives.
  - Make sure you understand the differences and relationships between a Literature Review and Secondary Research for your type of investigative approach.
  - Set up appropriate placeholders for your material as you gather it and a system for recording source references.

- **Primary research:**
  - Do you really need to do it? Identify what needs to be confirmed and what must be found as new. Check that the information is not already available from secondary sources.
  - Compare potential methods by breaking each into its component parts: what, who, how, where and when. Compare relative merits perhaps using a table. An approach like this facilitates a critical review of alternative methods.
  - Give details of your research targets and identify ways to approach them with reasons why they should help you by participating.
  - Run trials and use dummy data to test your methodology and its reporting before going live.

- **Feasibility and realism:** Stop and reflect on your proposed methods:
  - Are they practical?
  - What are the limitations and barriers?
  - What is the back-up plan if things do not work out?

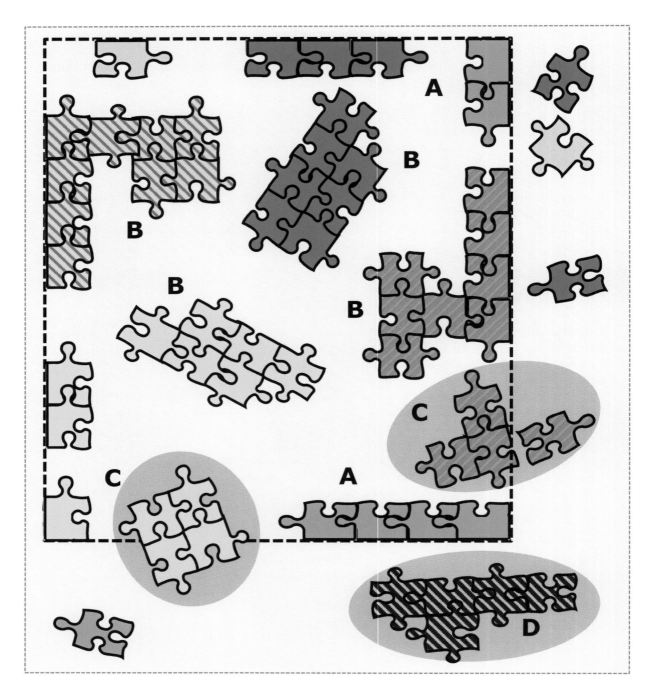

Figure 8.1   Literature Review Concepts

Chapter 8

Literature Review

The contribution of the Literature Review to the overall dissertation was introduced in Chapter 5: Dissertation Structure. This showed that its role and specific aspects will depend on the type of dissertation being followed. However there are some common features that separate it conceptually from other types of desk research. A dissertation report is a bit like doing a jigsaw. You are basically trying to complete a picture by putting pieces together using a number of different processes as shown in Figure 8.1. The Literature Review provides several functions:

A: It can be like the edges of the jigsaw creating a reference framework: an academic or rule based context that surrounds your area of interest.

B: Within it will be major blocks that are the theory or aspects of espoused wisdom related to your enquiry. Alternatively, where there is no specific theory, the major zones of pattern and colour are like different schools of thought, related but different ideas about the way things might be viewed. In controlled environments laws and regulations specify how things are supposed to happen.

C: The edges and recognisable blocks provide anchor points for your research, providing a framework against which you can align your findings, linking ideas together to form the big picture.

D: Unlike a jigsaw, it is possible that your picture lies outside the obvious boundary, but the Literature Review framework and its contained themes will still create a basis for discussion and comparison.

Creating a Framework

As a framework the Literature Review supports your dissertation in a number of ways:

- **Accepted theory:** Many disciplines are underpinned by established theory. You should identify the theoretical elements that are relevant to your dissertation themes. It is not necessary to reproduce the theory in detail, a reference is sufficient, but it should not be generic. Highlight any particular aspects of the theory that are critical to your ideas.

- **Espoused wisdom:** Formal theory does not exist for all disciplines, but the academic literature will provide commonly accepted opinions that are considered to be the way things work in your topic area. It is possible, especially in new and developing fields that the established view is open to challenge, but you will have a point of reference for any new findings or approaches.

- **Schools of thought:** Sometimes there are a number of different academic views. Typically they are all correct, each in a particular set of circumstances. You will need to choose the most appropriate ones for your investigation. This may not be perfect. Justifying your choices and critically assessing their significance is one of the ways that you can demonstrate analytical skills.

- **Rules and regulations:** In some environments the way things are supposed to happen is not based explicitly on theory or espoused wisdom but on official directives or legal requirements.

- **Starting points:** The Literature Review provides an overview of established ideas that you can accept as a valid starting points for your detailed investigation.

Combined, these provide a framework against which the dissertation can be developed and findings discussed. Lack of information may indicate that the topic has not been thoroughly investigated before, but often parallel fields can provide an outline for comparison.

Theory and Espoused Wisdom

Theory and accepted wisdom may be formally expressed as statements about how things work, as a set of rules or details of cause and expected effects. In some fields they are described as models and are often represented as diagrams. These may show accepted relationships, information flows as well as activity and process interactions. Identifying a relevant theory may not be sufficient; you will need to show how and where it is appropriate.

Consider an investigation of health and safety in the workplace where one of the themes is failure to use protective clothing. Motivation might be considered as a key factor with Maslow's Hierarchy of Needs identified as significant theory. Stating this is not enough, its application needs to be explained. Some students resolve this by describing the general theory in detail, perhaps presenting the standardised triangle diagram showing Maslow's need levels ranging from survival to self-actualisation. This uses a lot of word count and adds no value. Putting the theory description into an appendix might address the word count issue, but this is an unacceptable word dump. A reference is sufficient for well-known theory, but its relevance would still not be clear.

Better would be a recognition that health and safety relates to the first two Maslow levels: survival and comfort. This creates a more focused context for investigation. User awareness of danger could then be contrasted with their concern for comfortable work wear. This aspect of a critically considered theory would then be part of a valid framework for the investigation and discussions.

A review of text books relating to human resources would identify some themes in this example. A common view might have been that staff should be told what to wear in certain circumstances and disciplined in some way if they did not. This command and control view is either espoused wisdom or a statement of regulations indicating the way things are supposed to work. It can be used to guide the investigation perhaps by considering people's attitudes and responses to the imposed rules.

The theory, espoused wisdom and legislation provide a guide for the investigation and a framework for a critical review of the findings. The important thing is to identify theory, academic opinion or regulations relevant to your project. Drill into these with sufficient depth to find those aspects that support your stated aim and objectives.

Regulatory Frameworks

In some fields the way things are supposed to work is defined by a rule based system. These rules may be set by laws, regulations and policies that are mandated as working guidelines. Over time these get incorporated into procedures to form the operating practice for any given situation.

The original rules are analogous to the theory and the procedures similar to espoused wisdom, but the source material may not be academic. Nevertheless it is appropriate for the Literature Review. It will be found in official papers from government departments and accredited institutions. The operating practice will be found in semi-official handbooks and guidelines as well as in policy documents within organisations.

You may find academic work that discusses the rationale for the regulatory framework and its effect or other aspects. This material is secondary, describing situations related to the original official requirements. It could be used along with more general material as sources for Secondary Research since they are describing why the regulations were created and their impact instead of detailing the rules themselves. There is often a fine line between Literature Review and Secondary Research. You will demonstrate academic skills by differentiating between the two.

Schools of Thought

Some fields are characterised by a range of viewpoints. As an illustration, consider how tea is made around the world: hot water is poured over dried leaves – simple. Not so. In UK the water must be boiling, but in many countries you are given a cup of hot but not boiling water and a bag of leaves to dunk. Do you put in milk, first or last? Some prefer lemon. Making the perfect cuppa has a lot of regional variations and the **experts** will argue forever. None is wrong; these are all schools of thought, valid in specific circumstances each with their own disciples.

You may not have room in your literature review to present all variations. Pick out those that best suit your purpose, but do not be too narrow. Indicate the existence of other viewpoints but only in outline. Justify your selection, demonstrating reasoned judgement by explaining why a particular set was chosen. This could also be considered as part of your Discussion section so that your findings can be reviewed against a critically assessed framework. Digressing to discuss a variety of opinions in detail can confuse your presentation and squeeze out more significant material. An overview or summary list of other views is a reasonable approach perhaps in a table to save word count.

A Comparative Framework

Your Literature Review will become a multidimensional framework highlighting normal or expected behaviour in stated situations. As such it will provide both a guide for the investigative work and a set of reference points for the Discussion. It is therefore a good idea to group your material into topic categories that align with the main themes related to your aim and objectives.

Sometimes the theory, espoused wisdom or regulations contradict the indicated themes. Here your findings may lie outside the established framework which then acts as a mirror for an effective investigation and allows discussion based on the differences. A Literature Review structured in this way will provided a framework for the compare and contrast discussions.

You may also find ideas that do not match with your initial thinking. This indicates potential for further work or provides an opportunity for a reflective review of the dissertation process. Do not be too hasty to discard marginal material. Save this separately in case you need it later. As your project progresses you may want to reassess in and out of scope areas particularly when discussing your findings.

Qualifying Material for Literature Review

Your dissertation will need to explain how written sources are identified and selected. Putting this in your Methodology section as discussed in Chapter 7: Methodology is logical since the process is similar for several areas of your activity and only needs to be described once. However to be valid for the Literature Review, material needs to meet some specific requirements.

For ideas to be specified as relevant theory and for academic opinions to be counted as espoused wisdom they need to be accepted by a wide segment of the professional community. In the main, Literature Review material will be found in subject text books and professional journals that collate and summarise validated research activity. Typically these publications have a detailed review process before material is accepted. Ideas developed from research and observation will have been debated and critically analysed. The concepts are tested and refined. Unless the field is new or changing very rapidly it is likely that these sources will be found spanning a period of many years.

Initial ideas may be announced in contemporary media and examined, that is tested for accuracy and relevance, in research journals. Typically these publications are too early in the formulation process for this material to be considered as appropriate for a Literature Review. At this stage they are Secondary Research, but they may contain their own Literature Reviews which are potential sources or references to appropriate material.

Professional Sources

It is not necessary and often difficult to find the original publication for accepted theory. Typically you will find it in current text books. Academic text books are normally subject to significant peer review. The work is considered and approved by a number of established academic reviewers. Text books are often co-written by several authors with established reputations. In addition there is usually a significant audit trail, a list of references and notes that establish the provenance of the material. Similar safeguards apply to professional journals. Publication in these will be subject to scrutiny by subject area review panels made up of established professionals.

You should not rely on a single source. Try to find references from different authors, publishers or institutes. If these are well separated it is likely that their material will have come by different routes from the original theory source. This will give you more confidence that it is valid. Espoused wisdom is a little more difficult and you are likely to find wider variations. Even so you should consider publications and authors with established reputations. Finding more than one independent source gives credence to the stated views.

If you are unsure about a source discuss its suitability with the university library staff or with your tutors.

Identifying Key Themes

It is not possible to cover all areas of knowledge about your topic within your word count limit. You will need to focus. Develop your Literature Review by presenting theory and related views about the specific themes aligned to your main aim and detailed objectives. This gives structure to the section and will aid the later Discussion of findings.

Brainstorming and mind mapping techniques are good ways to identify relevant themes. Be careful not to start with too narrow a focus. Ideas from associated fields may provide valid comparisons. For example a student considering people movement across continents may consider road, rail or aviation themes but then be stuck in trying to identify appropriate theory. Recognising that they are all forms of transport might lead to a more general approach. Lateral thinking will also open avenues for consideration. A review of timelines leads to historical considerations and asking why people are travelling will identify a range of areas from vacations to economic migration. Sometimes to see things clearly you need to change your position and perspective.

Some findings will be clearly in scope while other are too far out. Reserve judgement on intermediate material; you may want to adjust your boundaries as your work progresses. This is one reason why it is important to write detailed notes and draft material as you go along allowing time for a focused edit later.

Literature Review vs Secondary Research

The word literature implies anything recorded, but a Literature Review is a particular selection from this well of information. It serves a number of specific purposes as described above with the focus being on how things are supposed to work in your chosen area. As such it has to be accepted by the professional community either as stated theory, articulated viewpoints or mandated policies. This does not mean that it is correct in every circumstance or that there is only one position. Identifying an appropriate consensus will provide a reference framework for your discussion.

In the context of your project, Secondary Research is material gathered by others relating to your selected themes. It is material that you might borrow, with appropriate acknowledgement, to support your argument. However it was originally gathered for a different purpose and its relevance, fit and reliability to your application should always be questioned. Useful material can come from a wide variety of sources some of which might not be particularly robust academically.

For example a source may have a research method showing considerable bias, but with appropriate cautions it may still be usable.

Theory vs Evidence

A consideration of your aim and objectives will lead to a set of themes for your searches. As you use these to look at various sources you will find a wide range of material that spans contemporary viewpoints, secondary research, theory or accepted academic wisdom and, if appropriate, rules and regulations. You should be ready for this, recording your selections in prepared files and folders under appropriate headings. In particular you should separate theory from evidence. Sources that indicate theory or espoused wisdom should go in your Literature Review file and elements of evidence in a Secondary Research file.

It is too simplistic to consider that everything in academic text books and certain professional journals is going to relate to your Literature Review. These will typically contain worked examples, case studies and reports of research findings that support the publication's purpose, but these are not Literature Review material. You should also be careful about using them as research evidence. This material is often selected and adapted for specific purposes and may be incomplete or an amalgam of several original pieces.

You should also be careful about reproducing the theory elements from these publications without careful consideration. Just because something carries a title: "Theory of xx", does not make it so. The authors may be extrapolating from other material to make points relevant to their field. Review the selected extracts and whenever possible find other sources with similar aspects so that you can effectively separate theory from evidence and opinion.

Conflicts and Alternatives

Sometimes there seems to be no academic consensus for your subject: not just diverging schools of thought but actual disagreements. Different circumstances can lead to contradictions and academic opinions may present a range of alternatives. A key point to consider is that any theory or espoused wisdom is likely to be considered correct or valid in a specific range of circumstances, but these may not fit your situation.

This is confusing, but it does give you the opportunity to demonstrate your cognitive skills by showing your thinking and reasoning processes as you choose the most appropriate for your purpose. You should select, with stated justification, Literature Review material that best matches your project and its specific goals. The fit may not be perfect, but this will give you a starting point for your investigations and subsequent discussions.

It is always possible that you are looking at something that has not been considered before or in a focused area that might be an exception to the established norms. In these circumstances you may not be able to find theory that comes even close to your requirements. This conflict is both a challenge and an opportunity. The best that you can do is to identify areas of theory that provide a contrast to your project. As you develop your themes and gather evidence you should regularly test that your area is really outside the accepted framework. In the findings discussion phase use the at odds theory as a mirror to reflect on your evidence in a compare and contrast process.

New and Emerging Fields

Sometimes your selected area is changing too quickly to have accepted theory or established opinion. It would be easy to assume that you are in a completely new area, but this is rarely true. Before deciding that there are no appropriate theories consider the essence of your subject. Henry Ford, commenting on the development of motoring, said that people did not want a car but a faster horse. Maybe your field is a novel solution to an old problem because of changing circumstances.

New and emerging fields have the capacity to make significant changes to the status quo. Initially email was no more than an electronic development of the postal system but led the way to broadcast, rapid forwarding and a lot more besides. By recognising underlying parallel aspects, theory that may seem dated or a poor fit can actually create a framework of principles that can then be investigated and discussed in the light of the new realities.

It may be appropriate to use one or two references from contemporary material to highlight a changed situation, but do not overdo it. Most contemporary material should be placed in your Introduction and Secondary Research sections. Combine the identifying references with an initial explanation that all of your Literature Review may not be a direct fit but a historical or parallel framework for the purposes of comparison. You will then have elements that will support analysis and discussion.

Discipline Specific Situations

All disciplines have their own areas of accepted theory and prevailing academic consensus. It is not unusual for students moving on to a specific Master's programme to have a background from an associated and sometimes a completely different area. Students who have studied or worked in the same field are more likely to be aware of some prevailing views, but their knowledge might be limited.

It is therefore important that you familiarise yourself with your chosen field by undertaking a significant amount of background reading. It would be risky to assume that you are familiar with the landscape and take short cuts by being very selective in your search for information. It is therefore a good idea to start reading and gathering material as soon as you can even if your selection criteria change later in the light of project approval or a revised aim and objectives.

You should also investigate how Literature Reviews are generally presented in your field. Particular attention should be given to the set requirements of your institution. Some expect detailed historical reviews while others favour broad descriptions of different schools of thought rather than a single approach. If the requirements are not explicitly clear then you should seek advice from your supervisor. The ideas presented in this chapter should provide you with areas for discussion so that you can decide on the most appropriate format, style and content for your Literature Review.

Literature Review: Case Study

A New Field

Business Studies student, Mubarak, was an early adopter of technology. He made significant use of web based resources. In the early days of e-commerce before the advent of Facebook® he recognised the potential for social networking to have a big impact on consumer behaviour. Already he was polling online interest groups and forums for opinions when he considered his own purchases. It was natural therefore that he would chose a Master's project that investigated the use of social media as a marketing tool.

His proposal was well considered with a clear structure except for one aspect. As the topic was so new, he argued, there was no established theory and so a traditional Literature Review was not practical. The best he could offer was a summary of contemporary articles from popular technical magazines and web sites. His supervisor advised that this approach would not meet the university's dissertation requirements and Mubarak almost abandoned his idea.

At a review meeting his supervisor asked for a more detailed explanation of social media. Mubarak described it as many online conversations between groups of individuals about topics of shared interest that might be initiated by an individual participant. He added that some of the "individuals" might actually be companies promoting their offers. The supervisor pointed out that this sounded like the traditional communication channel model and suggested his student should investigate this as potential theory.

Mubarak was dubious but agreed to go to the library to investigate. He found several business and advertising text books that described the communications model in great detail. One however had a simple diagram that stripped the model back to its core elements. Mubarak made a copy of this and while having a coffee in the library cafe he considered the model, marking up his observations. There were a number of basic similarities but also a lot of differences. Figure 8.2 shows his annotations.

An initiator sends a message, but unlike the traditional model this is then sent on to many others with multiple parallel paths and changing stories. Moreover, the system is a loop with clear feedback paths, it's multidimensional and it all acts at web speed.

This was the key to solving Mubarak's dilemma. Standard communication models and theories for commercial activity were based on certain assumptions. While this framework was not right for the new social media online environment it was a useful starting point. Mubarak was able to use the model and associated theory as a mirror to outline common areas and significant differences developing ideas about their potential consequences. In particular he considered the implication for the users of the much faster interaction times and the fact that many players and agents might respond with new or changing messages. His investigation also caused him to look at ideas he had not originally associated with his topic and he was able to find more background concepts that were relevant for his Literature Review.

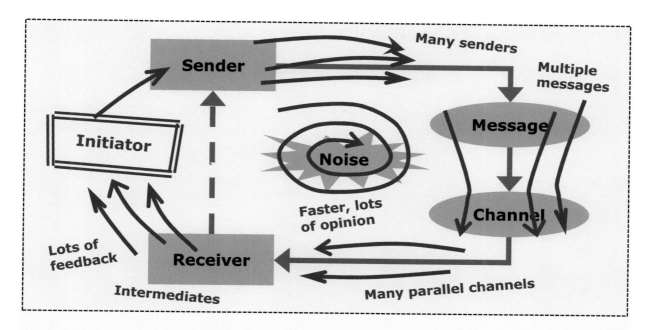

Figure 8.2   Old Theory in a New Field

This lead to some web based survey activity where he gathered opinions from other early adopters. He then discussed these responses with a focus group of non-technical university colleagues gathering their views on the possibilities and implications of social media. Mubarak used a reference to the Communications Model in his Literature Review and showed it with his annotations in the Discussion section as framework for a review of his research findings.

The outcome was a clearly argued and developed report based on a solid foundation. Not only did Mubarak get good marks, but the insights that he gained helped him start his career in this rapidly developing area. He successfully used his report at job interviews as evidence of his capability and understanding of the emerging field.

Observations

- Asking your supervisor for guidance is a good idea.

- Even new fields have some links to established theory.

- The accepted wisdom should be examined closely to identify areas of fit and difference.

- The Literature Review can inform research activity and is a framework for the discussion.

- The use of a reference to established theory and a diagram to show variations saved word count and was indicative of a critical review.

Literature Review: Good Practice

- **Purpose:** The Literature Review provides a framework for the Discussion of findings and can indicate starting points for research. Its format should be appropriate to the chosen type of dissertation.

- **Established material:** Focus on academic (peer reviewed) sources to identify theory and accepted practice in your selected area.

- **Accept limitations:** Provide a valid framework for discussion rather than trying to identify an exact theoretical match or a summary of everything written on your topic.

- **Schools of thought:** In certain types of dissertation a range of academic opinions needs to be considered. Explain and justify those you select.

- **Rule based environments:** In some fields the way things are supposed to work is governed by a set of regulations. Use these as part of your Literature Review framework.

- **Cross reference:** If possible identify a number of separate sources to support a given view.

- **Other views:** Present opposing and alternative views. This will provide appropriate material for your Discussion where the differences can be explored in the light of your own findings.

- **Define boundaries and focus:** Avoid a generalised approach. Concentrate on in scope aspects.

- **Structured presentation:** Grouping ideas into themes based on your aim and objectives will create a structure to guide research and discussion.

- **Justify use of non-academic material:** Use contemporary sources sparingly and only where they indicate changed situations or flag new areas for research.

- **Categorise carefully:** Some found material will be inappropriate for a Literature Review. Before discarding consider it as a possible contribution to your Secondary Research section.

Literature Review: Common Issues

- **Lack of focus:** There are many aspects to every topic. Avoid a broad brush approach. Focus on those aspects that are in scope defined by your aim and objectives.

- **Confused with Secondary Research:** The Literature Review should establish a working framework – the theory, accepted wisdom or regulations, for your area of investigation. It should not be confused with research evidence or data reports prepared by others.

- **Inappropriate literature:** Academic, peer reviewed publications, such as text books and professional journals and official regulations for rule based environments are the most common sources for a Literature Review. The inclusion of contemporary research and popular press material should only be used if they indicate a new or different framework appropriate to your topic. Historical material may still be valid, but you should justify the use of older sources.

- **Opinion and assumption:** Your topic may divert from accepted theory, but avoid jumping to conclusions. Collect evidence of accepted theory to create a framework for comparison in the later Discussion section.

- **Word count issues:** Prevent overruns by avoiding over description. Use references and diagrams with minimum description to highlight the key aspects for your investigation. Do not try to include everything written in your field. Show academic skills by being selective and justifying your choices.

Literature Review: Key Actions

- **Get started**: Read other dissertations and reports in your subject area even before your own project theme is finalised to understand how Literature Reviews are normally presented. In particular identify the type of dissertation that you will use and consider how the Literature Review fits to its structure. Make initial notes to inform your thinking about theory, schools of thought or regulatory frameworks appropriate to your chosen area.

- **Aligned themes:** Use your aim and objectives to develop a set of search themes for Literature Review material. Mind mapping and brainstorming techniques are a good way to do this.

- **Schools of thought:** When considering a range of views about your theme categorise them as in and out of scope with a justified selection of those chosen for development.

- **Create a reference framework:** Group your Literature Review material into topics to form a reference framework. Use this to guide your research and subsequent discussions.

- **Review with your supervisor:** Confirm that your ideas about material for your Literature Review, its styling and format meet the set requirements.

- **Cross check:** Confirm that you have more than one source for critical themes.

- **Recording and referencing:** Set up a recording system for the Literature Review (and Secondary Research findings) that includes detailed source referencing.

- **Focus:** As your Literature Review progresses you will identify new areas. Maintain your focus by positioning these emerging topics as in and out of scope. Review and revise as the project evolves.

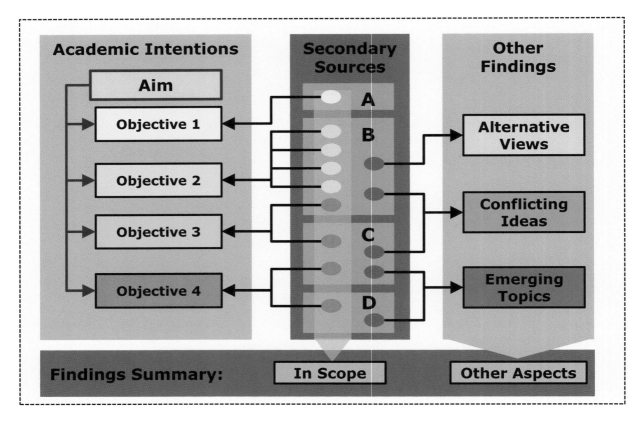

Figure 9.1   Secondary Research Concepts

Finding evidence to support the objectives:

Objective 1: If this is the first of a set of structured objectives it will typically set the scene and only needs basic support to be convincing. The single source (A) may be sufficient.

Objective 2: This seems to have a lot of support, but it is all from one source (B).This is being unduly derivative.

Objectives 3 & 4: These higher level objectives will be more complex and are supported by more than one source. Evidence from different sources reinforces your argument to give a clear and convincing picture.

Other Findings:

In addition to supporting the objectives, the various sources may identify alternative views, conflicting ideas and new or emerging topics.

Chapter 9

Secondary Research

In the previous chapter the Literature Review was identified as a process of finding and presenting the accepted wisdom relating to your theme. Secondary Research moves beyond a consideration of what is supposed to occur to investigate what actually happens in practice. It is about finding information based on existing sources that will support your dissertation intentions. A consideration of your aim and objectives will create lines of enquiry. You are looking for evidence. The challenges are to find it, validate its suitability, extract the relevant parts and then to fit them to your project.

Secondary Research Concepts

Secondary Research and its companion Literature Review are sometimes called desk research, but the process for gathering information can involve considerable legwork. Not just sitting while you surf the net but visiting libraries and archives as well as contacting organisations for information.

Supporting Evidence

Your starting point should be the aim and the associated objectives detailed in your Introduction. To achieve these requires a range of information and wherever possible you should identify supporting material from more than one source. Figure 9.1 illustrates the basic principles. In some cases a single source may be sufficient, but generally evidence from different sources reinforces your argument to give a clear and convincing picture.

Unduly Derivative

Using a lot of material from a single source is being unduly derivative and is considered academically unacceptable even if it is referenced. Use a diverse range of material to show professionalism and to avoid penalties. Sometimes you may find that there are only a few sources directly relating to a topic. You should acknowledge this and review the implications in the Discussion section. Even so you should be able to use a range of sources to support other aspects of your dissertation so that overall it is not considered unduly derivative.

The inclusion of exact source quotations should be treated with caution. These can have an impact, but too many can also be considered unduly derivative. In general you should not over use literal quotes but paraphrase the findings of others identifying evidence that supports your work.

Other Findings

In the course of Secondary Research it is likely that you will find a number of alternative views and conflicting ideas. This creates a temptation to start a discussion at this point in your write-up, but it is better to hold off until you have gathered all your evidence. Some new topics will also emerge. Integrate new in scope ideas into your research findings write-up. Out of scope topics should be set aside but do not throw the information away. Create a separate area or file to record these notes. You may find that as your project evolves they become relevant and therefore required.

Commentary vs Discussion

There may be a temptation to reshape the data as it is acquired with extrapolation to synthesise meaning, but you should exercise caution. There are dangers of selectivity and bias. It is important to hold back on discussion and analysis until you have gathered a broad range of evidence. Along the way you will also find alternative views, conflicting ideas and new topics. It is only after you have obtained a range of material and done some additional investigation in the form of Primary Research that full discussion can be considered. This will enable you to present a more structured Discussion chapter set in the context created by your Literature Review.

Your write-up of gathered secondary material should just present the bare facts. However some findings may be significantly unusual or unexpected. Perhaps the original data was collected for a special case that was outside the mainstream expectations and the scope of your project. You may decide that this material can be ignored, but it is better to demonstrate academic awareness by drawing attention to these anomalies. You may justify rejection of the material or its inclusion later in the more detailed Discussion section.

Finding Appropriate Material

Almost any type of source can contain information that is usable as Secondary Research evidence, but the original material is work done by others for reasons that may be very different from the aim of your dissertation. Its significance and reliability must be critically assessed to establish suitability and fit. Even if these are positive the information may be old and its current value open to question. At some point you will need to explain and justify your selections.

The general approach for choosing material is most effectively covered in your Methodology section as this will apply to all existing sources appropriate to your Literature Review and Secondary Research. As discussed in Chapter 7: Methodology, the initial ideas implied by your aim and objectives are developed to identify search vectors. These are topics or explicit data requirements that can then be used to generate key words or phrases that will drive your search for material.

Links to Aim and Objectives

Your aim and objectives provide starting points for the Secondary Research. The objective statement itself or a paraphrased version may be sufficient as a search phrase for finding support material in the basic cases. For more complex intentions it's much more of a detective story. Each objective will imply a need for a specific range and type of information. A consideration of these data requirements will suggest lines of enquiry. Brainstorming and word association around these will identify topics and phrases that can be used to facilitate your searches. This process expands your ideas and can easily lead to a wide range of material in related areas.

To keep things manageable it is important that you keep within the boundaries of your project. Your aim and objectives will help you decide what is in and out of scope. Resist the temptation to chase new ideas, no matter how interesting, if they are not part of your original plan. However keep a record of these potential avenues of enquiry. Sometimes there is a need to revise the scope of the dissertation in the light of findings or where difficulties prevent things going as planned. You can then return to these topics. They also provide some material for a reflective review on the dissertation process in your Conclusions where you may offer ideas for future development.

Parallel Fields for New Areas

In some cases the investigation seems to be in a new area that has not been covered by other researchers. There is then an inclination to skip desk work jumping straight into Primary Research. Students may express concern that there are no sources of evidence to support their ideas, but this is rarely the case. The problem may be that they are approaching the subject too literally, limiting searches to their explicit requirements. Expanding into more general but related lines of enquiry resolves this problem. There are usually parallel fields that provide relevant material.

Some fields are new with very little written about them. With some lateral thinking you should be able to identify related ideas. For example: what does this new area replace, improve or contradict? These associations provide direction for the search. They help identify material that can be used to compare and contrast to the new situation. This approach provides scope. You should also consider scale. Search for data that positions the new topic in terms of magnitude. Not everything can be measured in size as such but data can indicate its relative significance, extent and the degree of impact. The idea is to use secondary research to throw light on to the new area so that your objectives can be achieved.

Boundaries Implied by the Literature Review Framework

The overview outlined in your Introduction and developed in the Literature Review creates a working framework. The theme of your dissertation along with the theories, rules, espoused wisdom or a particular school of thought, define reference boundaries for the Secondary Research. It is not about limits. Keeping within these is not a requirement, but straying too far will take you away from your intended focus. Instead they give you anchor points where you can look for agreement, alignment or contradiction. It is not uncommon for a specific investigation to be a particular case that sits outside the norms of accepted practice. Use the topics from your framework to identify areas for investigation that will address your objectives. Look for evidence or any special circumstances that might challenge or only support particular aspects of the rules.

Source Categories and Locations

There are two main considerations when looking for Secondary Research sources: the type of information required and where it is located. The type ranges from basic data to detailed observations, from popular to the professional. Although a lot of data is available online, locations go beyond the web to the physical world of libraries, the media and organisations in general.

Having found the material its appropriateness must be considered in terms of relevance and reliability. These two are inter-related. For example a newspaper article may be highly opinionated with little supporting detail. This would seem to make it unsuitable for academic research, but it may be highly relevant in that it highlights a particular facet of your investigation. Hence you might include it but express caution in its use and if possible look for other more reliable sources for support. Anything and everything could be used if critically considered.

Source Types

Before diving into your search for material it is worth considering the type of information required to support each objective. This will prevent you from the pitfalls of quantity in a particular area while ignoring other equally important avenues. Data provides background facts, scale, associations and patterns that will inform your investigation and be the basis of your analysis.

- **Facts and figures:** Government at all levels, official public bodies, commercial organisations and charities produce a wide range of publicly available data. If it covers your area of interest it can be reinterpreted to suit your needs.

- **Analysis:** In many fields there are specific publications that report research activity. Many commercial reports will include detailed analysis that goes beyond the basic data reporting. Some of this will just be about the alignment of facts and figures, but others will include synthesis that makes use of historical trends or specific experience. These reports are often reviewed in the media.

- **Voice of experience:** Expert testimony, as limited responses to enquiries and as more fully developed opinions, are available in a variety of formats. Papers and summaries of discussion workshops around the themes of seminars, symposia and conferences are published in official journals. Submissions to trials, public enquiries and official proceedings are recorded as a matter of public record and often reported in the media. Experts, thought leaders and celebrities are interviewed in a wide variety of circumstances.

- **Media records:** Media ranges from entertainment to the highly specialised and includes sound and vision as well as print archives. There is a wide range of publications and websites that provide topic focused and specialist information as well as the general press and entertainment channels. In many fields there are specialist libraries and archives.

Locating Sources

It is too easy to think that all the information you need is available by simple web searches. A lot of material is not online or access is restricted in some way requiring membership, significant payments or approval. Your own institution will give you access to an extensive library system. As well as a wide range of books and papers appropriate to the courses offered it will have access to other resources including academic institutions, commercial surveys and databases. The access to these will have some restrictions based on non-commercial use. Seek advice from the library staff to understand what is available, how to get it and importantly what acknowledgements must be shown in your report.

You should also consider other external locations that may have material appropriate to your investigation:

- **Public and specialist libraries:** These can provide a wide range of commercial reference materials. In addition there are a number of national reference and specialist libraries.

- **Official archives:** Historical records exist in a multitude of areas from local parish ledgers to national registers; from newspaper cuttings to official government proceedings. Archives also include sound recordings, video and picture libraries. Since many of these records are not yet digitized, time is needed for searching as well as getting access. Having a clear idea of what you are looking for will optimise your time.

- **Representative bodies:** Trade associations, focus groups, societies, charities, government departments and larger companies all have resources available to their stakeholders. Some of the information is open to the general public. Some will give access or provide material specifically for student use.

- **Popular media:** These can be a significant source of news and views on every subject and will range from extremely biased individual opinions to very detailed and supported analysis. They tend to be very much in the moment and so you need to be constantly alert and on the lookout at anything and everything that is around you.

Access to some resources may require a letter of introduction to validate your education / research status. Your university librarian or tutors can usually provide these, but it can take time. Make your requests for access as soon as you can to avoid unnecessary pressure all round.

Relevance

It is very easy to get distracted by new ideas when searching for your material. A certain amount of serendipity, the discovery of things for which you were not looking, is appropriate, but you need to maintain a focus to keep your investigation on track. Good preparation will lead to a variety of topics that appear worthy of consideration. They should each be assessed for fit and relevance to your aim and objectives. Look for a range of material aligned to your identified themes. Different sources with similar information provide supporting cross references, but pick only the most appropriate to avoid excessive duplication.

Relevance does always mean agreement. Be open to alternative and contrasting views. It may be that you are identifying a different school of thought or things that relate only to your situation. Findings may not be exactly aligned to your area of investigation. You should record enough information from the source so that its inclusion can be justified and adequately reviewed in your later Discussion. Academically it is better to acknowledge different situations and justify following a particular line rather than just ignoring material that is inconvenient because it does not fit.

Reliability

Your findings may be in scope, but their reliability cannot be assumed. They will range from the professional, where the material has been peer reviewed or validated by a publishing panel, through to general statements based on assumptions and individual opinions. Selection or rejection should not be automatic. The methodology or sample groups of the professional material may be too different from your own to make it usable while a general magazine article may be unsupported but a very good fit to your area of interest. Critically review all your choices.

Consider the implications of reuse in your work vs its original intention. Is it too narrow or selective to be used? Was the data collected with a valid method? Does the author have a positive reputation in this field? How old is the source, does it still have appropriate meaning? If you want to include material where there are doubts, you should express caution about reliability. For example, up to the minute opinion pieces are particularly good for signalling new situations and changing dynamics, but reliability is suspect. Acknowledge this in your Discussion and if possible find other supporting evidence.

Particular care is needed with Wiki (What I know Is) web sites. These are open sources that allow alterations and updates. Some have been subject to malicious changes in the past. Most now apply filters and checks before entries are made or modified, but from an academic perspective they are still suspect. They are very useful for identifying material and some provide detailed source information. Use them as a searching tool to find relevant and reliable material, but using them as a main source implies a lack of academic care.

You should also be cautious with secondary information presented in text books. To illustrate a particular point authors can be highly selective, may extrapolate a bit far or merge a number of sources. This is a perfectly valid way to create a concise case study example, but the data may not be sufficiently reliable for reuse. If the topic is appropriate try and find the original sources so that you can make your own selections.

Structured Recording

As soon as you settle on a dissertation topic you will become sensitised to its themes and will tend to stumble across relevant articles. Avoid the frustrations of losing this material by preparing for it at an early stage. Set up a structured recording and referencing arrangement. This will serve you well once your organised search gets properly underway. It will help you avoid the chaotic and stressful situation caused by having a mass of disjointed notes. Their relevance is too easily forgotten even in a short timeframe. Organised and stored physical notes and electronic files that are backed up safeguard your efforts.

Draft Write-Up

Create an electronic record of found material as soon as possible. The files can then be backed up frequently as you make additions. Random electronic files are just as confusing as paper ones. Create order by preparing carefully named placeholder files. Put the topic headings from your search preparation into an electronic file. Do not worry too much about the structure. Detailed editing can be done later. The initial objective is to capture material in an ordered way under the identified headings. New themes will emerge and these can be added. Create a separate placeholder document for material that seems interesting but is considered out of scope.

Put your findings under the relevant headings as you get them along with their full source reference. Add notes and comments to help with your later editing. These might relate to unusual or unexpected aspects of the findings or a particular angle that you feel should be part of the later discussion. At this stage the document is a set of structured notes that you will turn into a crafted report. As such it will show you if you are over delivering on one area or leaving others with gaps. A regular scan of the placeholder document can help steer your Secondary Research activity.

It is practical to cut and paste material when the original source is in electronic form. Your initial editing should then extract the meaning relevant to your investigation. Otherwise your notes may become excessive in length almost requiring a second time consuming review. Avoid the temptation to use too many literal quotes. This can be considered unduly derivative and tends to eat up your word count. Shorten and focus to your requirements by paraphrasing the original.

Pointers for Primary Research

In some cases you may not be able to find secondary material for a particular topic creating a gap. You may also feel that certain aspects of your research findings are marginal in terms of their age, source reliability or fit to your specific theme. These are all flags pointing at potential areas for Primary Research. More generally, the Secondary Research activity will lead to ideas for direct investigation. Have a section in your placeholder document or a separated file where you can note these as they occur. These notes can then help you with your Primary Research planning.

Importance of Referencing

Acknowledging the work of others is a key academic requirement. Referencing your sources is straightforward if you do it up front and a nightmare if you leave it till later. Make sure you capture the full reference details as you make notes during your searches. Put a reference text tag at the start of each entry in your placeholder document. When you edit this into your final report you will need to adjust these to conform to the referencing style standards. As you add material to the placeholder document put its full reference in the correct position alphabetically in a draft references file.

This approach will ensure that all sources are referenced. It will help you avoid over reliance on a particular reference as you will immediately see if the source has already been cited. This may be reasonable, but you may also decide to look for alternative material to demonstrate a broader approach. Referencing helps others find your sources should they wish to look at them in more detail. As you proceed you may also need to revisit the original material to clarify a point or to make sense of notes that were too terse. Capturing the references in this way will enable you to do this if you need to go back to a source for more information.

Secondary Research: Case Study

Social Black Holes

During a break, Sociology student Liz flicked through some newspapers and magazines. She hoped to pursue a career in youth work and so was drawn to headlines about young people's involvement in crime and social issues. An interview in a women's magazine of a popular musician and philanthropist described her escape from a deprived childhood that had been limited by hardships and abusive relationships. It was not all study for Liz. Before going back to work on her dissertation an article about advances in cosmology that discussed the event horizon, a point where the pull of a black hole was inevitable, also got her attention.

Her Master's investigation was a broad review of contemporary social issues. She had noted that the general opinions and the political responses reported in the media about these tended to be simplistic. They were often based on emotion, lacking any real data or reasoned argument. She thought that she could investigate cause and effect more analytically to identify potential causes and solutions.

Liz's tutor pointed out that this was a massive undertaking way beyond what could be achieved in a Master's dissertation, but such research would need significant precursor investigations. A dissertation that characterised the issues in particular areas would be a significant contribution to a study of this type. Liz decided that she would take this approach based on the following objectives:

1. Identify a number of social issues involving young people to use as case examples.
2. Summarise the impact of these on society.
3. Outline current actions and initiatives aimed at dealing with the issues.
4. Review other opinions about the causes and solutions for the selected problems.
5. Make recommendations for a larger in-depth study.

Liz struggled to separate in her mind the roles of Literature Review and Secondary Research and sought advice from her supervisor. He pointed out that when there were a number of schools of thought these two dissertation elements often merged, but she should try to separate professional expectations from actual practice. With this in mind Liz decided her Literature Review should identify the rules and espoused wisdom in different schools of thought by collating details about the law, government policies and professional guidelines. To these she would add professional opinion about different approaches to the selected issues. She expected to find this information in official and professional publications.

For her Secondary Research Liz decided that data, current and historical, would provide scale to the identified areas. She would look for this material in official statistics. She also intended to gather wider public opinion as expressed and reported in the media.

Dividing the project in this way aligned her evidence gathering to her objectives. Objectives 1 and 2 were a development of her themes and could be satisfied by the popular and professional press. The approach chosen for the Literature Review and Secondary Research provided material generally aligned to objectives 3 and 4 respectively and could be expanded to consider actual practice and different schools of thought. Objective 5 implied analysis and synthesis from the overall findings. Liz was able to identify the types of information needed and potential sources by considering her objectives. She made use of university staff in the library and her department to make contacts in professional bodies and charities that were able to supply her with useful information when data was not available from university and public sources.

For her Primary Research she had already had contacts in the local social services and with a community police officer who were prepared to complete a questionnaire. Through her Secondary Research she had also made a contact in a charity that supported young people with social issues. She was unsure of the questions to ask. Her schools of thought approach was throwing up some diverse views, but the coffee break reading had given her an idea. She decided she would test the different espoused views with the professionals by asking them specifically about the boundary situations, the event horizon of social black holes. She would ask them to outline situations that sucked in the vulnerable and for examples of hope where people had somehow managed to escape.

Although only scratching the surface, Liz's report was praised for its focus and critically assessed review of a complex subject. She had created a valid structure with a convincing argument by appropriate alignment of her desk research.

Observations

- Liz used her supervisor as a mentor and coach to help her focus and manage the project.

- Although there can be a blurring between Literature Review and Secondary Research in some types of dissertation it is often possible to differentiate theory and rules from the practice.

- The progressive hierarchy of the objectives gave structure to the dissertation and provided indications for the type of material needed.

- Choosing a subset of examples or a case study approach reduces a huge topic to something more manageable while allowing the demonstration of academic principles.

- Awareness and a bit of lateral thinking can lead to wide range of valid ideas.

- Although a dissertation is academic some of the sources used may not be, but they are valid if used in an appropriate way and critically considered.

- Secondary Research can lead to meaningful ideas for Primary Research especially with a bit of lateral thinking.

Secondary Research: Good Practice

- **Focus:** Gather evidence to specifically address the topics implied by your objectives.

- **Data types:** Recognise that secondary material ranges from facts and figures to opinion, expert or otherwise. Chose appropriate material to support your investigation.

- **Source location:** Online searches will find a lot of material. Physical locations should also be considered. Knowing the types of data needed will help you find potential source locations.

- **Diversity vs selectivity:** A wide range of valid sources adds weight to your argument, but do not ignore findings that do not fit your expectations. Be prepared to present conflicting and alternative views. A consideration of these enriches the discussion that follows.

- **Critical assessment:** Consider the validity, suitability and limitations of all chosen sources. Explain and justify inclusion of marginal material.

- **Structured recording:** Anticipate write-up requirements. Create placeholder documents for material and notes. Back-up to protect your efforts. Do not throw interesting but out of scope material away. Have a separate file for this so it can be recalled if needed later.

- **Paraphrase:** A cut and paste approach can make initial data collection easy, but resist the temptation to collect many literal quotes. Paraphrase to save word count, to avoid being unduly derivative and to extract evidence realigned to your own investigation.

- **Accurate referencing:** Create a process and files for referencing of all sources.

- **Professional approach:** Be polite and professional when requesting data. Acknowledge all sources of help.

- **Flag unexpected results:** Separate data presentation from discussion, but comment on any unusual or unexpected results when they are recorded.

Secondary Research: Common Issues

- **Too wordy:** Avoid rambling around topics because they are interesting especially if they are out of scope. Being succinct means focusing on your theme presenting concise detail.

- **Misalignment**: It is not uncommon to research interesting but side topics that are out of scope. Use the framework implied by the Literature Review and your objectives to focus.

- **Unduly derivative:** Create a convincing argument by using a range of sources. Use literal quotes only if they are particularly relevant, otherwise paraphrase to extract the key points.

- **Unnecessary reading:** When you find a relevant source you do not have to read it all. Look at abstracts, synopses, tables of contents, chapter summaries and index entries to find the in scope material. Look around these to find any other material of interest and skim the rest to ensure fit. Reading it all is time wasting and leads to distractions.

- **Selectivity and bias:** It is important to be selective in your searches based on the requirements of your objectives. Within this framework present a range of material acknowledging any alternative views. Do not ignore things just because they do not fit.

- **Assumption and opinion:** Avoid preconceived ideas or jumping to conclusions. Instead look for evidence so that a convincing argument can be presented.

- **Lack of critical assessment:** The reliability and fit of sources to your requirements can vary significantly. Examine all material critically. This does not mean you have to reject any that are marginal. Justify inclusion and explain any issues in the Discussion that follows.

- **Premature discussion:** It is difficult to present a clear and convincing argument if you launch into discussion before all the research has been presented. Separate the presentation of findings from the Discussion section. However draw attention to any unusual or unexpected results as they are recorded, but consider the detailed implications later.

- **Referencing issues:** It is very easy to lose referencing detail. Plan and prepare a process for recording and keeping track of references right from the start.

Secondary Research: Key Actions

- **Preparation:** Examine the implications of each objective so that the research requirements are clear. Use a brainstorm or mind mapping technique to identify key words and descriptive phrases that can be used as search topics. Create a clear idea of the boundary between in and out of scope areas. This will enable a focused search.

- **Data types and places:** Considering the types of information required and possible locations where they might be found. Do not just rely on web searches.

- **Access:** Make requests for information or for access to sources as soon as possible. Ask your tutors and library staff for assistance and guidance on access issues.

- **Recording:** Set up a structured recording system and turn paper notes into electronic files as soon as possible. Detailed editing can come later. Back-up the files often as material is added.

- **Referencing:** Prepare and follow a process for recording references from the outset.

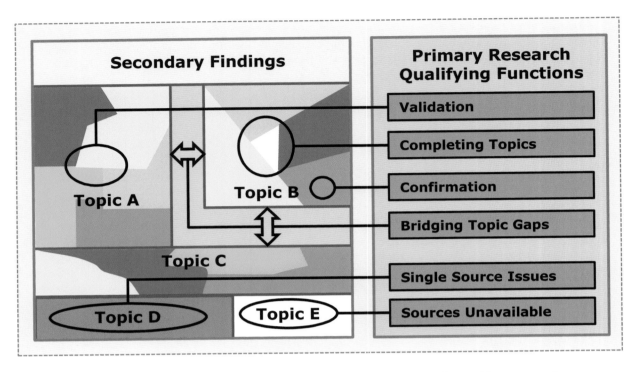

Figure 10.1   **Primary Qualification of Secondary Research**

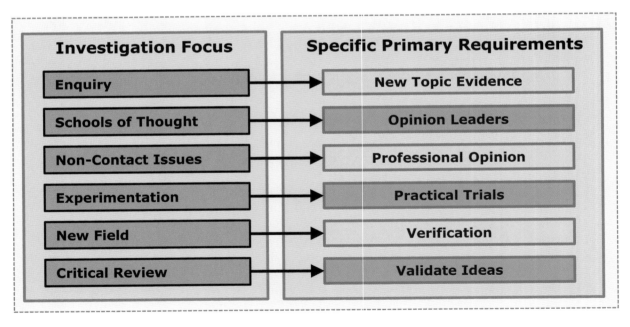

Figure 10.2   **Primary Research for New Material**

Chapter 10

Primary Research

Primary Research is an original investigation carried out to address the needs of the dissertation using a process outlined in the Methodology. It follows the desk based research and has two main functions: to support or qualify the secondary findings and to provide new evidence along specific lines appropriate to the type of dissertation used. Giving some attention to both of these aspects will enhance your narrative while demonstrating professional research skills.

Figures 10.1 and 10.2 position these two elements showing how Primary Research might be used to reinforce the secondary findings and find new material to support specific requirements in different dissertation approaches. Resource constraints, especially time factors, will limit the amount of Primary Research that you will be able to do and so the focus of the Primary Research should only be only on those things that are realistically achievable.

Implications from Secondary Research

It is unlikely that the Secondary Research will be sufficient to completely address your aim and objectives. A critical assessment of your secondary sources and a review of your initial findings will give you pointers for your Primary Research as shown in Figure 10.1. These will improve the quality of your evidence leading to a more convincing argument. You will also be able to identify areas that need additional material that can be provided by targeted attention, Figure 10.2.

It is important to recognise that qualifying secondary findings represents considerable investment and may not be fully feasible. It might require additional research approval as well as unforeseen time allocation. You will be well into your project before you realise that this support is needed. In these limiting circumstances it is better to demonstrate the principles rather than ignoring the issues. Try to address some of the problems with Primary Research and acknowledge the shortfalls where complete coverage is not possible.

Validation and Confirmation of Secondary Material

In most cases Primary Research is not about repeating the work of others, but sometimes your secondary material is doubtful due to age or inadequate alignment to your particular areas of interest and some checking is needed. In Figure 10.1 Topics A and B have some secondary sources of significant interest, but they may not be particularly robust academically. Investigations can test the validity of reported work and confirm that the material, originally recorded for different purposes, is sufficiently aligned to be usable. In some cases you may be relying on a single source or a narrow perspective as indicated by Topic D. Your own research can provide complementary evidence.

Identifying Gaps

Your project aim and objectives will have led you to a set of topics for the Secondary Research. As you develop these a number of gaps can occur. An area may not be completely covered as shown in the middle of Topic B. Likewise the individual topics may be narrowly defined and separated. In the illustration the gaps between Topics A and B and B to C create a disjointed overview. In some cases access to suitable secondary material may be restricted and not open for your use creating another gap, Topic E. Structured recording of your Secondary Research, as described in the previous chapter, will help you identify these gaps. A placeholder document anticipates required information and any missing elements soon become obvious. This then indicates problem areas that might be resolved with some focused Primary Research.

There will be areas that are very specific to your investigation relating only to your area of interest such that there are no appropriate secondary sources readily available to you. These gaps in knowledge are the areas normally associated with Primary Research, Figure 10.2, and are typically where your Methodology and approval requests will have been focused.

Realising the Methodology

Finding new evidence to address missing topics and to obtain information to meet the specific dissertation requirements is an involved process that is subject to a range of limitations and formal approvals. Your Methodology section should provide explicit detail of how you intend to implement the Primary Research taking these restrictions into account. Different types of dissertation, as outlined in Chapter 5: Dissertation Structure will require different approaches. There are a number of practical aspects that need to be considered so that the plans can be realised effectively.

You may have anticipated a number of Primary Research activities and obtained approval for them. These may not all be necessary. The Secondary Research may provide sufficient coverage for large areas, but this should not be an excuse to avoid Primary Research altogether. Instead focus only on those areas that will enhance your investigation and enable you to demonstrate research skills.

Choosing Target Groups

In many types of dissertation you will be seeking answers from one or more individuals. These are your research targets. Inevitably some will have more or better knowledge than others. It is not uncommon for the best to be the most difficult to access. Experts and senior people, for example, are typically very busy and are unlikely to feel any obligation to help you. Nevertheless it is worth trying to access the best sources of information. The PA to an executive or the department administrators are often easier to contact in the first instance. Also use your network of family, friends and tutors, to make contacts. A politely worded request for help with a clear but short explanation of what you are trying to do can bear fruit especially if you do not ask for too much.

This effort is time consuming. It is good to have a back-up plan that you run in parallel. Other people may be more accommodating, but you need to recognise that they may not have the same depth of knowledge to respond adequately to your questions. It is important that you consider who can answer your enquiries and at a level where you feel you can rely on the answers. Do not fall into the trap of thinking that if you ask enough people a realistic average response will emerge.

This highlights one of the difficulties of surveys and interviews with people you do not know. Are the respondents who they say they are? Are they realistic members of your desired sample group? You can guard against these problems by including some qualifying questions at the start and embedded within your queries. An initial filter may stop a lot of wasted effort, but some people, especially in anonymous surveys, will blag and continue. You will need to consider responses carefully to be sure that the participants are valid representatives that you can rely on.

Observations and Experiments

Choosing a target area is about finding who can provide usable information. In observation and experimentation methods the requirement is to identify where and how relevant material can be obtained. To get the best possible outcomes often requires the more difficult approaches. These carry higher risks of failure or resourcing issues. In general the **KISS** principle is good advice: **K**eep **I**t **S**imple **S**tupid. The Stupid part is not about you, or your ability but recognition that there are a lot of unknown variables and some things will go wrong. You need to have contingency plans.

Managing and explaining the trade-offs of all the methods used is part of demonstrating the research related skills associated with the dissertation learning outcomes. A simple method that helps you get sufficient information will demonstrate the principles. You can then review its effectiveness and limitations in the Discussion section to further illustrate your knowledge and understanding of the processes involved.

Plan for Success

Primary Research represents a major investment. If things go wrong or the information is insufficient then you will rarely have time to start again. There are a number of things that will minimise this possibility. Allocating some Primary Research effort to qualifying the secondary information, as discussed above, improves your data and will allow you to demonstrate the principles of good research with the integration of secondary and primary investigations.

Chapter 6: Introduction advised you to create a set of structured and progressive objectives. Aligning the original research to these will build from some simple activities to the more complex. This increases your chances of getting some valid work completed. It takes away the all or nothing scenario. Shortfalls with the later objectives can be discussed in a reflective way to highlight your understanding of research activities and the difficulties they present.

Recording Results

Preparing and implementing a research method can be exciting, but managing the resulting data flow can be overwhelming. Worse is the later realisation that something is missing and that you cannot go back. To avoid this possibility and to effectively record meaningful results you should consider the quality and quantity of your findings and how they are to be arranged.

Quality and Quantity

Quality starts with appropriate questions and lines of enquiry. Chapter 7: Methodology discussed the importance of preparation to identify what you want to know and where it might be found. Pitching to the right audience or observing in the right areas will generate reliable material. Clearly articulating who or what should be included and screening tests to cut short or weed out inappropriate responses will enhance the value of the retained findings. To avoid a criticism of bias be transparent about the inclusion criteria both to your research participants and in your report write-up. Show that you are homing in only on data appropriate to your objectives.

The quantity of material should be sufficient to support meaningful discussion. You may not be able to get enough to present detailed statistical analysis of your findings. This may take more time than you have, but beyond a certain point you will be able to talk about indications and trends as well as the difficulties caused by a relatively small sample. In other words your research may not be definitive, but your demonstration of the learning objectives for the course will be possible.

Result Capture and Placeholders

Although you will not know the actual findings of your Primary Research until it is done you can anticipate the nature of the outcomes. The preparation for your surveys, interviews, observations or experiments will provide templates for expected responses. Think also about how quickly the information arrives and how it will be logged. Things happen at a rate determined by the participants. Online surveys are in electronic form and may come in quickly, but you can unpick them at your own speed. For other situations your recording process must be able to keep up. This can be greatly facilitated by having pre-prepared tick boxes and tally sheets.

Test your result capture mechanism with trial runs. You can do this with friends who respond to your enquires as if they were the real participants. For this the responses do not need to be accurate. You just need to be given a range of responses at a realistic rate so that you can stress your recoding process to verify it is fit for purpose. For non-contact and experimentation situations you can test your process with initial observations and trial runs.

Converting written responses and recorded results into electronic form as soon as practical will let you protect your investment with electronic back-up. Think about how your data will be used later and prepare appropriate placeholder files as data repositories arranged and formatted to facilitate presentation and discussion. Test these by using a set of dummy data. This preparation may seem like a lot of work, but it will help you fine tune the investigation, spotting missing elements before rather than after the event making the later stages of presentation and analysis much easier.

Barriers and Limitations

Primary Research is by its very nature highly variable and unpredictable. It may seem straightforward in principle, but in practice there are real barriers to overcome and areas of compromise and difficulty that will limit your investigation. The important thing is to recognise any difficulties and to reflect on their impact.

Problems of Access

You will often have to compromise between what is practical and available against an ideal target group or location. Getting access to individuals can be difficult and time consuming. Asking nicely is an important first step. Take care not to over sell your research. It may seem like a major piece of investigation to you, but promising to provide earth shattering findings to a senior executive is unrealistic.

Most people are kind and willing to help if you are honest and open with your approach and realistic about what you are trying to do. Asking for a one hour interview this week will nearly always be impossible. Fifteen minutes in the next month stands more chance. You challenge is to be prepared to make the short time count. If they say OK come tomorrow you need to be ready. It is also a good idea to have supplementary questions lined up. They may commit to only fifteen minutes, but once they meet you and learn more of what you are doing you may be given more time.

You will face similar issues when requesting access to staff for surveys or interviews and to areas for observations. In all cases you need to be explicitly clear about what you are asking for and what you will do with the data. Some organisations will want formal non-disclosure agreements or other forms of reassurance. If your initial request indicates clearly that you are only using the information in an academic exercise and not for commercial purposes this may be sufficient. You are not an authorised representative of your institution and should not sign agreements that commit the whole university to some legally binding restrictions without seeking advice. Previous students will have faced this difficulty and so your supervisor or library staff will be able to advise you and can often provide wording for a suitable letter that has met the needs of external organisations and your university in the past.

Time and Place Constraints

Many dissertation themes are international in that they relate to situations across the globe. With modern communications, especially the internet, it is possible to gather information from far and wide. However some things may need first hand observation, a presence in a particular region or direct contact with locals. You will not have a travel budget or a lot of time to go visiting and so time and distance limitations need careful consideration.

If lucky you may have a local contact who can act as an agent on your behalf, but you will need to be explicit with your instructions. You will need to demonstrate that this is not a joint investigation or that you are using the original work of someone else. A safer plan is to use alternatives. Wide ranging secondary information and primary material acquired through available channels might provide a general picture. You could then limit detailed specifics to areas that are accessible to you. This general overview, with a local focus such as a case study, will let you demonstrate the principles and show that if you had the resources you could conduct a more extensive investigation. The limitations of this approach and the potential future opportunities should form part of your Discussion or concluding review.

Primary Research: Case Study

Practical Realities

The participants in Gordon's MBA cohort were sponsored by their companies as part of their professional development. For their dissertations they were expected to investigate a strategic theme relating to their own organisation, identified with the help of a sponsor from within the company's senior management team.

Most of Gordon's organisation had a history of a market leadership, even dominance in their chosen sectors, but one division was experiencing significant structural change in their market place. No longer the leader but a market challenger, the division was struggling. The director sensed that the company's history mis-set expectations about how they should develop products and engage with potential customers. He asked Gordon to use his dissertation to examine the impact of organisational culture in these circumstances with the hope that the findings might help improve strategic planning and facilitate change management.

Gordon's tutor advised caution. There was a significant temptation to focus only on the business imperatives ignoring the importance of addressing the more academic requirements of the course. To address this Gordon decided to establish a general overview with objectives to understand differences between market leaders and successful challengers. His Literature Review created a reference framework around company culture and senior management practice. Secondary Research provided examples of organisational behaviours within this framework that pointed at potential ways forward as well as identifying some that had led to company issues.

Gordon's intention with the Primary Research was to then understand his own company's current position in the light of this framework and some contemporary examples by considering established practice, perceived wisdom and professional attitudes of the division's senior management team. It was hoped that critical factors impacting change initiatives could then be identified.

The target group consisted of 42 senior managers located internationally. Gordon had met only a small number of the group and was concerned that many would be unresponsive. He asked one of the company's senior executives if he would endorse the activity to encourage involvement. Approval for the investigation was readily given, but the executive would not insist on participation. He was concerned that this might be used as an excuse to avoid other operational priorities.

Gordon had the authority to attend a number of internal business conferences and events scheduled for Europe and intended to use these as an opportunity to meet a large proportion of the target group. The company also had well established teleconferencing facilities and so virtual meetings were a possibility for discussions with the rest. Based on these arrangements Gordon decided on a structured interview / survey approach and prepared a set of questions and templates for recording the replies, leaving room for supplementary questions and answers. As part of the preparations and to encourage the participants to think about their responses, the question list was sent out prior to the intended meetings.

Things do not always go to plan! A difficult economic climate caused the company to cancel a number of events and to limit international travel. Gordon was only able to meet five out of a target group of 42. The required number of teleconferences jumped to 30 plus. The time and the logistics as well as the reluctance of the participants created significant barriers. Instead Gordon asked the group to respond to the information that had already been sent out. This was not a well-structured questionnaire but a list of open questions. Dealing with the responses was then very difficult. They varied from short, almost cryptic, answers to several paragraphs of comment. In all cases they did not correspond to the original plan for data capture and presentation.

After considerable thought and experimentation a coding scheme was developed so that the diverse answers could be mapped into a structured set of weighted opinions that could be presented graphically and analysed. The danger of researcher bias was considered and fully discussed. Although only 19 out of the 42 managers responded there was enough material for reasoned analysis to demonstrate the academic principles involved and to provide some insights to the sponsoring manager.

Observations

- Despite sponsoring interests, academic requirements have precedence over commercial considerations. Supervisor input ensured that this was recognised by the student.

- The coherent structure was established. The Literature Review and Secondary Research created an academic framework and view of contemporary practice against which the target situation could be investigated with Primary Research.

- Although small, a precise target group was identified that allowed the demonstration of a valid research process. Even with a low response rate the basic academic principles could be shown.

- Access to the target group and engagement with them was based on clear plans about how the responses would be collated and presented. Permission and support were obtained for the group contact. Events, that might have been anticipated, knocked the plan off track.

- The primary data management issues created further opportunity to demonstrate critical research and analysis skills as the problems of access were resolved.

Reflection

- **Contingency:** This example from the author's own MBA shows that many problems are actually predictable. He now realises that he could have anticipated these issues and prepared for them by considering different scenarios with contingency plans for adverse situations.

- **Smart thinking:** It is good to learn from one's mistakes but smarter to learn from the mistakes of others. This is why it is a good idea to discuss your plans in detail with your supervisor who has seen all these problems before.

Primary Research: Good Practice

- **Positioning:** Primary Research should support your objectives, fit within the framework of the Literature Review and complement the Secondary Research.

- **Effective resource usage:** Consider Primary Research as the utilisation of scarce resources; your time and energy. Use it to validate established themes within the context of your investigation, to expand specific areas of selected interest and to explore identified gaps.

- **Approved methodology:** Your initial preparation should have outlined potential research requirements and appropriate methods when obtaining ethical and other approvals. Keep within the boundaries set. Request additional approval if it turns out that there are further requirements, but only if you have time and this is absolutely necessary.

- **Supervisor guidance:** Review your plans with your supervisor and consider the given advice carefully.

- **Trial runs:** Test your methodology by running a trial with a team of helpers who behave like active participants. For experimental methods test the various stages with dummy runs.

- **Appropriate participants:** Consider your targets carefully and critically. Make sure that the participants are valid for the method and your research requirements.

- **Professional engagement:** Approach potential participants in a professional and polite way explaining your purpose and requirements simply. Thank people for their help.

- **Anticipate outcomes:** The actual responses are unknown, but their structure is set by the way data is collected. Plan for this by creating templates and a placeholder to capture your primary data in an organised way.

- **Recognise limitations:** The research method used may not be ideal. The number and quality of responses may not be what you want. Identify these different categories of limitation and critically assess their impact to demonstrate knowledge and judgement skills.

Primary Research: Common Issues

- **Too much haste:** Primary Research can seem like the most important part of your project, but do not be too hasty to get it started. Detailed preparation and alignment with the other dissertation elements will lead to better outcomes that are more easily managed.

- **Straying off track (1):** Formal approvals are there to protect your participants, the university and you. You must keep within the approved boundaries.

- **Straying off track (2):** Even within an approved method it is all too easy to ask inappropriate questions or follow irrelevant threads. Make sure that you focus on the stated requirements of you project implied by your specific objectives and academic requirements.

- **Disjointed positioning:** Primary and Secondary Research should be complementary and sufficient to address the objectives of your project. Make sure that these two areas work together so that your research is sufficient and effective.

- **Realistic expectations:** Knowing where the required information is and who has it are only the beginning. You need to get access. It is hard to persuade others to participate. Ask nicely and you may be lucky, especially if you are honest and realistic about your requirements. It is rare that others will consider your research as important as you do.

- **Over optimistic:** Your research will rarely go as expected. Eliminate as many issues as possible by using trial runs and initial experiments to stress the method to find its weaknesses. Review your plans with your supervisor to get experienced advice.

- **Responses vs results:** These are not the same. In anonymous surveys, especially online, you may get many inappropriate replies. Have some qualifying questions and filtering to keep the quality of the gathered data as high as possible.

- **Problems and limitations:** These are inevitable and should not be ignored. Recognise them and discuss their impact critically to demonstrate knowledge and skills.

Primary Research: Key Actions

- **Alignment:** Consider your objectives and the degree to which the Secondary Research has covered these. Identify areas that need confirmation as well as gaps that can be addressed by the Primary Research.

- **Focus:** Direct the Primary Research at key areas. Avoid redundant questions and themes unless these are needed to confirm established ideas with respect to your particular focus.

- **Stress tests:** Use test runs and trials to identify issues and limitations in your methods before going live. Check that your recording process can keep up with the data flow.

- **Consider outcomes:** Anticipate the nature of your findings and plan how these will be recorded as your research progresses. Create dummy charts, placeholders and templates to record your results.

- **Critical review:** Note any issues and barriers as well as considering the veracity and validity of findings. These notes will form the basis of the critical review of your methods in the dissertation Discussion section.

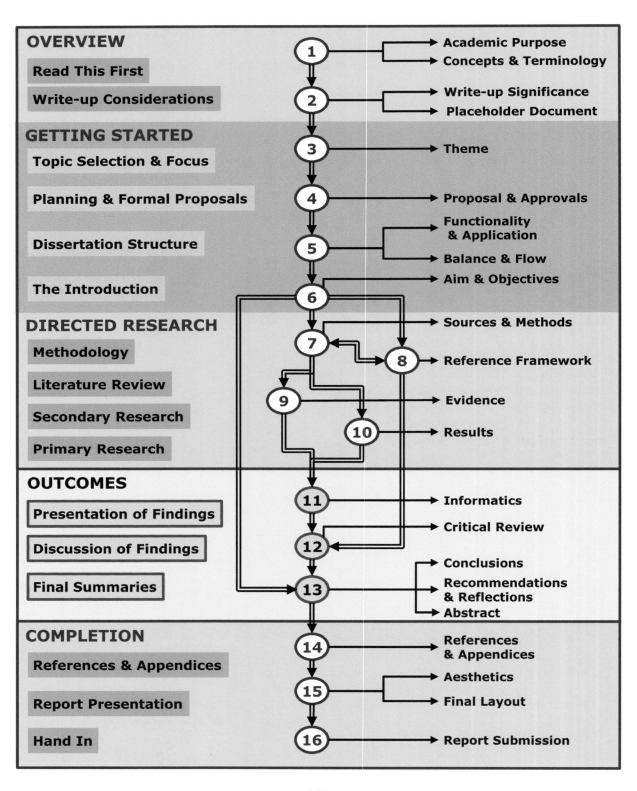

OVERVIEW

Read This First

Write-up Considerations

1 → Academic Purpose
   → Concepts & Terminology

2 → Write-up Significance
   → Placeholder Document

GETTING STARTED

Topic Selection & Focus

Planning & Formal Proposals

Dissertation Structure

The Introduction

3 → Theme

4 → Proposal & Approvals

5 → Functionality & Application
   → Balance & Flow

6 → Aim & Objectives

DIRECTED RESEARCH

Methodology

Literature Review

Secondary Research

Primary Research

7 → Sources & Methods

8 → Reference Framework

9 → Evidence

10 → Results

OUTCOMES

Presentation of Findings

Discussion of Findings

Final Summaries

11 → Informatics

12 → Critical Review

13 → Conclusions
    → Recommendations & Reflections
    → Abstract

COMPLETION

References & Appendices

Report Presentation

Hand In

14 → References & Appendices

15 → Aesthetics
    → Final Layout

16 → Report Submission

138

OUTCOMES

The early dissertation activity details the aim and objectives and sets the project in context. The process of investigation, its methods and the gathering of evidence, then follows. A range of outcomes, information and results from the research activities, are generated. These findings must then be presented in a coherent way so that they can be discussed and appropriate conclusions made.

Outcomes: Section Summary

Chapter 11   Presentation of Findings: Students often find that when they then come to write up their findings sections they use a disproportionate amount of word count and over describe the raw data. An appropriate use of charts and other graphical tools can address this issue, enhancing the clarity of the basic results and synthesised ideas. Effective presentation of findings saves word count and facilitates a more focused Discussion.

Chapter 12   Discussion of Findings: It is a good idea to separate the presentation of the found evidence and research results from their Discussion. All the elements of the dissertation project can then be considered together enabling a more holistic approach. This allows you to critically review the whole process and its outcomes to draw meaning from the investigation without being side tracked with detailed data explanations.

Chapter 13   Final Summaries: The dissertation has specific intentions detailed in the Introduction. It is normal to present a Conclusion that summarises the key activities and findings in relation to these.

It is common to reflect on the overall dissertation process and where appropriate make recommendations for further work and improvements. Sometimes this reflection is required as a separate chapter.

At this point the investigation is complete and so an Abstract that gives an overall summary of the whole work can be written.

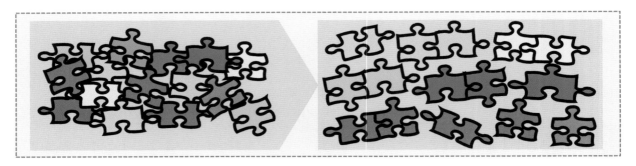

Figure 11.1   Data Sorting Concept

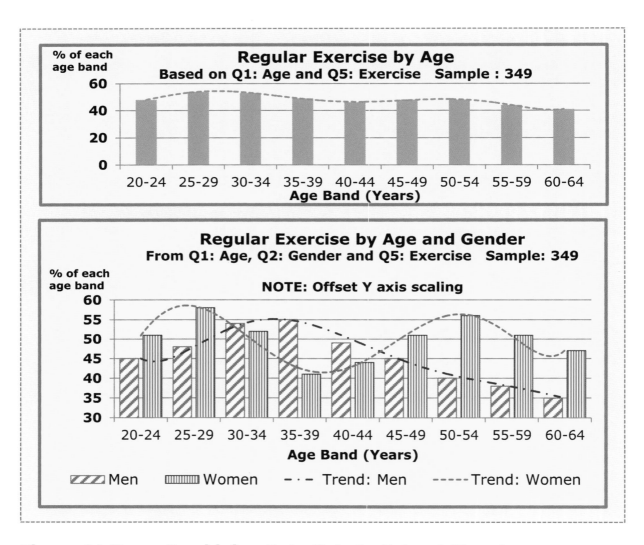

Figure 11.2   Combining Data Sets to Extract Meaning

Chapter 11

Presentation of Findings

Your dissertation investigation will create a great deal of information that will need to be organised and aligned to create a meaningful story. Again, it is a bit like a jigsaw, Figure 11.1, with pieces that cover different topics that somehow need to be separated, sorted and linked together. Unlike a jigsaw there can be more than one configuration. Putting the pieces together in structured ways will then allow different pictures to emerge such as the combined data charts of figure 11.2.

The process of creating these pictures or stories is the role of the Discussion section. Before this can happen all the pieces must be turned over to reveal their detail. Hence it is important to present all of the findings in only basic arrangements with limited combinations prior to alignment, extrapolation and interpretation.

Presentation vs Discussion

As data is gathered a number of themes will quickly become apparent. At the same time there will be anomalies and contradictions. In some cases it will be clear that there are misfits due to errors or limitations in the acquisition method. It is very tempting to start discussing these straightaway. This can be counterproductive as later evidence may clarify the picture.

Avoid Description of Results

Findings from desk research and data from primary investigations should therefore be presented in a structured way but as found. **"What"** should be separated from **"So what?"** The latter will form part of your Discussion. Data and results should be presented in their basic form in the appropriate chapters for Literature Review, Secondary and Primary Research. However it is reasonable and important to flag unusual or unexpected results as they are presented. A review of these anomalies can be incorporated into the later considerations of issues and limitations.

Over description of findings will lead to word count issues. Dissertation guidelines will typically advise you to be succinct. Keeping it short and precise is a challenge. There is often a tendency to describe findings in detail. Remember that your write-up is a professional report. In some disciplines there may be an expectation for flowing prose and essay style presentation, but in most cases a business like format with short sentences and paragraphs as well as tables, bullet lists, charts and diagrams is more appropriate and acceptable. Grouping topics under headings and arranged in logical structures as described in the Literature Review and Secondary Research chapters will facilitate a concise and organised summary of your findings.

Even so the research results need to be detailed and explicit. This can be a challenge when presenting data from surveys, interviews, experiments and observations. Charts and tables can be effective for the presentation and comparisons of large amounts of acquired data. Clear annotation reduces the need for lengthy text descriptions. It is too easy to squander 10% to 15% of your word count in elaborate explanations of the data that are no more than wordy duplications. As shown in Figure 11.2 charts and tables can be almost self-explanatory. Let them do the talking.

Findings from Secondary Research

It may be tempting to present a review of each secondary source separately. This approach can be useful in some types of dissertation. It is valid when reviewing schools of thought or sets of experimental methods with only a few sources for each. In more general cases this approach can create a disjointed view that relies on the reader's ability to extract meaning. Instead it is usually more appropriate to group the Secondary Research findings into identified working topics that will provide a relevant structure to guide your narrative, making things clearer for the reader.

Identify Themes

For your investigation you will have identified a range of themes. As the Secondary Research proceeds, you will discover more. It makes sense to present the findings in associated groupings. The preparation of a placeholder document will focus your efforts and will help you collate the found material. Initially this is likely to create an unbalanced write-up. Some sections will have many more entries than others often with significant duplication.

At this stage avoid consolidation and editing out of material. Instead make use of headings and sub-headings to revise the grouping of themes and associated topics. You may identify a number of alternatives in terms of the logical relationships between ideas. Avoid describing these in too much detail. The objective at this stage should be to sort the information into a manageable format and to identify alternative arrangements. It can be helpful to summarise the choices in a diagram or table as this will provide a pointer for the subsequent Discussion. At the very least make separate notes about your observations. These will help you structure your Discussion section later on.

Align to Objectives and Literature Review Framework

It is easier to compare and contrast material and relate it to expectations if you use headings derived from your Literature Review and objectives. These themes will have been identified earlier and used for searching and as headings in write-up placeholder documents. Carrying the same themes forward through the results presentation chapters to the Discussion section creates a coherent structure. However new topics will have emerged and you may also realise with hindsight that the flow is not as logical or progressive as you would like. This is especially true when anomalies and alternatives are identified.

Once all the material has been gathered, review your initial ideas on themes and structures. This may require some edit to the earlier chapters so that there is alignment across your work. Avoid excessive rework effort by holding back until you have completed your investigations, primary as well as secondary. Capture yout thoughts about changes by writing notes in the placeholder files. These will guide you so that you can make a final edit to arrange and consolidate the material.

Identify Anomalies

Some results may be unexpected or extreme in some way. For example you may identify contrasting or alternative points of view. It is appropriate to flag these anomalies in the presentation of your findings as and when they occur so that the later review can give them some attention. Often they are pointers to new lines of enquiry. You will need to make some pragmatic decisions. Will you have enough time to develop these new themes? In some cases you will have to hold back, recognising that this is unfinished work. This can then be considered in the Discussion and Conclusion sections in terms of limitations and recommendations for improvement to the process or as ideas for further investigations.

Findings from Primary Research

Primary Research findings are usually very ordered since they are the responses to predefined questionnaires and interview prompts or the output of planned experiments or observations. The working templates that provide a framework for the data acquisition also imply a structure for the presentation of the basic results. These should be shown first. Derived results that are developed by combining or taking subsets of the original data should then follow. Where the primary material is quantitative, it is both practical and word count efficient to present results as charts or tables.

Use of Appendices

Some dissertation guidelines will ask you to place all illustrations, including charts and other images, in a separate appendix at the end of your dissertation. If this is not specified then it is much better to place them close to the body text that relates to them. This makes it easy for the reader to follow the arguments and serves to break up the text into manageable pieces. Having to repeatedly flick to a set of diagrams at the end of the work is extremely irritating for the reader. However the diagrams need to be of a reasonable size so that the detail is clear. It is not uncommon for students to make these too small to be effective. On screen they can be enlarged, but in a printed document the detail may be lost. This may be why the end placement is specified by some institutions. There are other aspects where the use of an appendix is appropriate.

Blank versions of your data capture guidelines, such as questionnaires or observation tally sheets, can be usefully placed in appendices. It is also helpful to include some examples of completed forms. In many cases it is practical to collate all of your acquired data into lists, tables or spreadsheets so that these can also be presented in appendices. These appendices are not strictly necessary for the dissertation argument. You should flag them clearly with a pointer in the main report, but do not expect them to be read in detail. Their purpose is to give your report credibility by providing evidence that the work was actually carried out. Putting all of your raw results in an appendix also creates a source of information available to other researchers. This is particularly useful in departments where on-going research is encouraged along certain lines. Your supervisor can advise you if this is worthwhile or needed.

Dealing with Issues

It is not uncommon for there to be redundant, unusable or anomalous, even unreliable data, in your captured results. Even though you may have to reject material it should not be ignored. It is confusing for the reader when a question is presented as part of a survey or a test is indicated, but then there is no data to show that these things happened. Instead show the data that was obtained or give an explanation of why it has been rejected. Stick to basic facts and leave the more detailed discussion to a later section where the significance, implications and limitations of the missing or rejected material can be reviewed in the context of the overall findings.

Themes and Alignment

For clarity of presentation there should be alignment between the primary data collection method and the presented results. Keep to the same sequence with headings that match those used in your questionnaires, interview prompts or data gathering guidelines. Using numbering alone is not enough. Repeat the section questions / titles in full. If this is too wordy paraphrase the topic; Q5 - Age, Q6 - Income … A title in addition to the numbering adds clarity and reduces the need for repeated and frustrating cross referencing to a template in an appendix as the report is being read.

However this structuring will be designed to suit the Methodology that addresses the practicalities of data capture. The sequencing may not fit easily to the themes and topics derived from the aim and objectives or the framework created by the Literature Review. This mismatch can create pressure to add explanations and discussion to the basic primary data presentation, but it is better to wait for the full Discussion chapter where these can be considered alongside material from other parts of the investigation.

You may decide to create new viewpoints by combining data from several questions or from a subset of the overall material. This is valid and should follow the initial basic data presentation. In your write-up make it clear how the derived material was created by indicating which original material was used as its source.

Presenting Data in Charts and Tables

The large amount of data generated from Primary Research is often most easily presented in some form of chart. There is a very wide range of display formats and styles available. Avoid gratuitous embellishment. Follow the **KISS** principle – **K**eep **I**t **S**imple **S**tupid. The Stupid part is about recognising that even if the viewers are capable, they do not have your level of knowledge about the subject. You need to make it explicit and clear for them.

In some courses, aesthetics, the use of images and their visual impact in the report, is part of the assessment. These particular requirements are discussed in Chapter 15: Report Presentation. In all cases, illustration styling in terms of fonts, colours, legends and scales, can make a big difference to understanding, while a consistent approach creates an air of professionalism. This section is not a complete review of presentation techniques. Its purpose is to highlight some basic principles of effective presentation and to discuss some pitfalls that are common in dissertation submissions.

Clarity of Information

At first sight, the chart in Figure 11.3 has a lot to recommend it. There is a large difference between the two columns implying a significant finding from the research.

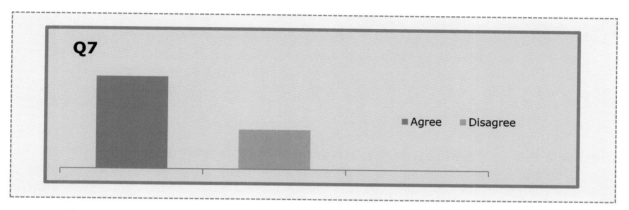

Figure 11.3   Simple Data Presentation

Closer examination shows that there are a number of easily corrected issues.

- **Title:** It is not clear what the data represents. We would have to search for the questionnaire, perhaps in an appendix, to understand to what Q7 is referring to.
- **Legend:** The legend detail is too small for the columns to be reliably identified.
- **Colours:** You might think that it would be better to use different bright colours for the columns and background, but if printed or photocopied in monochrome for a reviewer they may appear like this. To a colour blind person even a coloured image might appear to be undifferentiated. Make sure the information is discernible in all circumstances.
- **Scale:** The columns may actually be only one count different. Without a vertical scale we cannot tell. Also there is no information about the total number in the survey.

Chart Type

Various chart types are designed to present data in different ways. The choice of which to use should be made carefully to support your intentions. There also practical considerations. Changing a vertical bar chart to a horizontal one can make it easier to label sections with long titles. On your computer screen the image may be very clear. Give some thought to how it will appear on the printed page. Make sure it will be big enough to adequately convey the information.

Figure 11.3 was economic with the use of available information. As well as the Agree and Disagree respondents there might have been a number of Unsure / Do Not Know replies. Figure 11.4 addresses this and some of the other identified issues. The title is expanded to explain the question. The shading patterns can be differentiated by a colour blind person and will be clear even on a black and white photocopy. The legend is larger so that the elements can be more easily identified.

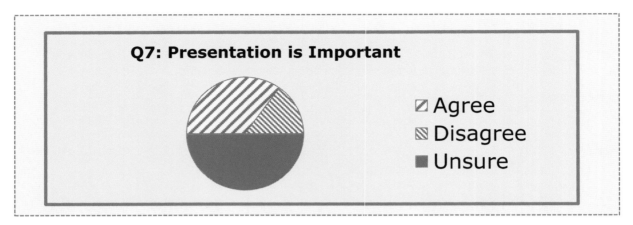

Figure 11.4   Selecting an Appropriate Chart Type

A different chart format has been chosen. Pie charts should be used when the data represents a complete set of information. The slices indicate the proportions for each sub-set category. Clearly half the respondents are unsure and this is a potential limitation when the findings are considered in detail. Things are no longer as certain as Figure 11.3 implied, but we still have no scaling.

Scales and Other Information

Figure 11.4 would still need a lot of text description to provide a complete picture. In Figure 11.5 more detail has been provided. A subtitle indicates the overall sample size and the fact that 100% of it is used in the chart. Each segment of the pie is annotated with the count and the percentage. Similarly, adding axes and numerical scales to bar charts and graphs will make the detail explicit.

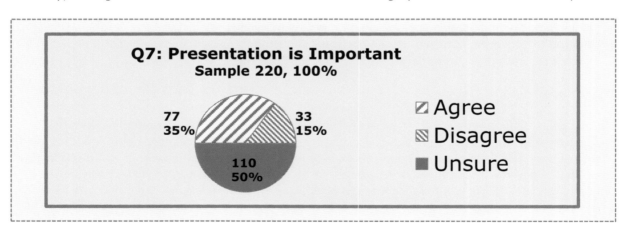

Figure 11.5   Adding Scales and Other Information

Adopting the small changes as indicated above reduces the requirement for a detailed description in the body text when the results are presented. The charts and their legend do the talking so that word count usage is optimised. Instead of describing the findings, the word count can be used to indicate the activity flow in acquiring it and the identification of anything unusual.

Style Over Substance

The range of chart options for data display can be seductive. Figure 11.6 shows part of a student's findings from a survey. The two questions are similar in that the participant is asked for agreement to a statement. Some of the pitfalls highlighted above have been addressed. There is an explanatory title, detail of the overall sample size and the data elements are clearly identified by the x axis labels.

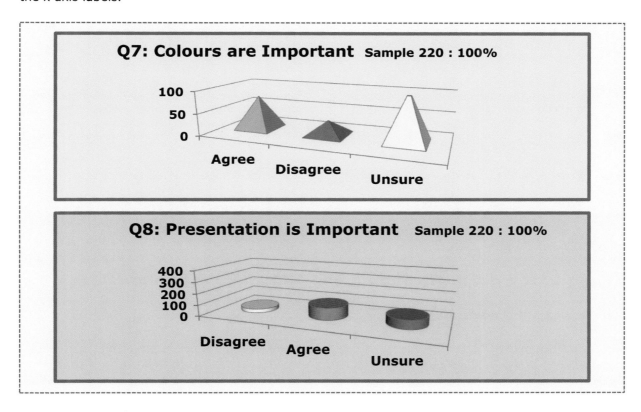

Figure 11.6   Gratuitous Styling and Inconsistent Formats

However the use of styling is somewhat excessive. Different formats are used for no real purpose and the sequence and colouring of the elements in the two charts is different. The three dimensional style adds unnecessary complication since it impossible to gauge the height of the individual elements. Even though the sample sizes are the same, different scaling is used. This compresses the information in the second chart, Q8.

Often there is value in comparing responses to different questions as part of the Discussion. This is not so easy when the scaling is different and almost impossible when the charts are not aligned. Figure 11.7 shows how this might be done. In these examples the two charts should normally be in pie chart format as they cover complete data sets. However, the aligned two dimensional bar chart format makes it possible to compare the responses to the two questions. The scaling, legend colouring and sequence are the same and so comparisons are much easier.

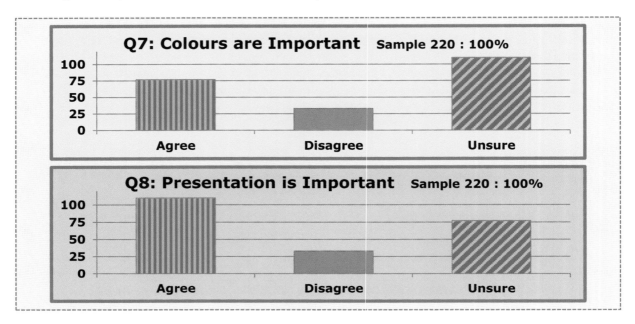

Figure 11.7   Simple Styling and Alignment for Comparisons

Combined and Derived Data

Survey participants and the data collectors can be confused if several points are combined in each question. For simplicity, data gathering exercises are usually structured so that each question focuses on only one topic. This generates raw data that by itself may not be useful. It is only when combinations, or derived data sets are created, that meaningful information starts to emerge.

Once all basic data has been presented it is reasonable to then combine data sets to pull out more involved information. For example: Figure 11.2 at the start of the chapter shows a street survey by a social studies student aimed to identify lifestyle and activity changes across the working age range. The intention was to ask the same number of males and females in each of a set of age bands a series of demographic and lifestyle questions. In practice the numbers participating in each band varied, but presenting the data as percentages for each sub-group normalised the information enabling comparisons. The top chart in Figure 11.2 combines two questions to show who regularly exercised. This was valid but not very informative. Combining with a third question, Q2 Gender, and presenting a clustered chart with trend lines shows significantly different patterns of behaviour for men and women. In this case the information is amplified by using an offset in the chart and is clearly indicated.

In this example data from several questions were combined and presented using a specific charting option. This turned the basic, single element questions, into a meaningful and differentiated presentation. Without the chart a lot of word count would be used just describing the raw data. In this case it was valid to present the combined chart in the Primary Results section as this was the original intention. In other cases ideas emerge as the results are being considered and the most appropriate place for derived and combined findings will then be in the Discussion section.

Tabulated Data

Another way to show a lot of related data is to present it in a table. These are particularly good for summarising the data from questionnaires and tally sheets to collate information from surveys and observations. In this format they could be placed as an identified appendix to provide evidence of research and as a source for other researchers. Specific data can then be extracted for the main body of the dissertation perhaps to be presented as derived charts.

Although tables are an easy way to present a lot of information, not everyone is good at extracting the detail from them. Figure 11.8 shows data collated from a company's annual financial reports. The student was examining historical data to identify the impact of strategic decision making in a high street fashion retailer. A table contains a lot of information, but its implications can be hard to see. However this could be a good starting point for chart preparation. Subsections can be used to produce a number of related charts with a common X axis, the financial years in this case.

Annual Revenues by Division - $1,000s										
Financial Year:	**2005**	**2006**	**2007**	**2008**	**2009**	**2010**	**2011**	**2012**	**2013**	**2014**
Children's Wear	100	110	120	110	110	120	180	230	270	280
Women's Wear	60	70	90	120	150	180	240	270	280	290
Men's Wear	260	260	240	220	180	140	80	100	170	160
Services	10	15	29	25	30	60	120	180	220	250
Totals :	430	455	479	475	470	500	620	780	940	980

Figure 11.8   Tabulated Data

Tables are obvious formats for quantitative data, but can also be useful for presenting qualitative information. This will work well if the data has an obvious structure as the table will indicate its form but only if the information is compact. Be careful not to be too terse. Truncating information so that it fits neatly into the available column and row spacing can obscure its meaning. Use bullet point lists or short paragraphs with headings if the information needs longer descriptions.

Combining Charts and Tables

As shown in Figure 11.9 a lot of information can be conveyed in clustered or stacked charts. These separate out the subset elements throwing light onto the variations they relate to and are good to indicate relative trends and positioning. However they can be difficult to read since the individual data sets are not aligned to the axis scale. When a lot of information is packed into a small space accurate comparisons of size are difficult to make. This is the opposite problem experienced with tables where the numbers are clear but their relationship is not.

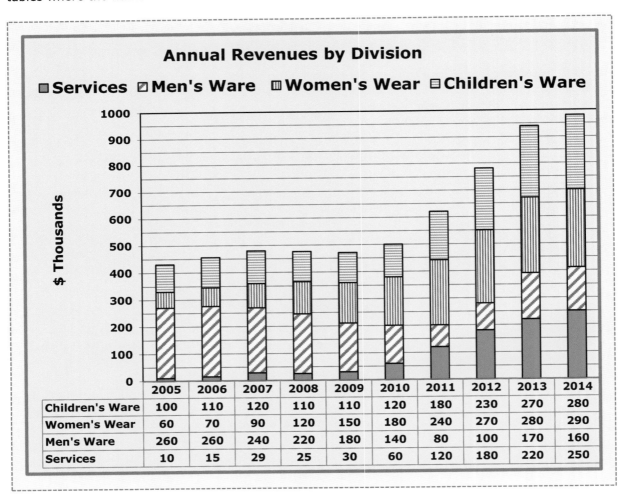

	2005	2006	2007	2008	2009	2010	2011	2012	2013	2014
Children's Ware	100	110	120	110	110	120	180	230	270	280
Women's Wear	60	70	90	120	150	180	240	270	280	290
Men's Ware	260	260	240	220	180	140	80	100	170	160
Services	10	15	29	25	30	60	120	180	220	250

Figure 11.9   Combining Charts and Tables

Combining a table with the chart addresses these issues. Figure 11.9 shows the data from the table in Figure 11.8 in a stacked bar chart that indicates the timeline changes and trends. The chart options allow the table to be aligned under the X axis so that the actual values are clear for each column.

Bullet Lists

More involved information can be effectively presented in bullet point and list formats. Consider these as expanded single column tables. Arrange the headings and contents into logical groupings sequencing them in a progressive or meaningful way. This creates a structure and flow to your information that is easy for the reader to follow, demonstrating a critical and analytical approach.

Each entry in the bullet lists should be relatively short, one or two sentences. If more is needed then consider a series of short paragraphs with headings instead. This will give you more room for explanation. The headings will also make it easier for you to arrange the material so that your argument flows convincingly.

Consistent Styling

The various chart and table options provide a wide range of information display choices. These are most effective when consistent styling and formats are used. This makes it easier to compare information across a number of displays. Colours, shading, legends and title fonts should all be considered. If appropriate use exactly the same axes for charts based on common data such as the age range groupings or financial years in the charts shown above. Changing the vertical scaling of the derived chart in Figure 11.2 by offsetting the zero point was a conscious and indicated decision that enhanced the detail. Instead of trying to imply skill by arbitrarily using different chart styles show real capability by making the different formats support your argument.

It is worth creating a style sheet for result presentation as part of your overall write-up preparation. This will then serve as a reminder as your project progresses. The aim with these styling considerations is to make things clear to the reader, but it is also of value to you as you consider your findings. Patterns and relationships are more easily seen and explained if you have a consistent approach to displaying the information.

Presentation of Findings: Case Study

A Pasty Presentation

Dissertations are normally assessed independently by two markers; the supervisor and a second tutor who usually has no contact with the student. It is unusual for the tutors to disagree widely about the merits of a dissertation submission. Their marks are usually very close. After all they have to follow the same grading criteria. This is the scheme that is normally given to the student along with other aspects of the dissertation requirements paperwork. A final mark is then agreed by the tutors often by taking an average of their individual assessments. However, this is not usually done when the differences are significant or they cross a grade boundary. In these cases the tutors will have a more involved discussion in the process of agreeing a final mark.

In Martin's case the separation was considerable. His supervisor, the first marker, thought that the work was almost an A grade distinction while the second marker rated it only as a marginal pass. How could there be such a difference of opinion? The problem was presentation.

Business study student Martin had concentrated on Human Resources, HR, for his Master's degree. His dissertation was a comparative study of incentive schemes for senior management across different industries. He was a diligent student and had consistently gained high marks in other assignments. However the dissertation was challenging. He found writing hard. He was well organised with a good plan for his write-up, but getting the words to flow was not his forte. He was more comfortable texting and this influenced his style.

Martin had a disciplined approach to the gathering and recording of his research. He reviewed most of his sources online cutting and pasting material into holding files for editing later. For Primary Research he asked a group of senior HR managers to help. He contacted them through a relative who was an HR director. His aunt participated in a number of business forums and she asked her contacts to complete Martin's short questionnaire. This was organised through an open online facility and a few others outside the group also contributed. Some were clearly not genuine responses. Martin had set some filtering questions and was able to weed out the phoney responses.

Concerned about the write-up, Martin spoke with his supervisor for advice. An early draft was reviewed and the problem became clear. The cut and paste material had hardly been edited. It was still in the various fonts and styles of the original extracts. It was well referenced but tending to be derivative. Martin's supervisor advised him to paraphrase using more of his own words based on the selected material. He also reminded Martin of the dissertation styling guidelines that specified a font style and size that should be used for the report. Their discussion was all about the presentation of written material. The presentation of findings in tables and charts was not considered. Martin had a lot of these and this is what gave the second marker his concerns.

It was clear that many of the Secondary Research charts and tables had been lifted directly from web sources. They were all properly acknowledged, but the styles were all different. Some were elaborately journalistic designed for visual impact while others were more basic. A number had additional content that was not part of Martin's theme. The cut and paste approach created difficulties with sizing and clarity. Some images were too small and fuzzy in a lot of empty space. Martin's own data charts were more clearly presented but styled in similar ways to some of his secondary sources. There was no consistency.

The chart and table presentation issues caused the second marker to look at the text in closer detail and he concluded that this was also not far from a cut and paste job. He felt that this approach was somewhat derivative and therefore lacked the merits for a high mark. Martin's supervisor had noted the variable data presentation, but argued that the grading criteria did not actually allocate marks for presentation. It clearly was not impressive and so fell short of an A grade. However the supervisor was aware of the considerable effort that Martin had made and could see that although a lot of the Secondary Research was presented in a somewhat derivative way the rest of the report showed a clear and logical argument.

In the end the tutors agreed that the report was not as convincing as it could be. The poor presentation indicated weaknesses in transferable skills and some issues with understanding of the requirements for an academic report as described in the grading criteria. However on consideration the second marker was persuaded that the work had significant academic merit and was convincing in terms of the data collection and interpretation. A high intermediate mark close to the supervisor's original assessment was agreed. The both noted in their feedback that a little more attention to the presentation might have moved the mark to an excellent grade. The work clearly had potential.

Observations

- Marking is not an arbitrary opinion. Markers have to follow a set procedure aligned to a defined set of grading criteria. These are usually available to students as part of their course and dissertation documentation.

- Even if there are no specific requirements given for data presentation it must meet accepted academic standards to be clear and convincing.

- Your tutors will give you good advice in response to your queries, but they are not editors of your report. You must take responsibility for its style and content.

- Source material was written and its images styled for particular aims that may not align to your dissertation objectives. Only relevant data should be extracted and you should consider redrawing it in a way that supports your principal themes.

Presentation of Findings: Good Practice

- **Set guidelines:** Make sure your layout and styling conforms to set requirements.

- **Avoid over description:** Describing results uses a lot of word count unnecessarily. Present them succinctly in easily assimilated formats such as charts and tables or bullet point lists.

- **Simple and consistent:** Use the most appropriate chart format and styling. Be consistent with fonts, colours, scales and legends. Avoid over-elaborate embellishment.

- **Illustration placement:** Locate diagrams, charts and other images in the body text close to where they are discussed unless your institution specifies otherwise. This makes it easy for the reader to follow the arguments and serves to break up the text into manageable sections. Having to repeatedly flick to a set of diagrams at the end of the work is extremely irritating for the reader.

- **Logical sequencing:** Use your objectives and Literature Review themes to create structure for the presentation of findings. For Primary Research results follow the question sequence and headings used in surveys and interview templates.

- **Clear relationships:** Use numbering and titles for charts that link to the information source by matching titles to survey questions. For derived charts indicate in their title blocks which original sources have been combined.

- **Hindsight editing:** New ideas and topics emerge during your investigation. As part of your overall editing process review the earlier chapters, Introduction and Literature Review. Make sure the new topics are covered and positioned appropriately. This will ensure that the overall report is consistent with a logical flow.

Presentation of Findings: Common Issues

- **Overly descriptive:** It can take a lot of word count to describe a set of results and even then the picture may not be clear. A simple chart or table can make things explicit, but do not spoil this by then adding a wordy description.

- **Disjointed sequencing:** When the narrative jumps about inconsistently it is difficult to follow the argument. Well-structured objectives and identified themes from your Introduction and Literature Review should create a logical framework for the results presentation.

- **Insufficient headings:** Even if findings are presented in the same sequence as an original survey it can be difficult to understand the material. Simplistic headings such as Q1, Q2, Q3 ... followed by the outcomes do not indicate what the results are about. The reader must flick back and forth from the results section to the original questionnaire, perhaps in an appendix, to see the relationship. Using both the numbering and the actual question or topic as headings eliminates this frustration.

- **Diagrams in appendices:** Putting all illustrations in a separate section at the end of the report makes it very hard for the reader to follow along due to the constant switching back and forth. If you are not sure how to embed a chart or other image in the text find someone to help you. Many institutions have student services that will help with such problems.

- **Assumption and extrapolation:** When a lot of data is presented the reader may not realise that there are gaps. Worse, if gaps in data have been bridged without supporting evidence then the work has moved into the fiction category. You must base your presentations on actual evidence, highlight gaps and explain any shortfalls.

- **Inappropriate styling:** Using a different style for each chart demonstrates capability (you are able to do it) but not competence (you do not appear to know what you are doing). By choosing the most appropriate format and by using a clear, simple and consistent styling you will demonstrate professionalism and logical thinking.

Presentation of Findings: Key Actions

- **Prepare for success:** Before you gather any data consider how you will record and present it. Placeholder files with prepared headings are good for text details. This includes initial preparation of tables or bullet lists. For numerical data prepare chart or table templates. Verify that you are using the most appropriate format for your data presentation so that they clearly convey meaning and understanding.

- **Confirm format validity:** Test your charts and tables with dummy data that can be replaced as your results come in. This will let you check styling and axes. Make sure that they are appropriately titled and fully annotated so that the data stands on its own. This reduces the need for wordy descriptions.

- **Expect the unexpected:** Have a notes file to record observations and detail of anything unexpected or unusual. Review this material in your Discussion section.

Discussion Context		
Project Overview	Review of background and intentions	
	Impact of approvals and scope boundaries	
	Relative value and positioning of sources	
Framework Summary	Selected theory / schools of thought / regulations	
	Prevailing opinions and assumptions	
	Identified issues and limitations	

Review of Objectives (or Themes)	
Collation of Evidence	Present in a coherent and logical sequence
	Develop viewpoints from all of the evidence
	Consider the degree of completeness for each
	Explain significance of information gaps
	Identify anomalies and alternatives views
	Justify selection of particular viewpoints

Project Effectiveness	
Overall Aim	Evaluate achievement against expectations
	Limiting factors and incomplete investigations
	New areas with potential follow on work
Methodology Review	Reflections on selected approach
	Practical difficulties
	Areas for improvement

Figure 12.1   Discussion Write-up Plan

Chapter 12

Discussion of Findings

The Discussion chapter moves the report from presentation of evidence to an explanation of its significance. To do this you will need to consider the original intentions and the academic context. This will require a review of the whole project. It is not just what you found in your research, but also a reflective consideration of how the project was conducted and what can be learned from your approach.

Discussion Write-up Plan

The Discussion write-up should consider the findings from the whole project. This includes a reflective and critical review of your aim, objectives and investigative approach as well as the consideration of your research results. You will have a lot of material to work with and need to be careful not to repeat the earlier presentation of basic information. A write-up plan such as the generic one shown in Figure 12.1 will help keep things focused and manageable. This can be adapted to suit most types of dissertation.

Discussion Context

Before any detailed review of your findings can begin you will need to consider the investigation in terms of the background to your chosen theme and the selected academic framework. These create a context for the discussions that follow. Your Introduction should have described an area of focus for the project as well as outlining the aim and objectives. The Literature Review will have provided a reference framework for the whole investigation by identifying selected theory, schools of thought or regulatory environments as well as prevailing opinions and assumptions. The Discussion should not repeat this material, but the choices made should be critically summarised so that the findings can be understood in context.

From the outset you will have imposed restrictions and limitations set by the approval process as well as chosen boundaries implied by your area of focus. You may have selected particular schools of thought to define an angle of approach and these will also provide evidence appropriate to your investigation. An initial discussion of the relative value and positioning of sources with a consideration of any issues and barriers will add clarity to the Discussion creating a context for the review of your research evidence.

Objectives Review

The objectives review represents the major part of the Discussion section. The research will produce multiple strands of evidence and typically these will have been presented in separate chapters in sequential groupings based on the acquisition methods. The Discussion should have a more holistic approach with a structure linked to your objectives. Each objective can then be critically reviewed based on the available evidence from multiple sources. If the objectives were arranged in a progressive hierarchy, as previously suggested, then following their sequence will bring coherence, logical order and alignment to your review.

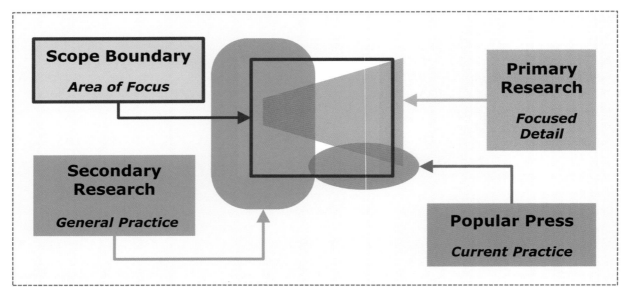

Figure 12.2   Positioning the Research Evidence

The Discussion should be differentiated from the presentation of research evidence and findings by comparing and combining information to create a view point for each objective. Deductions can be confirmed through linkages and cross references. You should draw on various research elements to address the objectives as well as highlighting other points of interest. Figure 12.2 positions the different sources of information, some of which will lie outside the boundary set by your area of focus. There will also be gaps and anomalies. Findings that are unexpected or unusual should be identified and their significance considered.

This review will also identify new or changing situations that create alternative views for a particular objective. You should use the evidence to justify a preferred choice or provide explanation to why different aspects are valid. If there is insufficient evidence to position the differing views they should be highlighted indicating that more work is needed to resolve them.

Project Effectiveness

With the benefit of hindsight it is appropriate to reflect critically on the overall project and the methods used. The dissertation aim sets a high level goal for the investigation with the objectives as its component parts. Having reviewed the evidence supporting individual objectives it is appropriate to consider the project as a whole to obtain a picture of its effectiveness. The impact of limiting factors and incomplete investigations should be discussed so that you can evaluate your achievements when set against the original intentions.

In some types of dissertation there may not be a set of objectives for review but a single statement of purpose. Ideally evidence for different aspects and viewpoints of your theme will have been presented earlier in separate Literature Review or research chapters arranged under a number of headings. The Discussion should not repeat these findings. Instead it should review them considering their relative merits, justifying preferred views or the selection of particular options, so that an overall evaluation of the project aim can be made.

Often new areas of related but out of scope ideas will be identified. It is unlikely that you will have sufficient word count to develop these fully. The overall review can position these, identifying potential for follow on work. In all cases, for both in and out of scope findings, make sure that the Discussion is evidence based using only your reported material and not personal opinions.

In some courses the dissertation requirements call for a more personal reflective review of the project as a separate section. If this is not a listed requirement then the Discussion provides an opportunity to critically evaluate the project methods by reflecting on the approach used, the sources found and the way information was obtained. Significant aspects would have been outside your control and a review of the limitations and practical difficulties is appropriate. You should also be open and reflective about your own approach. Try to avoid negativity. Instead demonstrate learning by identifying areas where you could improve. Discuss how aspects could be more effective if a different approach was used, perhaps if more resources were available, or identify specifics where the benefits of hindsight indicate areas for development.

Evidence Based Discussion

Your research review will require a point of view, a reference framework, against which findings can be positioned. The Literature Review provides this by identifying relevant theory, regulations or espoused wisdom and it applies to all aspects of the investigation. In many cases this is a consensus about how things should happen. This does not mean that your findings have to agree. You may be looking at a particular special case or considering a new field where the theory is not fully developed. The importance of the reference framework is not that your research fits inside it, but that you have a something against which it can be compared.

In some fields there are alternative points of view or schools of thought. In these cases the different opinions contribute to the secondary evidence. For the purposes of discussion you may choose to align with one viewpoint or some combination of them. Your Discussion should justify this choice based on evidence. In fact all of your Discussion should be evidence based, but various factors create gaps and other issues that will require that you make considered judgements.

Anomalies and Issues

Sometimes findings do not conform to expectations. There may be assumptions in the initial topic review; indications from other aspects of the research or implications from your reference framework. Whatever the cause you may have unusual, unexpected or contradictory results. Check your findings for errors and mistakes in recording, but do not automatically assume that the problem results are wrong.

It could be that your investigation has covered a number of specific areas where each has its own norms that are not the same as in the more general situations. You may have a biased method such that data is acquired from one particular group, area or in a particular way that yields a different spectrum of results. This is not necessarily a fault. It could be an intentional part of your investigation to look at certain selected areas. Whatever the situation you should acknowledge the anomalies and try to offer some explanations. If you are not able to do this then the issue is a flag indicating an area for future work and could be part of your recommendations.

Positioning Research Evidence

The relative merits of your research material and its value as evidence supporting your investigation should be considered. Figure 12.2 shows a typical relationship between secondary and primary findings. In this case the secondary material had been split into two. The more academically robust Secondary Research is used to indicate general practice based on the research of others. Material from the popular press and other academically weaker areas is also used to show current practice or to indicate trends.

The Primary Research, your own original material, is also shown with two aspects. Part of it overlaps or duplicates some of the Secondary Research and the popular press material to provide corroboration of these findings in your specific area of interest. In addition the Primary Research provides new and separate information directly related to your aim and objectives.

As well as overlaps that provide support or contrasting views there are also gaps where there is little or no evidence for particular parts of the investigation. If carried out effectively most of the dissertation findings will be in scope, sitting inside the boundary defined in your Introduction. Inevitably though there will be some aspects that spill out into other potentially interesting areas.

The Discussion should consider the merits of the different sources and their relative positioning, identifying gaps and significance of out of scope findings. It is unlikely that there will be sufficient space to develop these areas, but their presence should be noted.

Holistic Overview

The focus should be on the in scope areas in the context of the reference framework with a holistic overview of all the findings. That is, all threads of the investigation should be drawn together for joint consideration. This implies that the Discussion sits round both the scope boundary and the Literature Review Framework as shown in Figure 12.3. Some investigations will have findings that are in scope but outside the espoused wisdom or regulations. As discussed in Chapter 5: Dissertation Structure and Chapter 8: Literature Review, this offset will lead to aligned, non-aligned and complementary findings. The Discussion should consider all of these aspects and is therefore represented in Figure 12.3 as an outer framework.

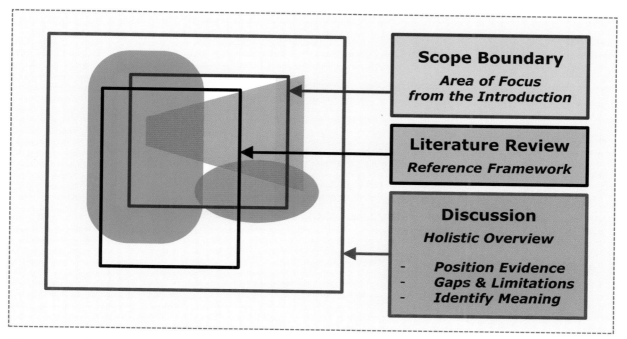

Figure 12.3   Holistic Overview

At this stage you should be arranging your findings to support the specific requirements of each objective. Do not jump to premature conclusions. Use evidence from different sources, secondary and primary, to support your argument leading to a justified point of view. In some cases you will identify alternatives and the Discussion should weigh up the pros and cons for each. All of this should be considered against your reference framework. You may confirm alignment or use the framework as a mirror to debate contrasts.

Information Gaps

It is not uncommon to realise at this late stage that data is missing leading to gaps in your investigation. If practical and you have time you can attempt to remedy the situation by further data gathering. Sometimes the issue is an incomplete Methodology. You should not undertake new Primary Research if it has not been previously sanctioned with appropriate ethics and other approvals. Better to acknowledge the shortfalls with an indication of how the situation might be overcome with more time or resources and then to discuss the impact of the issue.

You may be disappointed in that you do not have sufficient material to fully support an idea or to confirm some hypothesis. This is quite common and you need not be frustrated. You may have intended to interview someone, but they were not available or there may have been a poor response to a survey request. These are normal issues and it is valid to discuss the difficulties of acquiring information and the limitations that this creates.

One way to avoid the disaster of a failed investigation due to gaps in the research is to have a progressive hierarchy of objectives as discussed in the Chapter 6: The Introduction. You should have sufficient material to complete the process for the basic objectives creating evidence to argue that with better resources the higher levels would have been achieved. In the end it is about demonstrating a range of skills in a research context.

Even without gaps problems can arise if you only have a limited amount data. Do not jump to conclusions by extrapolating from a limited base. At best this is informed opinion and at worst just guesswork. The Discussion should consider the actual findings in the light of the realised practicalities of your Methodology. If a certain situation is indicated then say so, but beware of absolute certainty unless your data is very robust. Better to say that there is a trend towards a certain position that could be confirmed with more work and additional data. You may not be able to fix a problem of gaps or limited data, but critical reflection is part of the process, providing you with insights on likely outcomes or how the overall approach could be improved.

Limitations

It is important to recognise and be realistic about the limitations of your project. You may not have sufficient material in terms of depth or breadth to fully meet idealised objectives. This is only a failure if you delude yourself by claiming too much from the findings. Instead demonstrate an understanding of the research process and cognitive skills by critically reviewing what you were able to achieve. Identify any restrictions and indicate their significance.

Consider limitation from different points of view. There are those things that restricted the investigation such as approval boundaries: an investigation relating to children might have been conducted by talking only to adults related to the area of interest. There may have been access issues: ideally you wanted to talk directly with the managing director, but the best you could achieve was a middle manager. The response from your sample group may have been disappointing: the survey returns came in too slowly to meet your time restrictions. There are other resource limitations, not least your own capabilities as a researcher. Categorizing the issues demonstrates understanding. Other skills are shown through critical review and judgement as the impact of these barriers and your way of dealing with them are considered.

Identifying Meaning

All being well you will have enough material to address your specific intentions. You should move beyond basic data presentation to justified interpretation. This requires that you present the evidence from a range of findings to support a position for each objective. As indicated in the Knowledge Cascade in Figure 2.3 you a trying to move from data and information to knowledge and wisdom. This can only be done if the findings are considered holistically. Evidence must be taken from a range of inputs and considered together. This will require critical analysis and the synthesis of material from different sources and areas.

Critical Analysis

Critical analysis involves several considerations. First, is the data valid and secondly, has it been interpreted correctly? In other words can you rely on what the findings say and is there only one interpretation or are there other possibilities?

Data validity will depend on its provenance and its fit to your requirements. You should consider how the information was obtained and the reliability of your sources. With survey data how consistent are the responses? Is there strong agreement or a broader spread? Do you have confirmation from several sources? Here you need to exercise caution. It is not unusual for contemporary secondary sources to be based on the same original historical information. This is not corroboration but repetition. However if each author has added to the original, based on their own work or experience, then the supporting argument is stronger.

You will not be in a position to check everything in forensic detail and so will have to exercise academic judgement based on the evidence. It starts with your original selection of sources and continues with a considered evaluation of what they say cross referenced to others. Your own questions and their answers should be a good fit to your topics, but the secondary material was gathered for other purposes. How reasonable is it to reassign their findings to your requirements? This is something that should be justified and any limitations or issues identified and assessed.

Having established the credibility of your information, you need to think about its interpretation. Your earlier planning may have created templates for data presentation based on an assumption about what the findings will say. Be careful not to blindly follow the path that was laid out. Look at the data carefully. Sometimes the actual findings from some of the sources will imply a different route. Be open to alternative interpretations justifying the selection of a particular line. This is critical analysis

Synthesis

The objectives and issues around your topics can be too complex for a single data set to be used as the defining answer. You may need to combine, select or extend from a set of findings. There are two basic scenarios: deduction and induction.

Deduction: Imagine that you have two sets of data A and B where:

$A = (x + y)$ and $B = (y + z)$ x, y and z are the detailed data elements.

Only the y data from each set is common. Deduction uses only this element. The other components are eliminated, but they should not be ignored.

Selectivity is a well-known ruse to get to the opinion you want. To avoid an accusation of bias you must pull out the information desired while justifying the exclusion of the other elements. Suppose you want to consider only students in your study. Identifying them by selecting an age range may seem innocuous, but you need to justify the chosen boundaries carefully. You might think that those over 21 are working age adults, but some people study till they are older or start later. You may be creating artificial separations. Justify your selections and consider the implications of the unused elements.

Induction: The same data sets A and B are considered, but elements are not rejected. Instead A and B are used to imply a new situation C where:

C= (x + y + z + ?)   where ? indicates other unknown elements.

This is combination and extrapolation, but take care not to jump to unreasoned conclusions. For example: all of a survey's respondents were students with over 80% worried about tuition fees. Secondary research shows that young people spend a high proportion of their income on fashion related items even foregoing regular meals or buying text books. You might conclude that some young people are choosing between higher education and fashion. This may be true, but the extrapolation is highly dubious.

In general using subsets of data is valid, providing the significance of the eliminated information is considered. Pulling together separate sets of information to characterise a new scenario requires careful justification with enough supporting evidence to show that the extrapolation or combination is a valid and reasoned argument.

Implication for Recommendations

Recommending actions in response to particular situations may be one of your higher level objectives. Some of your research activity will be directed at finding information so that you can address this intention. In addition other ideas for suggestions will come out of your investigation even if you are not explicitly looking to offer advice. These are only valid if they are evidence based and the indications are strong. Avoid expressing opinions if you do not have sufficient material to back up a recommendation.

Ironically it can be valid to make some recommendations when the data is weak or out of scope. In these cases the focus is not interpretation of findings but a reflection on your research process and recognition that it could be improved by following a suggested alternative path.

Out of Scope Indications

Inevitably your investigation will have some aspects that stray outside your area of focus. In general you can ignore material that is significantly out of scope concentrating on your main theme. You have to be disciplined. You do not have enough space to go off at a tangent no matter how interesting the information is.

However some side topics will be closely related to your investigation. If they relate directly to your objectives, it is reasonable to reconsider the in and out of scope boundaries. If the application to your investigation is not that strong it is better to park the material. Instead of ignoring it, use the

Discussion to highlight its existence. You may then choose to include it in suggestions for follow on investigation.

Process Considerations

Things rarely go to plan and the plans themselves are restricted by a range of limitations and circumstances. Hindsight is a wonderful thing and as you come to the end of your project you will realise that you could have done things differently or anticipated and managed particular situations better. Many courses encourage a reflective review and recommendations for improvement to the dissertation process. Sometimes this is required as a separate chapter. As you consider the findings, the effectiveness of the process in acquiring them can be highlighted and critically considered.

There are two principal perspectives: did you do the right things and did you do things right? The first part includes limitations to the dissertation process outlined above, but you should also consider your own judgements. On reflection could you have followed a different methodology, used another sample group or anticipated issues that held you back? The second part is a reflection on the actual methods used. Were they appropriate and effectively carried out? Use part of the Discussion to highlight potential areas for process change as well as improvement.

New Areas for Investigation

Sometimes the research identifies aspects that had not been considered in the dissertation planning. It will not be practical at this late stage to incorporate these new topics. Your research may also stop short of developing a complete picture due to the boundaries that you have set, but the findings may indicate other avenues for consideration. The Discussion should draw attention to these new areas so that recommendations for further investigation might be made.

Discussion of Findings: Case Study

The Ethics of Motivation

Naadir's family came to the UK as refugees along with thousands of others who had been ordered to leave Uganda. They had nothing, but with the help of friends they were able to set up a small general store that provided income and work for the family. As well as the more usual merchandise, a range of ethnic products to meet the needs of a changing community were offered. From these lowly beginnings Naadir's grandfather created a thriving enterprise importing and distributing traditional African and Asian foodstuffs and goods.

When he was old enough Naadir worked in the family business, showing commitment and capability. It soon became clear that he was the natural successor to his grandfather. With this in mind the young man worked and studied hard. He went to university to do a business degree and later undertook a Master's course in Strategic Management.

Naadir was well informed, following politics and business in the popular press and trade publications. These coupled with his knowledge of his family history made him very articulate and opinionated about international affairs. He was particularly interested in the way companies in supply chains treated their workers. He had observed that generally the working conditions were hard and the pay and conditions poor. He wondered how these impacted an organisation's performance.

For his dissertation he decided that he would review different management styles in the light of growing requirements for corporate social responsibility, CSR, under the title: The Ethics of Motivation. His aim was to answer the question that became his subtitle: How should companies treat their workers to get the best performance? He identified two principal schools of thought based on opposing views: some work to live while others live to work. The former seemed to imply laziness and therefore a need for incentives such as rewards or pressure to perform. The second appeared to centre on motivation factors that catered to an individual's need for personal growth.

Using his suppliers as a sample group Naadir created a survey for managers to identify their attitudes and experiences, with a particular focus on how they treated their own suppliers and workers. His supervisor queried this choice with concerns that it might not be a reliable or representative sample. Naadir did not get on well with his supervisor and ignored his worries. He was adamant that the findings would be of use both for his academic studies and for the business.

The survey produced rather bland results. Naadir had expected a wider range of responses and wondered if the replies were entirely honest. He had also scheduled an interview with his grandfather. It seemed that the old man had experienced a much wider range of conditions and expressed the opinion that business relationships, as in life, should start with respect, dignity and trust. Afterwards they discussed Naadir's project in detail. The student was worried that he would not be able to complete it as his limited survey findings gave him little to discuss. Grandfather pointed out that Naadir did not have to like his supervisor, but he should be professional about it and seek his guidance.

It was a hard lesson for Naadir, but he met with his supervisor, apologised for the previously dismissive attitude and asked what he should now do. It was suggested that the survey responses might be based on what the suppliers thought Naadir wanted to hear. After all they were anxious to hold onto their contracts. He advised Naadir to present the information as he found it; this would demonstrate the principles even if the outcomes were biased. The desk research, especially the contemporary material from the popular press, would provide information that could be used to illuminate the different schools of thought. The Discussion would not produce a definitive answer to the original question, but a reflective review would recognise the difficulties in carrying out this type of research.

The final submission was criticised for expressing strong opinions without supporting evidence. In particular there was nothing of substance to support the premise that the survey responses were not truthful. On the other hand the markers recognised that the principles had been adequately demonstrated and praised the student for his critically assessed and reflective review of the dissertation process and the student's awareness of his own limitations. They indicated that the consideration of the survey process as an example of the problems associated with management and motivation showed skilful synthesis of the findings.

Observations

- The narrative should always be evidence based. Naadir had strong opinions, perhaps based on real knowledge, but these were not always supported with evidence. His suspicions about the survey should have been presented as a concern rather than a fact.

- Naadir realised that a professional working relationship with his supervisor was more important than friendship. His tutor gave him good advice which he eventually followed.

- It may have been that the respondents were not convinced that the survey responses would be anonymous. This barrier should have been considered beforehand, but Naadir had to go with what he had and review the implications afterwards.

- Demonstrating the principles of good research was more important that getting definitive answers.

- Naadir recognised his own limitations and reflected honestly on their impact.

Discussion of Findings: Good Practice

- **Context:** Setting the scene by reviewing the in and out of scope boundary and selected academic framework clarifies the Discussion focus and purpose.

- **Holistic overview:** Pulling together material from all aspects of the investigation will create a coherent and convincing argument.

- **Aligned structure:** The aim and objectives provide a structural framework for the Discussion creating a meaningful flow.

- **Critical assessment:** Comparing and contrasting findings with theory, espoused wisdom or regulations and considering relative merits and fit are part of the process of critical review.

- **Develop meaning:** Sometimes it is easier and more word count efficient to use diagrams to elaborate on findings. Derived charts based on sub-set and combined results can help develop ideas once the basic data has been presented.

- **Evidence based:** Rely on your actual data taking your discussion only as far as it will allow. Do not over extrapolate, speculate or make assumptions.

- **Gaps and anomalies:** Explain any gaps in topic coverage, missing results or shortfalls in data collection. Recognise anomalies. Explain them if you can and indicate their significance.

- **Acknowledge issues:** Identify any issues with your methodology and general research approach, highlighting their impact on your investigation.

- **Open ended:** The discussion should identify a range of ideas and may well present alternative explanations. While it is reasonable to indicate a preferred view, leave the selection and justification of a particular line to the Conclusions section.

Discussion of Findings: Common Issues

- **Disjointed sequencing:** The Discussion will be confusing if it does not have a recognisable structure. An opening paragraph should set the context followed by an objective lead review. If you choose to use a different flow explain the topic sequencing first.

- **Plugging gaps:** It is very tempting to go back to try and get missing data. Do this if you can, but only if you have time and approval for the revised Methodology. The new material should be presented in the correct area of your report not in the Discussion. Usually there is insufficient time after a shortfall is discovered. Quick fixes at this stage lead to unreliable data. Better to show professionalism by recognising the issues and discussing their implications.

- **Over extrapolation:** Stretching results to cover a gap or to address a specific point is not synthesis but creative writing. Keep within the limits set by your data.

- **Repetition:** Avoid repeating the findings. The Discussion is about extracting meaning from them to support your objectives.

- **Opinion:** Points raised should be based on the evidence presented not your own viewpoint. Selections and choices derived from your material should be justified.

- **Limitations and bias:** Failure to recognise and critically consider your approach and findings indicates a lack of skill. Be open about issues and the limitations they create.

- **Over delivery:** Sometimes there is a shortfall in the completion of objectives and those that are achieved are then over described. Be succinct. Critically review why information is missing and its implications rather than over delivering on your successful outcomes.

- **Focus:** It is appropriate to recognise out of scope material and associated ideas, but these should not be discussed extensively. Focus on the in scope topics.

- **Lack of reflection:** Projects and the methods used can all be improved. A Discussion is not complete if you do not reflect critically considering how well the project was conducted in terms of the activities and your part in it.

Discussion of Findings: Key Actions

- **Coherent structure:** Review your Introduction and Literature Review to remind yourself of the investigation purpose and context. Make sure you use appropriate headings across all data findings and discussion areas to create a sense of structure and purpose that align with your aim and objectives.

- **Identify gaps:** Have you got the resources and approvals to cover missing areas at this late stage? If not write an explanation that considers the implications of any gaps.

- **Evidence based:** Make sure that the Discussion is based on actual data. Confirm that any synthesis and extrapolation is supported by stated evidence.

- **Differentiation and critical assessment:** Avoid repetition of earlier material. Instead confirm that the Discussion pulls ideas together and considers their merits based on cross referenced findings and logical extensions.

- **Reflection:** Review the whole dissertation project considering the effectiveness of the approach in terms of identified limitations, methods used and your own actions.

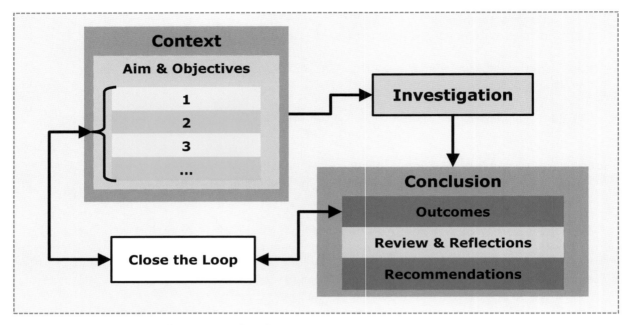

Figure 13.1   The Conclusion In Context

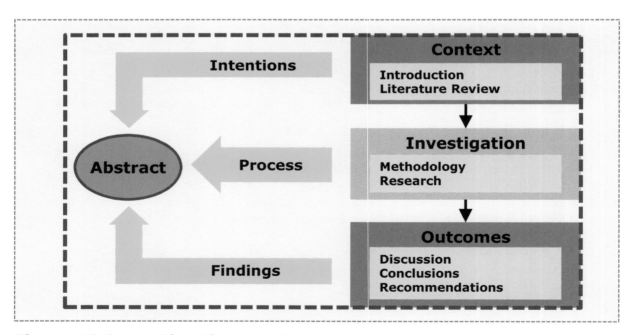

Figure 13.2   The Abstract Structure

Chapter 13

Final Summaries

You and the readers of your report need to know that your investigation is finished and what the outcomes were. A dissertation is complex, multifaceted and often ambitious. It is unlikely that everything intended was fully realised, but Conclusions can be drawn from the research findings and subsequent Discussion.

Incomplete work, issues and limitations inherent in your research should be identified and considered with reflections about how the processes could have been improved. In addition related topics with potential for further investigation may have been identified and can form the basis for additional recommendations.

It is conventional academic practice to provide an Abstract. In the future, your research may be of use to others in their investigations. An Abstract, a summary of your dissertation's intentions, process and findings, gives a complete overview and is a useful filtering tool that enables others to decide if your work is of use to them and worth examining in more detail.

The Conclusion

As shown in Figure 13.1 the Conclusions should be drawn from the complete investigation and related to the original objectives. Its primary task is to identify explicit outcomes and make relevant observations. These will have been identified in the Discussion where explanations and alternative views should have been explored. Do not repeat these or introduce new topics. Instead a summary of the key findings related back to the aim and objectives should be provided. The various threads should then be drawn together to present insights and set the ground for recommendations. The Conclusion should finish with a summary of realistic suggestions to improve the project process as well as identifying potential areas for follow on work.

Close the Loop: Outcomes vs Objectives

The Conclusion must be based on the actual information presented. If the findings offered a choice of views then it may be appropriate to favour one based on the context of your particular investigation. This means that it is very important to acknowledge the original intentions. The linking of outcomes to the original aim and objectives is called closing the loop; did you do what you set out to do? There several scenarios:

- **Achieved ... found this:** The objectives are reviewed and the findings presented as a completed activity.

- **Not achieved ... because**: It may be that you just had too much to do and it was not feasible to complete a stretching objective. You have shown an understanding of your topic by having the objective in place and can indicate that completing it could be the basis for future work. On the other hand the objective may not have been realistic or valid. In these cases your Discussion should have offered explanations and this can be recognised in the Conclusion.

- **Partial ... implications:** Sometimes things are not clear cut. You may have insufficient evidence or it could be that there is a range of valid outcomes in different circumstances. Your Discussion should have identified the issues and considered possible approaches to deal with them. The Conclusion should summarise the situation and, if there is sufficient evidence, offer a judgement on the most appropriate alternative in the context of your investigation.

Some types of dissertation do not have a set of formalised objectives. Instead there may be a statement of intent with related actions to address an area of interest. These can typically be broken down into components and used as a structure for the Discussion. You can use the same structure for the Conclusion following the process described above. In the end it is about demonstrating analytical and critical thinking based around the aim of your project to reach relevant conclusions.

Insights and Observations

The detailed study of your theme will have been guided by your aim and objectives but these were proposed at the outset before you really understood the nature of the subject. It is likely that you will have covered areas that go beyond the initial ideas or will have investigated specific topics to a greater depth than anticipated. This broad coverage with some areas of great detail will lead to insights and pertinent observations.

This may seem an ambitious idea, but insights do not have to be earth shattering or particularly revolutionary. They can be as simple as the things that you have noticed that others would overlook. Through your investigative work you will have developed some expertise and detailed knowledge about the particulars of your field. You will be in a good position to see the wood through the trees to present or explain the big picture. Take a little time to reflect on your project and its findings. Are they broadly as expected or are there some nuances that have only now become apparent? There are various possibilities:

- **The sum is greater than the parts:** You started with an area of interest and an aim to investigate a particular aspect. To guide this you may have set some goals or objectives. Individually these may have been achieved, or at least addressed, and when considered together does an overarching idea or thought emerge that was not initially considered?

- **Light bulb or eureka moment:** As you consider the various project elements together things may suddenly become clear. Why things work the way they do, cause and effect relationships stand out or explanations of the complex are actually quite simple. These are examples of the clarity that can come with hindsight.

- **New schools of thought:** You may have thought that you were investigating a very particular situation only to realise that it has a wider, more general, application. You may have identified a new scenario or school of thought that sits alongside more established or accepted ideas.

- **Accepted ideas are invalid:** Your work may challenge historical thinking showing, at least in your particular area of interest, that it is wrong, invalid or inappropriately applied.

- **Identified parallels:** It is often assumed that new fields require new thinking, but you may have found that established ideas with some minor modification are a good fit. The insight is not necessarily the application of old theory or ideas to a new situation but understanding what needs to be adjusted or adapted to make them work.

- **Rogue results:** Unusual findings, anomalies and misfits can be indicators of a new or hidden situation or suggest a different hypothesis.

- **QED:** *"Quod Erat Demonstrandum"*, literally *"that which was to be demonstrated"*, is a statement that you have done what you set out to do. It is easy to get lost in the detail of individual findings and objectives. It is appropriate to indicate that together these demonstrate your original premise or validate your intentions, the aim of your project.

Insight vs Intuition

A consideration of the list above may well lead you to valid insights, but be careful not to confuse these with intuition. As you gather information your brain may make connections that are subconsciously leading you to convictions, things you are certain about without knowing why. This is intuition, implied knowledge without the detail to back it up. In daily life it is a powerful force but not academically sufficient for a dissertation. You need explicit evidence.

Insights must be based on the material presented, sometimes with a justified extrapolation, or they could be speculative where the reasoning is argued and supported by evidence. You may have additional material that for some reason was not presented. If you use this to formulate an idea then your statements will appear to be without foundation. Likewise your dissertation may be centred on strongly held beliefs that you have developed over the years. Presenting ideas from this background will seem like unsupported assertions that are no more that personal opinions. For an observation or insight to be in your Conclusion the supporting material must have been present in your Findings or developed in the Discussion.

Recommendations and Reflections

Recommendations can come from two main areas. They can be suggestions that relate directly to your investigation theme or they can be considerations about how the project process could be changed or managed better.

The nature of your investigation may lend itself to producing a set of recommendations as an outcome. In fact this can be a valid objective in some studies. They can arise as specific points of interest or insight but must be based on the actual evidence of your research. Be cautious about absolute advice. You findings need to be very robust for you to suggest that a particular action is the way forward. If this is not the case then it is better to suggest that the findings indicate that a specific response might be appropriate or that an idea is worthy of further investigation.

Some recommendations come from interesting but under developed findings. Often these have fallen by the wayside because they are out of scope for the main project aim. They represent potential areas of interest where there is an indication that various actions would be worthwhile. Without sufficient evidence to make anything but a tentative suggestion, the best recommendation in these circumstances is that they are areas worthy of further study.

Inevitably you will have encountered limitations in the execution of your dissertation and will have made compromises in your Methodology or areas of investigation. The implications of these should have been covered in earlier sections of your write-up. Hindsight is a wonderful teacher and so recommendations relating to process improvements are a valid contribution to the concluding section, but you should be realistic. Suggesting that vast resources be deployed to address a topic of minor interest shows a lack of understanding. Recommendations about improvements to the project implementation should be consistent with the nature of your studies and its scope.

A critical reflection about your experience of the dissertation process can also be a valid element of your Conclusion. In some cases it is a specific requirement of the course and will then be presented as a separate chapter. It is reasonable to include thoughts about the investigative process and its imposed restrictions and compromises. In this type of reflection the main focus should be a personal one. Be succinct and focused. These projects are hard for everyone. Avoid a broad brush approach and identify the one or two things that had the greatest impact for you. If you were to do it again what would you do differently? What are the most significant things you have learned about doing a project of this scale? What have you learned about yourself?

Do not forget the dissertation learning objectives. Make sure that your recommendations and reflections demonstrate knowledge, understanding and critical thinking. You need to maintain an academic professionalism right to the end.

Summary of Key Outcomes

If it has not happened naturally as part of the Conclusion flow it is a good idea to present a closing statement. This should be a summary of the key outcomes and an indication of how close the project came to delivering the intended aim. It is effectively the QED statement described above. It is not necessary to repeat earlier information in detail, but a couple of sentences are an effective way of closing your report, indicating clearly that you have finished. This also provides a framework that can be expanded slightly as the last element of the Abstract.

The Abstract

It is conventional practice with academic writing to provide an Abstract. This is a high level summary of the whole work. It provides a synopsis that will help other researchers and scholars decide if the work is of value to them and therefore worth reading in full. For a dissertation the Abstract also serves as a big picture guide for your markers. The initial overview provided by a clear Abstract will put your work in context, helping them follow and understand what follows more easily.

The Abstract should be based only on the presented work. It should not contain new material or include elements that were not used in your main report. It is a very good final check for you and an initial check for your markers to test that your report is coherent and logical. showing how initial intentions flow through actions to deliver concluding outcomes.

Writing the Abstract

The Abstract can only cover the presented project if it is written at the end when everything else is finished. Although written last it should be placed at the front of your report. It is a good idea to anticipate its write-up as you proceed by preparing notes. These can serve as a useful review of each section as they are completed.

As indicated in Figure 13.2 the Abstract has three main parts:

- **Intentions:** The principal theme with its aim and key objectives should be summarised with some basic justification based on the context that is usually set by the Introduction and Literature Review.

- **Process:** Outline what was actually done based on detail from the Methodology and the specific investigation processes used. This will depend on the type of dissertation and will indicate where information was found, with some detail of your target groups and your experimental approach. This part will briefly summarise how the research was conducted.

- **Outcomes:** Present a summary of key findings and recommendations derived from the Discussion and Conclusion.

These three elements give a high level overview of the whole dissertation. They should be brief; a taster of what is to follow. The Abstract should be short, one or two pages at the most. Some dissertation requirements specify a maximum length. Check for any specific requirements and common practice for your course. The detail needs to be sharp and succinct. Limitations and assumptions are not normally discussed beyond setting the basic context of the study.

The Abstract stage is not the time to start revising your project, but preparing it may highlight some discrepancies and flow issues that impact the quality of your argument. Minor editing revisions at this stage are reasonable if you have time, but you must then check that the Abstract reflects only what is in the main report.

Final Summaries: Case Study

Concluding Assumptions

Business studies students, Mary and Ben, were both interested in consumer behaviour. Mary was passionate about the environment. She tried to be green in her everyday life and wondered why others were not so committed. She felt that people wanted to be good citizens, but that business did not make it easy for them. To test this hypothesis she decided to research consumer attitudes to environmental issues and to investigate how companies presented themselves in terms of their impact on the planet.

Her supervisor warned her that this was a very big topic and that she should narrow it down to a manageable area with a set of progressive objectives to critically examine the issues. These would let her develop the ideas in stages, taking things as far as she could within the time and resources available. Mary decided to narrow her focus to clothing purchases using her student colleagues as the study target. Her hypothesis and broad research area remained the same. She did not propose a detailed set of progressive objectives.

Companies' green credentials were identified through their annual reports and press releases. Primary Research was demonstrated by a questionnaire circulated to her peer group about their behaviour relating to clothing purchases. After a lot of hard work she was very disappointed that her project failed. The feedback indicated that the work was largely descriptive and assumptive with very selective research. The markers felt that there was insufficient evidence for her Conclusions and Recommendations with a tendency to frame questions and lead the participants in a direction favoured by the researcher. They said that she was uncritical about the company reports failing to recognise that companies would write these to show themselves in the best light.

It could be said that she was trying to persuade people to be better citizens. This was a worthy goal based on a significant assumption that people wanted to be good consumers and would be if only they had appropriate information. She jumped to this conclusion without actually using her research to test the idea.

Ben was also interested in social aspects of consumption. He noted that many of his student colleagues spent a significant amount of money on clothes, favouring low cost, fast fashion, brands. Ben was an avid reader of the financial and business press and knew that these companies made extensive use of outsourced manufacture in Asia where there had been many supply chain scandals. Human rights, exploitation of children and deaths in factory fires were among the issues. He decided to investigate the impact of these reports on consumer attitudes using his peers as his research group.

Gathering data about supply chain issues was a straight forward secondary research exercise. However he did not feel so confident about the right sort of questions to ask his target group. On the advice of his supervisor, Ben decided to gather a few friends as a casual focus group so that he could explore potential avenues for his research.

Almost straight away he found that his whole idea was built on a very weak foundation. He had assumed that his colleagues would be as well informed as he, but few of them followed the popular press, let alone the more analytical business reports. He realised that it would be difficult to test a reaction to the supply chain issues if his sample group was not aware of them. He was now in a difficult position with little time left. He decided to revise his ideas to focus on where the group got information relating to their purchase decisions and how it influenced them. At the end of his personally delivered survey he posed a question about the potential impact of bad news using an image from his Secondary Research to stimulate a reaction.

While the dissertation did not go as planned, Ben was able to demonstrate the principle of a critical and analytical approach. He was able to draw some justified conclusions from his findings and related these back to his original and revised intentions. He was able to make valid Recommendations for future studies to improve and develop his work. He passed with a good mark.

Observations

- Both students worked hard, but this is not enough. The research and its report have to meet the academic requirements of good research practice with unbiased review.

- Mary had assumed a particular scenario, presenting a journalistic view rather than a critically examined academic report. Ben was open and more aware, realising that he had made an initial assumption about his target group's knowledge. He realigned his objectives to the situation so that his overall flow was convincing.

- Ben revised his objectives in the light of his initial findings. His Conclusions closed the loop by referring back to both the original and revised intentions and he reflected on the changes he made. Mary assumed a general hypothesis and just repeated this in her Conclusions.

- Ben's Conclusions and Recommendations were solid, based on actual evidence. Mary's were more an expression of her own opinions and wishes rather than information derived from the research evidence.

- Both students received good advice from their supervisors. Mary did not really follow it. She reduced the scale of her investigation by narrowing her sample group but not its scope. She still wanted to change the world.

Final Summaries: Good Practice

- **Succinct summaries:** The Conclusion and Abstract should be brief, focused reviews that summarise only the main points of the project.

- **Conclusion content:** The focus should be on the key findings with appropriate recommendations and reflections about the whole process.

- **Close the loop:** The Conclusion should refer back to the aim and objectives from the Introduction, indicating the extent to which they were achieved.

- **Potential development:** Incomplete or underdeveloped points of interest can be identified in the Conclusion as potential areas for further work.

- **Reflective view:** The one and only area where you can express your own opinions freely is when you reflect on the dissertation process. Some courses require this as a separate chapter. Otherwise it is appropriate with the benefit of hindsight to make comments in the Conclusion section indicating how you might have done things differently.

- **Exercise caution:** Express certainty only when the evidence is very strong. Where it is weaker or incomplete, moderate your language to identify possibilities or indications rather than certainties.

- **Abstract function:** The abstract should provide a summary of the complete work: context, initial plan, what was actually done and the key findings. This should have just enough detail for a reader to decide if the main work is of sufficient interest to be read in full. It should provide a high level overview of your complete project for the dissertation markers.

- **Evidence based:** All conclusions, recommendations and the Abstract should be based only on the presented evidence.

Final Summaries: Common Issues

- **Late additions:** Adding new material to the Conclusion shows very poor organisational skills. If you realise that data is missing at this late stage it is probably better to acknowledge the shortfall with an explanation in the Discussion section. If you have time for fill in research, it should be added to the appropriate earlier sections.

- **Extended analysis:** The Conclusion should summarise earlier material and discussions. It should not add to the debate. If a new point of view occurs to you, consider adding it to the Discussion if you have time.

- **Lack of focus:** The Conclusion should state how well the original aim and objectives were achieved. Failing to do this indicates a weak and incomplete academic argument.

- **Stretching the truth:** Do not jump to conclusions or fill in the gaps. You may have found evidence for an idea, but be sure that it is robust enough before you make absolute statements. If the evidence is weak or incomplete, the indications can be acknowledged with a suggestion that further work is needed.

- **Unsupported opinions:** Expressing ideas as conclusions or recommendations without the supporting evidence in your report shows lack of cognitive skills. It is reasonable to give personal opinions on how you conducted the project and what you might have done differently, but even these ideas need to be based on presented evidence.

- **Wordy repetition:** The Conclusion and Abstract should be brief summaries. A lengthy cut and paste job on earlier material does not read well, wastes word count and is unlikely to meet the requirements for a succinct and coherent report.

- **Incomplete Abstract:** The Abstract is more than an introduction. To be of use to others who might consider your work as a reference, it must summarise the whole project: its purpose, activities and key findings. It should be brief; a taster of what is in the main report. As such it serves as a high level overview of what is to follow.

Final Summaries: Key Actions

- **Review your initial intentions:** Make a final edit on your Introduction and Methodology. This is not about making things perfect with a direct fit to the actual work done, but it is appropriate to make sure that the whole report has a coherent structure. For example some objectives and research activities may have been just too stretching and not even attempted. Better to remove them or tone them down, possibly moving them to recommendations for future work.

- **Reality check:** Verify that conclusions, recommendations, reflections and the Abstract are all based on the actual work done and not some wishful thinking.

- **Linked and logical flow:** Confirm that the concluding material refers to the original aim and objectives. Verify that you have been consistent with topic flow so that your report has a clear and logical structure.

- **A clear finish:** Make haste slowly. You have almost finished, but do not rush the end. Review the set requirements and check that your work has addressed them. Is all the material in the right place? For example: is there a requirement for a reflective review as a separate section; are you digressing into further discussions; have you found new or missing material? Make sure you put everything into the correct sections so that the Conclusion is a clear end to a well-structured investigation.

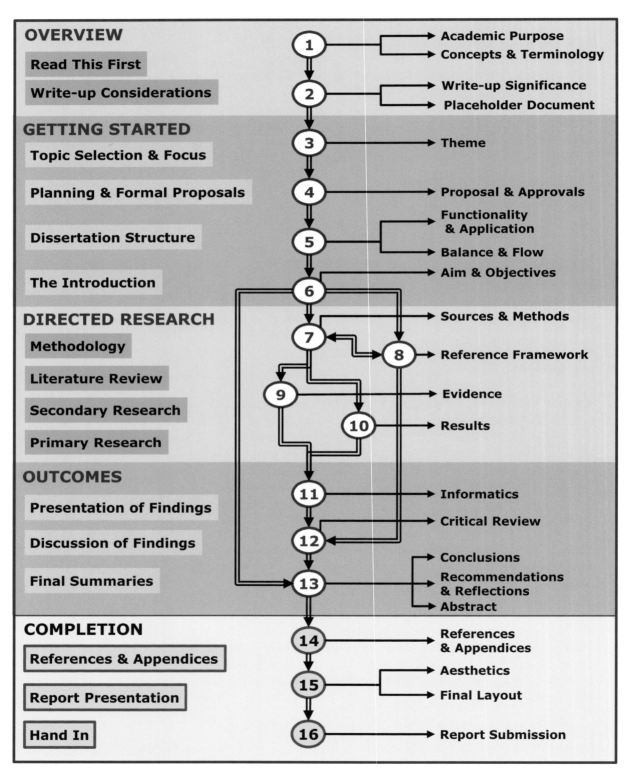

COMPLETION

At this stage the dissertation is almost finished. The investigative activity should be complete and the write-up in an advanced stage, probably as a set of chapter or section drafts. These need to be put together to form a convincing report that meets the academic requirements in terms of content, flow, layout and general presentation.

You also have to submit the report following the prescribed procedure or it will not be marked.

Completion: Section Summary

Chapter 14   References and Appendices: Your final edit must be within the word count limit making an appropriate use of appendices. The most important of these is the references list. Careful checking is needed to ensure that the body text tags and the listings match. Other appendices should be clearly identified in the main text and should serve specific purposes and not just be a deposit of interesting material.

Chapter 15   Report Presentation: Some consideration needs to be given to the final layout and presentation of your report. In many cases the basic styling is specified and needs to be confirmed. Some courses go beyond this requiring a more significant visual impact that is part of the assessment criteria. Even where this is not a requirement the general look should be considered so that you present your work as positively as possible.

Chapter 16   Hand In: Last minute checks should be made prior to submission to verify that you are conforming to all the set requirements. Hand in instructions are usually very specific and time limited. You must submit something on time following the correct procedure for your work to be marked and a grade awarded.

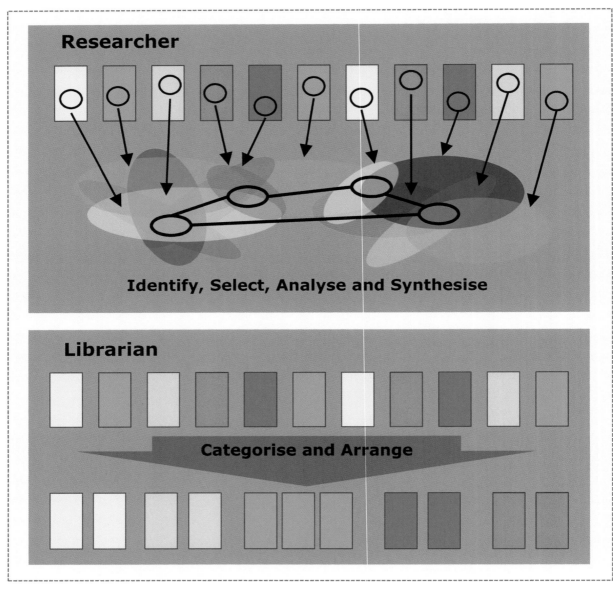

Figure 14.1   Researcher and Librarian Roles

Researcher: Identifies and selects sources, analyses findings and synthesises meaning

Librarian: Gathers material together and arranges it in a catalogued order

Chapter 14

Referencing and Appendices

Completing a Master's dissertation requires the activities of both a librarian and researcher to acquire and manage information. Figure 14.1 indicates the differences between these two roles. For most of the project you will have been a researcher identifying, selecting, analysing and synthesising data to create meaning appropriate to your theme. In the final stages your role shifts to that of a librarian. You must arrange and categorise your material with reference listings and organised appendices to create a coherent report that addresses the set requirements.

The layout of the main body of the report has been discussed in earlier chapters and should now be complete or at least in a final draft stage. To this you must add front and end material. In particular you should give careful consideration to references and other appendices to ensure their accuracy and validity in supporting your submission. Chapter 5: Dissertation Structure cautioned against the over use of appendices, especially if this was an attempt to control your word count, but some are needed as evidence of your activity. The most important of these are the reference lists that identify other people's work on which your argument is based.

Reference Requirements

It is normal in academic work to provide source information to show where your information came from. No matter that you developed this into your own ideas it is still necessary to acknowledge the work of others that formed the foundations on which you built. References also provide an evidence trail that lets others follow your research in detail with the possibility that they might develop it along different lines in their own work. It is therefore important that there must be a direct connection between the reference tags in the text body and the full details in the reference listing so that others can get back to the original source.

References are also a useful way to reduce word count. They can be used as a short form for established theory, ideas, schools of thought and regulations, avoiding the need for elaborate explanations in the text. Even so there should be some indication of the subject matter. A terse reference tag and listing is not sufficient.

Getting the right number of references is a balance driven by the requirements of each report section. A Methodology chapter may derive all the discussed options from a single well regarded text book, but a similar approach to Secondary Research would be considered highly derivative even plagiarism. On average one reference per hundred to two hundred words is typical. Some disciplines and research areas will require more.

The quantity and quality of the identified sources gives examiners some indication of the depth and breadth of your investigation. You should avoid gratuitous over delivery, but too few indicate weak research. Examiners also check for alignment of text tags and listing entries, doing spot checks in both directions. This is a good indicator of the thoroughness and care that has been applied. Text tags without a corresponding listing, list entries with no mention in the body text and errors in formatting are red flags that will cause concern about the quality and completeness of your work.

Referencing Conventions

Each institution has a preferred referencing style. This will be specified in the dissertation guidelines and must be followed. Most universities produce a handbook or provide a link to an online source that describes the required layout conventions.

It is vitally important that there is a unique link between your text tags, the reference identifier in the body of your work, and the full entry in the appendix listing. Problems can arise when there is no clear indication of author or publication date, a not untypical situation with online information. The web addresses are often too long to be practical text tags. Using an abbreviation or substitute is acceptable, such as Web1, Web2 …. but only if the listing contains this tag in the appropriate alphabetical position in front of the full source identification.

Citing different authors with the same name from the same year or multiple publications from one author in the same year can also create confusion. Most conventions specify the use of some form of numbering to differentiate these, for example (Smith[1] 2012), (Smith[2] 2012). The numbering should not be forgotten in the alphabetic appendix listing.

Reference Lists

The dissertation guidelines may specify a number of different reference lists. It is common to separate references for written sources from illustrations and other types of media content. The context will usually give a clear indication to the reader which list should be consulted. Some students will go a step further to list books, journals, magazines and web sources in separate lists. This may stem from their own recording processes, but it is infuriating for the report reader. Often the context and text tags do not give a clear indication and several lists may need to be consulted before the full source detail is found. It is better to put all of the references into a single alphabetic listing except where there is a specified requirement for separation.

Some organisations like you to differentiate between explicitly cited works and any general background material that was used to inform your activity. Other institutions prefer a single combined list. Be sure to conform to the set requirements. The source listings may be called References or Bibliography. There seems to be no clear convention in the use of these terms. In the absence of specific guidelines it is suggested that the title References be used for cited work and Bibliography for general background and uncited works. In other words two quite distinct lists.

Plagiarism Checks

It is dishonest to claim the efforts of others as your own. Using their ideas as a starting point or combining various works to synthesise a new theme can only have academic integrity if the original sources are cited. Plagiarism is unacceptable and may lead to severe penalties, but the nuances of referencing are a minefield that can catch the unwary. Universities make extensive use of plagiarism checking software such as Turnitin®, often providing students with facilities to check their own draft work. Final submissions may then be submitted through the system or be checked independently. High similarity scores are not unusual. Acknowledging the work of others through extensive referencing only partially addresses the issues. A high score made up of many low value matches is common. After all you will be referring to many established areas and a lot of students are likely to be covering similar topics using the same sources.

Literal quotes and a cut and paste of selected phrases from a source will lead to high individual similarity scores that are a cause for concern. This approach can make you look lazy and is inefficient in terms of word count with extraneous material that is not directly relevant to your report. Paraphrasing – using your own words, overcomes these issues. Use literal quotes only when you require the impact of the original wording. High match scores may also indicate that you are collating a lot of material from only a few selected sources. Even if these are referenced you may be relying too heavily on someone else's material. This is being unduly derivative, not cheating as such, but academically unacceptable. It could lead to loss of marks or penalties. In your investigation you need to be a researcher looking for linkages and meaning and not a librarian organising the work of others.

You may have earlier coursework that is entirely your own that is appropriate to your dissertation. In this situation the previous material should be considered like any other source. You should reference it and extract the key points for use. Recycling of large sections of work done for another activity as if it were new is not valid and may be considered as plagiarism.

It is a good idea to check your draft material if the facility is available. If you find high matches that you are not able to remedy or that you do not understand consult with your supervisor for advice. There have been cases where a student's work had been copied by others without them knowing. At the assessment stage it was not clear who produced the original. Bringing matters to your tutor's attention early on, especially when coupled with your own notes and diary, will protect you from unfair accusations.

Appendices

It is inevitable that you will identify a lot of interesting material in your studies. Not all of it will fit into your main report, but it is hard to let all this work go to waste. Guidelines typically indicate that appendices are not included in the word count and so the temptation to add the extra material in an appendix is strong. This might seem like a good solution, but it is inappropriate. The use of an appendix for excess material shows an inability to demonstrate academic judgement. Unless an appendix is needed and adds value, cut it out or incorporate the key information that it contains in a different way.

Valid Appendix Usage

Dissertation guidelines may call for specific appendices and you may wish to add others. In general, use an appendix when its content is needed, but where this is too long or too detailed to be included in the main body without disrupting your narrative. In many cases the appendix is not an essential read, but serves as evidence that you have actually carried out the stated activities giving credibility to your work. Figure 14.2 shows valid usage and also indicates alternatives if an appendix cannot be justified for inclusion.

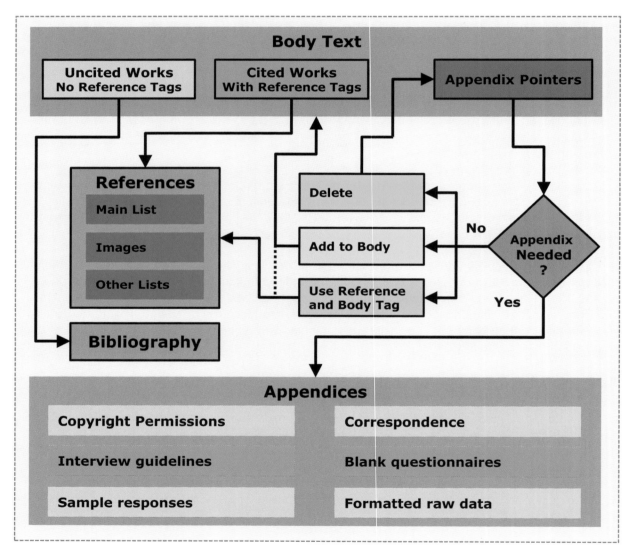

Figure 14.2   Valid Appendix Usage

Typically, appendices should acknowledge the work of others used in your report and also provide evidence of your own activities:

- **References Lists:** These are a particular form of appendix as discussed above. A single listing of sources cited in alphabetical order based on the text reference tags is the minimum requirement.

- **Permissions:** Group together any formal approvals given for the use of legally protected work such as copyright material, trademarks and intellectual property.

- **Correspondence:** Show requests and responses relating to investigative activities such as asking for site visits and engagement with staff members.

- **Templates:** Blank research templates such as survey questionnaires or interview check sheets are easier to show than describe.

- **Completed Responses:** Demonstrate activity by including sample copies of some actual participant returns. Note: Take care to protect promised anonymity.

- **Results Data:** Consolidated raw results arranged in spreadsheets or tables. Your report may focus on the extracted results, not these details. The reason for having them is to provide evidence that the research was actually done and to provide a secondary source to others.

It is important that you draw attention to each appendix. Indicate its existence in the body text with a little information about what it contains. The reader can then decide if they wish to look at it in detail. At the very least they will recognise that you have evidence to back up your story.

Appendix Alternatives

Before you rush to include other appendices stop and ask yourself why you need them. If you want one because you worked hard on the information but the content is not part of your selected in scope material then leave it out. If on the other hand the material is relevant then why is not it in the main body of your work? Dumping material by telling the reader to *"See Appendix X"*, but providing no detail in the text body is actually a statement that you want to include the work, while trying to avoid the word count implications. Your examiner may not accept this and could still add the appendix to the overall word count taking you over set limits.

Sometimes information is needed as evidence or proof of activity, but it does not need to be read in detail. It would spoil your flow if the material was in the main text. An appendix may seem the obvious solution but can still be word shedding. As an alternative consider using a reference. Some things do not need detailed explanation; accepted theory, established schools of thought and regulations for example, you just need to apply them using a reference as an identifier. If this is not possible consider putting the material into a separate side text box, table or diagram that is called up in a main paragraph.

References and Appendices: Case Studies

The following examples of reference and appendix usage highlight some typical problems seen in dissertation submissions.

Extensive Research

Yang indicated in his dissertation Abstract that the findings were supported by extensive research, but he had only 25 references listed for a 10,000 word report. Clearly more sources had been consulted as there were text tags in the main body that had no corresponding entry in the listings. The reference list was divided into three separate sections covering books, journals and websites. There was no differentiation in the text tags. Checking the references during the marking process was a tedious exercise.

Yang was a bit disorganised. He had not kept track of his sources adequately when writing his drafts. At the final edit stage he did not have enough time to find the sources again and had to rely on his limited notes containing basic lists. The actual research and discussion were sound, but one marker failed the work initially. Her view was tainted by the poor quality of the far from extensive referencing. The other marker argued that Yang had nevertheless demonstrated the basic learning objectives, just. They agreed a low pass mark.

See Appendix X

Criminology student, Lorna, tried to characterise criminal activity on a scale ranging from social obligation – gang membership, through employment – the professional law breaker, to one off moments of madness – crimes of passion or negligence. She then used this spectrum as a basis for a survey about social attitudes to punishment.

Overall it was an ambitious but well-structured investigation that considered many aspects of social behaviour. She identified a range of theory and relevant schools of thought in her Literature Review. It was her practice to make detailed notes as a way of consolidating her learning and so it seemed natural to include descriptions of the espoused wisdom as appendices. Her main body text said: "See Appendix X" each time she introduced a new element.

The second marker was from another university where there was no tolerance for using appendices for word count shedding. He argued that the effective length was way over the set limit and that references should have been used instead of detailed appendices. The first marker pointed out that it was normal at Lorna's university to allow significant use of appendices; in fact some tutors encouraged it. Lorna had followed normal practice and so a good passing grade was agreed.

In Love with the Research

A Business Studies group specialising in HR were asked to focus their dissertations on changing work practices. Adam decided to look at the benefits and issues of home working with a review of its history as well investigating current practice through an online survey. His tutor advised that the historical focus should be limited to providing only a background context.

Adam obtained nearly two hundred replies to his online survey. This was more than enough material for his dissertation. He extracted data from the returns under several headings without providing full details of the original questionnaire.

He had already found a lot of information on cottage industries and historical working methods. He found the parallels between the western industrial revolution and the rapid industrialisation in some developing countries fascinating. He was reluctant to let the historical perspectives go after his hard work and felt that it would make an interesting appendix. It was a substantial historical review, equivalent to 18% of the dissertation target word count.

The dissertation failed by a few marks. It was assessed as being too descriptive, journalistic, lacking focus or critical review with no credible evidence of the survey detail. It was penalised for significantly exceeding the word count limit due to the use of an inappropriate appendix.

High Similarity Score

Cindy was concerned about a Turnitin® score of 32% when checking a draft submission. Most matches were less than 1%, but a few were over 5%. She knew she had not copied other people's work. Her supervisor pointed out that the course requirements defined a narrow field with other students following similar projects. A lot of low level matches were to be expected, but the bigger ones were a concern. These were identified as literal quotes. Cindy felt that they made an impact, but agreed their length could be considerably shortened and in some cases replaced with her own paraphrased comments.

It was clear to her supervisor that she had been thorough with the referencing process using a wide range of material. He advised her to make only a few minor changes. In her final submission the Turnitin® score was still high at 25%, but her work was praised for providing extensive evidence in support of her arguments.

Observations

- The number and range of references as well as the use of appropriate appendices impacts the credibility of your report and has a significant influence on markers.

- Low level similarity matches are normal. Higher value ones are a concern.

- Appendices are not the place for out of scope material or the reproduction of established theories, schools of thought or the presentation of formal regulations.

- Institutions may have similar guidelines, but practice can vary. Your supervisor is the best person to advise you on these.

References and Appendices: Good Practice

- **Demonstrate academic skills:** Use references to demonstrate your capability to find, compare and collate sources of information.

- **Professional acknowledgement:** Provide source details for images and permissions to use copyright material and other intellectual property.

- **Conform to set requirements:** Always follow set guidelines for referencing style, number of reference / bibliography lists and the use of appendices.

- **Alignment:** Make sure that there is a one to one correspondence between text tags pointers and the reference listings and that all appendices are clearly indicated in the main body text.

- **Mix and match:** Avoid reliance on one source. Use a range to support the argument.

- **Paraphrase:** Avoid long literal quotes unless they add particular value to your report.

- **Alternatives:** Use a reference instead of an appendix or extensive body text for established ideas such as accepted theory, schools of thought or regulations.

- **Evidence of primary research:** Use appendices to show blank survey and structured interview templates along with completed examples. If practical, present all raw data in an appendix as tables or spreadsheets.

- **Unpublished work:** It is best to paraphrase the work in the main body with a reference tag. The reference listing can then give background detail indicating that the work is unpublished.

- **Clarity and flow:** If you need to provide some detail but are concerned that this interrupts your flow, consider using a side text box, chart or diagram instead of an appendix.

References and Appendices: Common Issues

- **Ignoring requirements:** References must be used. Support all aspects of your work with appropriate source information. Guidelines may specify that certain information be presented as an appendix and not incorporated elsewhere.

- **Unduly derivative:** Multiple use of one source implies a narrow approach and lack of critical thinking. Use a mix of sources rather than repeated reference to just a few. Long passages of direct literal quotes indicate a lack of originality and use up word count.

- **Poor alignment:** There should be no missing text tags or listing entries. Each appendix should have a pointer and some basic information in the main body text about what it contains. Otherwise it may be ignored.

- **Multiple lists:** You should not provide reference lists in different source categories unless specified by your institution. Instead provide a single alphabetical list.

- **Random material:** Appendices should serve a clear purpose. They are not supposed to be a library of interesting but out of scope material.

- **Word count dump:** Just because appendices are not included in the word count does not give you a free hand to dump material in them. If it's relevant it should be in the main body and counted. You may be penalised for the misuse of appendices.

- **Describing accepted wisdom:** Established theory, schools of thought or regulations may be new to you, but do not always need to be explained to others. Use a reference instead. If readers want more information they can look up the source.

- **Lazy illustration:** It can be difficult getting images aligned within the associated area of text, but putting all diagrams in an appendix is lazy. It makes it hard for your reader to follow. Switching back and forth to the images is irritating. Place all images in one appendix only if this is a university requirement.

- **Dissertation by numbers:** If the main text says: "See appendix 1, 2, 3 …." in sequence without any other details then they should all be included in the word count. This approach indicates an inability to create a structured argument that flows convincingly.

References and Appendices: Key Actions

- **Set requirements:** Confirm that you are following your institute's guidelines for referencing style, list requirements and the use of appendices.

- **Finalise the reference lists:** You should have kept a record of all your references and these should now be edited into the final lists. An effective process for managing and editing the master list is described in Chapter 2: Write-up Considerations.

- **Cross check:** Scan your finished write-ups as part of proof reading to match reference tags and appendix pointers to their full entries.

- **Analyse similarity scores:** Critically assess your referencing before the marker does. Take appropriate action to deal with any high level matches. Discuss concerns with your supervisor.

- **Critically review the use of appendices:** Have you shown sufficient evidence of your activities? Are all the appendices needed? Could you use a reference instead or should the material be in the main body?

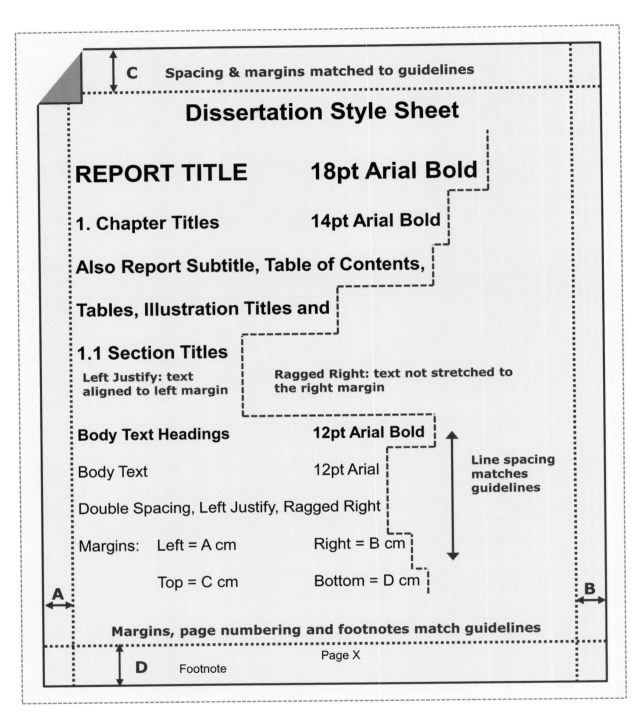

Figure 15.1   Style Sheet for Dissertation Set Requirements

Chapter 15

Report Presentation

Most universities specify dissertation layout requirements to ensure a consistent format that is easy to read and mark. In general the visual appearance is important and in some programmes it is also an assessed element. In these cases additional guidelines for styling and the use of illustrations may be given. Conforming to the set requirements is a basic skills test, but you will still have a lot of latitude in how your report looks. You should avoid a style over substance approach. A well-presented report will have an immediate appeal. Getting the look right inspires confidence and implies that you know what you are doing.

Making a Good Impression

You should consider the impact of your report. Your argument needs to be convincing; not just the written content but also its presentation. How it looks can affect the attitude of your readers. Poor layout and inappropriate use of images can be discouraging or distracting so that what you are trying to say gets lost or distorted in the effort to untangle it from a confusing presentation. Even before a word is read you should try to make a good impression.

A solid mass of text is daunting. It can be broken into more accessible pieces with paragraph breaks and headings that guide the reader. Illustrations, tables and bullet point lists also serve to set the pace and break up the narrative. Your report should look right and be easy to follow. This implies a need for a clear and structured layout. To ensure conformance to requirements and consistency across your report it is a good idea to create style sheets.

Figure 15.1 shows an annotated style sheet for a typical set of format requirements. The font style, size, spacing and margins are reproduced exactly as required. This gives you the written instructions complemented by a visual form that matches the guidelines. Create a second sheet for your own styling decisions. Include information on how you will use bullet points, position and size of illustrations and the format and spelling of key words and phrases. Have print outs of these style guides nearby as you do your writing. They will serve as a reminder of requirements and will keep your own choices consistent across the report. As your work progresses add items to the second sheet as you come across them to serve as a final proof reading checklist.

It is also a good idea to create standard templates for charts and tables. These can be prepared as you get ready for results recording. The principles are discussed in Chapter 11: Presentation of Findings. In addition to thinking about how data will be presented, spend a little time considering the overall visual impact so that your report has a common look and feel. Similar data elements presented in the same way in terms of labels, styles, colours and shading make it a lot easier to compare findings.

Consider the Readers

The appearance of your report can have a big impact on the reader both in terms of attitude to your work and also to their understanding of your material. It is in your own interest to make things easy for your markers to follow. Good work buried in a poor presentation may be overlooked. Markers are not motivated to deconstruct complex presentations. You need to make things clear.

A well-presented report is also a valuable tool after your degree is finished. It can be an impressive demonstration of your capability if shown at interviews for jobs or further studies. It is unlikely that the work will be read in detail, but a quick scan of a professionally presented document can say a lot about you and how you work.

It is also possible that other researchers will be interested in your area of investigation. The Abstract will indicate if the report is relevant to their studies. A review can then identify material of interest, but only if there are clear headings and results presented in easily read charts and tables.

Editing Considerations

It is usual to number chapters and the major sections:

1. Chapter Title
1.1 First Section Heading
1.2 Second Section Heading

and so on, but where do you stop? After a few levels the numbering looks inelegant.

1.2.3.4 Chapter, Section, Subsection, Paragraph

This is taking things too far. Better to stop at two levels and use unnumbered bold or italic subheadings for parts within the sections. Be careful with word processing applications that set levels automatically. They will happily run on to multiple levels without considering the overall look. A style sheet that defines the heading structure can serve as a reminder to keep things consistent.

Editing and rearranging material can be problematic. Saying that there are three main points to consider and then listing four confuses the reader and undermines your credibility. You probably caused the issue by repositioning material in an edit. The difficulties are compounded when wordy labels are used: firstly, secondly … eleventhly, becomes a nightmare to edit as the labels may be across several pages of text. Better to separate the topics into unnumbered paragraphs. If the points are short then consider using a bullet point list. If they are long, use a subheading for each. This reduces the need to renumber each time you move something as you edit your work.

It is normal to use cut and paste as you bring material together and arrange it, but this can lead to abrupt changes in fonts. Computers can have a mind of their own in this respect and so you need to be on your guard. Large sections in different fonts can imply that you have "borrowed" material from other sources and might be considered cheating if they are not correctly referenced. When you move material by cut and paste make sure the typeface and line spacing remains consistent.

Commercial work usually has even left and right finishes to the blocks of text. This left-right or block justification is best avoided even if the dissertation guidelines are not explicit. Most computers will add spaces to get the line lengths even but unlike specialist publishing systems they are not subtle and the result can be difficult to read. The uneven gaps seem like the writer has a stutter. Applied to unusually structured text, such as the way references are listed, can lead to very large gaps making things ugly and confusing. Left justified, ragged right avoids this problem.

Writing Considerations

It is normal for professional reports to be presented in an impersonal detached way. Avoid personal pronouns by using a third person style to achieve this.

Change from: to:

    My research ...   The research ...
    I interviewed ten people.   Ten people were interviewed.
    I found ....   The dissertation found ...

The project is a major undertaking and should be described, but your report should not be a saga. However it has some similarities with a journey or expedition. Your text should indicate that you are looking forward with future plans or are considering what happened by considering the past while much of the material will be described in the present tense. Getting tenses right or at least being consistent adds clarity in separating intentions from actualities.

The word count limit is often a challenge. Your write-up must be succinct, that is brief and to the point. Adopting a professional business style should achieve this. You need to strike a balance between terse and flowing prose so that your meaning is clear. Avoid flowery filler phrases that add no value. Your report will have more impact without them. Over description, especially of presented results, and needless repetition eat up word count. Avoid detailed descriptions. Say why charts and illustrations are there, but then make sure they are clear enough to tell the story for you. Say things only once and put them in the most appropriate section. Planning and then editing your layout will help you achieve this.

Proof Reading

It is important and practical to do your write-up as you go along. At first it is better to capture ideas even if the structure and writing quality is not the best. Editing and proof reading should then follow in stages. As discussed above rearrange material into appropriate sections and eliminate repetition. At the same time you will be able to tidy up your language so that it flows more clearly. It is a good idea to then leave it for a while, at least a few days, before final checks.

Proof reading is more than the correction of errors. It is about the appropriate use of language and the overall flow of your narrative. If you are not a native speaker it is a good idea to get someone to read through your draft to advise on language and styling. Their job is not to help you with content but to point out inconsistencies in the presentation and misuse and confusion in your rhetoric. They should be a native speaker so that they can recognise words, phrases and idioms that are used incorrectly. It is better if your helper is not familiar with your subject so that they concentrate only on the language used. By following their advice you can improve your written style or at least avoid confusing misuse of language.

Read Aloud Test

Spotting typing errors, spelling mistakes and the use of similar but incorrect words is very difficult. Figure 15.2 shows how the brain is remarkably adaptable. Most people can read the distorted text without too much difficulty. Figure 15.3 has the corrected version. It is obvious that there are problems when there are so many mistakes, but the translation still contains at least three errors and these are much harder to see.

Reread the text in Figure 15.3 but this time say it aloud as if presenting to an audience. It is very likely that you will now find the mistakes. Reading aloud slows you down and engages more of your brain. Hearing your own words will create a second version of the text that stops your brain from forcing corrections so that mistakes can now stand out.

The read aloud test also gives you an overall feeling for the content and flow. If it is difficult to read, the structure is not right. If you get breathless then the sentences are too long or lack appropriate punctuation. To be effective you need to speak up, whispering is not enough. You will need to find a suitable place to do this. The university library is not the place. You may need to warn your neighbours in case they think you are going mad, but this method is highly effective for a final polish of your work.

Word Count Check

Once you have completed your rearrangements and corrections it is a good idea to review word count allocation. Check the overall figure against the limit set by your university guidelines. Also look at the split between sections. This is probably your last chance to make adjustments. A well-presented report needs to have a good flow and balance between chapters.

If the count is significantly low you should consider adding more material if you have time. Ideally you should have saved items that were previously considered marginal and these can now be added into the correct sections. If you are over the set limits you will need to make some tough decisions about cutting some things out. Better this than losing a significant percentage of the marks or worse facing disqualification. If you are way over the limit and feel the structure is tight then review your objectives. Can a later one and its associated material: research, discussion and conclusion, all be removed to meet the word limit? If you have written in short paragraphs with a consistent structure across the report you will be able to this quickly. Once done scan the whole report to remove any inconsistencies or disconnects.

Wirtnig a diserstatoin is esay. It is teh rearsech adn ifonrtimaon gtaheirng taht is dififluct. Yuo jsut hvae to ptu pne to ppear or get tinypg on yuor copumter. It nedes smoe onisargation adn pistersence. Hanvig a denefid paln is a good ieda. A cealr sucttrure an d ligocal folw cerate a good iressmpion. The rorpet may not need to be oinrigal btu it shulod be yuor own wrok. Yuo msut rebmemer to awlecknodge the eforfts of ohters by aropppriate reenfercing. Donsemtrate acamedic priplncies by fidning, colalting a nd anysaling inormfation aronud yuor secteled theems. Meka srue yuo sumbit on tmie.

Oh, tehre is aslo the salml isuse of poorf redaing!

Figure 15.2   The Brain is Amazing - Typoglycemia

*Most people can read this text despite the jumbled lettering of each word.
Over the page is a translation.*

Illustrated Reports

In some courses where design or illustration is important there can be a requirement to present reports using a range of techniques and imagery where the presentation creativity is as important as the content. A discussion of these is outside the scope of this book. However requirements for investigative projects in fields as diverse as physical geography and fashion management may indicate that your report should be illustrated. Even if it is not a requirement you may wish to use images to enhance your presentation.

The use of illustrations requires consideration in terms of their value and effectiveness. The project requirements may provide guidelines that specify how the material should be presented. You should take care to follow these directions. At the very least there must be a clear reason for using the images so that they support your written argument. Normally the image should be flagged within the body of the text in a similar way to appendices; indicate the image or figure number with some comment about its content or reason for being there, but avoid over description.

Writing a dissertation is easy. It is the research and information gathering that is difficult. You just have to put pen to paper or get typing on your computer. It needs some organisation and persistence. Having a defined plan is a good idea. A clear structure an d logical flow create a good impression. The report may not need to be original but it should be your own work. You must remember to acknowledge the efforts of otters by appropriate referencing. Demonstrate academic principles by finding, collating a nd analysing information around your selected themes. Make sure you submit on time.

Oh, there is also the small issue of proof reading!

Figure 15.3   Typoglycemia Translation

The text is now clear, but there are still at least three typing errors

Illustration as Story Telling

It is said that a picture paints a thousand words. Optimising word count is one good reason for using an illustration. The detail in an image can present information efficiently, but the benefit is easily lost if it is then over described. Captions and the body text should make it clear why the picture is there, but the picture itself should provide the detail. Illustration can provide a lot of information in ways that are easily absorbed. Various forms of chart, flow and relationship diagrams can serve to scale and contrast your findings. Before and after pictures illustrate changes. A collage of images can replace "etc" or long-winded descriptions when outlining a range of situations.

In some cases your narrative will be trying to set a scene. You may need to present a range of situations that are difficult to describe fully. A picture can tell the story for you. For example: contrasting traffic flows in a city centre and in the countryside might seem easy to portray, but readers' preconceived notions may inhibit their understanding. Imagine a picture of a single car in a deserted business district next to office blocks being held at an unused pedestrian crossing. Compare this to a crossroads traffic jam in a rural village centre. Pictures like this would reset the reader's thoughts as you investigate the benefits of smart traffic control signals in a human geography dissertation. The story told by the pictures can quickly reframe the normally assumed narrative.

Visual Proof Reading

You should try to strike a balance between your text and the number of illustrations used. Too many gratuitous images are distracting if they serve no real purpose other than making your presentation look pretty. To be useful they must be clear and large enough for the detail to be seen. Even then you need to take care that the original image has enough definition. Making a pixelated image larger does not make it clearer. Particular care is needed when cutting and pasting images from online sources. The original may contain text or other features that you do not want or they may scale to an inappropriate size for your report.

Beyond this obvious checking of quality, visual proof reading is needed to ensure the images do what you intend. A good start is to ask your friends to look at the pictures and tell you what they see. Do they interpret things the way that you expect? Even with agreement about the representation a closer look is called for. The brain is very good at ignoring small details and at fitting things to recognised patterns, not always the ones you want.

Once again the read aloud test is effective. In this case the technique is to systematically scan the picture, describing out loud everything you see in it. This will make you look right into the fine detail of the image without assuming a big picture interpretation. Only then will you notice aspects that might not be appropriate. While doing this you can also consider the impact of colours and contrast. Will a person with a visual impairment, such as colour blindness, see what you intended? Do the colours have a cultural significance that you had not considered? Will it photocopy in black and white effectively?

This test is fine for individual illustrations, but you should also strive for a consistent look and feel across your report. You can set this with your own charts and diagrams but may have limited choice with found images. Select carefully, thinking about their style and format, so that your overall presentation is harmonious. This demonstration of aesthetic skills will be more important in some courses than others. The main thing is to be positive in your choice of suitable images.

Acknowledgement and Permissions

You should not assume that you are free to use found images. In general many sources, especially online sites are happy for images to be used for one off academic purposes providing acknowledgement is given. Universities often have copyright arrangements that facilitate this. Get advice from your library staff about what you can and cannot do. Even when you reproduce a diagram yourself it is polite at the very least to acknowledge the original producer. Copying visual material without proper acknowledgement and permission is just as bad as copying text.

It is normal to list image sources separately, either in a table as part of the contents section or in a separate appendix. Often this is a dissertation requirement and the format of this may be specified. In some cases you may need to obtain formal permission to use an image. Details of these permissions should also be listed in an appendix.

Report Presentation: Case Study

Dissertation Styling

Heart Sinking Presentation

This long meandering paragraph of over 300 words is not an untypical submission. Before reading, consider its appearance and general appeal.

1. Introduction to Home Shopping

1.1   Background to Home Shopping

1.1.1   Shopping from Home in Context

1.1.1.1   History of Home Shopping

In the beginning before the world wide web and the internet age people could do some shopping from their homes, staying in and not needing to go out. Recreational buying, www.buyingfromhome.com and Peterson (2012), is not new. www.beforecomputers.co.uk/home_shopping identifies five different ways. Firstly some tradespersons had standard home delivery service, www.howweusedtodoit.com/shopping. Multitudinous types of requirements including milk, bread, soft drinks, coal to name but a few were often brought by van or lorry or even by a boy on a bicycle to the door. Secondly while circulating the shops people could order in the retailer for home delivery. Meat and groceries were specified in the shops and the order made up on the set day to be delivered by a boy on a bike with a large basket. Thirdly was the representative who came door to door on a regular basis taking orders. Typically household cleaning goods, brushes and polish etc., were sold this way. Orders were placed and brought on the next order seeking visit. Avon, the cosmetic company, continues this style of service to this day, (Woman's Weekly 2015). Fifthly is the encyclopaedic home catalogue listing multifarious items containing wide range of products. Indeed, everything for the home a householder might need from furniture to cloths. Furthermore, these were often offered to the costumers with easy weekly term payments, a form of hire purchase. Sixthly there was mail order that was like the home catalogue shopping only different as there was no catalogue but adverts in the papers and magazines. These had order slips that were filled in and sent off so that the goods could be returned to the sender. Fernlow (2013) confirmed all of these five methods and identified modern equivalents either the same or similar but via an online process.

Succinctly Put

The revision below shows how the paragraph could be edited down to less than 170 words with a more effective and appealing layout.

1.0   Introduction: Home Shopping

Home shopping has always been a feature of commerce, (Webref-1), (Webref-2) and (Peterson 2012) identify some traditional ways:

➢ **Home Deliveries:** Traders brought goods as varied as milk and coal to the home, (Webref-3).

➢ **In Store Ordering:** Requests were made for home delivery while shopping. Butchers and grocery stores typically offered this service.

➢ **Door to Door Representatives:** Agents offering household necessities such as cleaning products would call on a regular basis presenting goods and taking orders that were delivered on the next order seeking visit. Avon, the cosmetic company, continues with this style of home service, (Woman's Weekly 2015).

➢ **Home Catalogue:** An encyclopaedia of goods listed everything a householder might need from furniture to clothes. The customer was offered weekly term payments, a form of hire purchase.

➢ **Mail Order:** Coupons placed or printed in magazines and newspapers offering home delivery.

Fernlow (2013) confirmed all of these methods and identified modern equivalents that use traditional and online processes.

Observations

- A significant word count reduction is achieved using a sharper writing style that cuts out over description, redundant headings, verbal numbering and superfluous filler phrases.

- Style and Clarity were improved. The text is changed from first person to a third person professional style. The examples are clearly differentiated by using a bullet point format. Inconsistent and erroneous verbal numbering is avoided.

- The problem with the long web address is solved by using the dummy reference text tags, Webref-1, Webref-2… These can then be placed in the alphabetically ordered listing where the actual full web address can be given.

- The use of left only instead of block justification helps to avoid ugly blank spaces in some lines. Using paragraphs and a bullet list make the end result much easier to read and it has a lot more impact.

- In the revised version it was easier to spot errors. Costumers was corrected to customers, cloths changed to clothes.

Report Presentation: Good Practice

- **Professionalism:** A well-presented report with appropriate illustrations gives a good impression, implying that you know what you are doing.

- **Set requirements:** Any styling and layout considerations should be in addition to and not a replacement for the pre-set dissertation requirements. Take particular care to conform to the guidelines for fonts, page sizing, margins, spacing and page layout as well as overall word count. The ability to follow instructions is one of the skills tested.

- **Style sheets:** Use a style sheet aligned to the set requirements and another one for your own layout decisions. These serve as reminders and proof reading checklists to ensure consistency.

- **Numbering:** Keep it simple using only a few levels. Use numerical notation for chapters and major sections. For subsections and key points use bold or italic headings.

- **Paragraphs:** Break the text into short paragraphs to separate ideas and to improve readability. Long blocks of text are discouraging; individual themes are easily overlooked.

- **Tables, charts and diagrams:** These can provide a lot of information in a word count efficient way and add interest. They also break up the text, improving readability.

- **Visual story telling:** Illustrations can convey some information and ideas more effectively than text providing the images are relevant and clear.

- **Acknowledgements and permissions:** Appropriate recognition should be given for all image sources in addition to text referencing.

- **Read aloud test:** Proof reading is more effective if you read your work aloud as if to an audience. The same applies to illustrations. A detailed verbal description enables you to see into the fine detail of the images. In a silent review your brain fills in the gaps, skips sections, corrects mistakes and creates meaning when there may be multiple problems.

Report Presentation: Common Issues

- **Rambling prose:** The report should be succinct: short and to the point. Flowing prose that reads like a saga is an ineffective use of the limited word count. It is difficult to extract key points from undifferentiated text. Break the text into themes and ideas by using short paragraphs and headed sections.

- **Filler phrases:** Resist the temptation to use meaningless phrases that soften your prose – to name but a few, in this day and age, firstly, lastly … These waste word count. It is acceptable and a positive attribute in most reports to have a business like, even punchy, style. Only use joining words, and, or, but, when their inclusion adds impact.

- **Styling changes:** Abrupt changes in font types and sizing imply cut and paste issues. These can be the result of casual indifference to editing and presentation or may indicate something more serious such as copying the work of others.

- **Block justification:** Trying to line up text to the left and right margins typically involves adding spaces arbitrarily in each line. The computer will do this for you, but the result can look messy and be difficult to read. Unusually formatted text such as the references listing can become significantly distorted. Unless advised otherwise use only left justification.

- **Images in an appendix:** Positioning charts and other illustrations within the text at appropriate points can be tiresome; the computer tends to shift things around, but it is worth the effort. Putting all the images together in an appendix may seem like a solution, but this is then extremely irritating for your reader who will then have to flick back and forth.

- **Gratuitous images:** Peppering your report with images is only worthwhile if they have relevance and meaning that works in tandem with your text.

- **Inappropriate image styling:** Images need to clear and large enough when printed to be effective. Just because there is a wide range of style choices for data charts do not feel that you have to use them all. Ideally they should have a consistent style. Cutting and pasting from online sources can lead to poor resolution and irrelevant text with clipping or large areas of background. Verify that the image you get is what you want.

Report Presentation: Key Actions

- **Reader reaction:** Does your work look right? Is it well presented and easy to read with clear images? Ask friends to scan the work to give a reaction.

- **Proof read:** Systematically proof read your work. Not a casual scan but a detailed review to sharpen your prose, to get material appropriately positioned and to find and fix typing errors. Apply the same attention to all your charts and illustrations. The read aloud test is an effective process for doing this.

- **Conformance:** Once you have finalised all your changes, verify that you have met the set requirements for the text layout and for the use of images. This requires a systematic review of all the material checking fonts, spacing and margins. Confirm that all image sources and permissions are listed.

- **Back-up:** Save historical versions of your work before you edit and correct them. Sometimes you realise that you need to go back to an earlier version and it is easier if you have a hierarchy of dated revisions instead of only one that has been repeatedly overwritten.

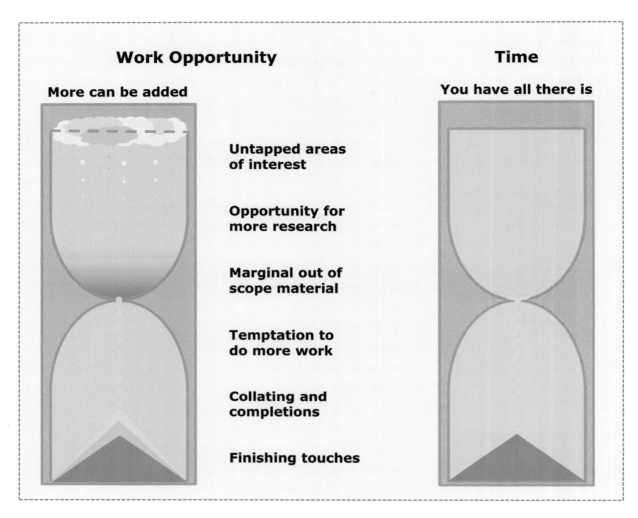

Figure 16.1   The Sands of Time

Work Opportunity: *There is always more that could be done.*

Time: *You have all there is, no more, no less. It will run out.*

Chapter 16

Hand In

It is important to realise that the investigation will never be finished but your investigative report must be. It is a bit like an open ended egg timer, Figure 16.1, where you can pour in more sand. You can always do a bit more reading, carry out a bit more research, look for another reference or add more illustrations. The list is endless. The research and your presentation of it will never be complete or perfect. You can only do your best in the time available. There is a deadline and you must meet it: no ifs or buts, it is not negotiable. The time will run out.

Regardless of how you work, at some point you must finish the write-up and prepare it for hand in. Then you must actually submit it. The hand in process will be precisely defined by your institution. Make sure you know what you have to do before you have to do it.

Submission is not quite the end point. Until your work has been assessed and the marks validated it is possible that you may be called for an interview. In some courses this is normal. You may be expected to attend a viva to present and discuss your project. In a few cases there may be concerns about your report and you might be asked to attend an academic integrity interview.

Assembling Your Report

Smaller files that were more easily managed must now be integrated into one for submission. The last chapter discussed the presentation of your report and the process of checking it. You may have done this for each of the parts, but the process of combining them can introduce issues. Computers seem to be very good at "*helping*" you in ways that are not always expected. Review the final document carefully. Make sure the process of combining files has not upset page numbering and repositioned images. Do you have all the necessary sections in order and listed correctly?

The submission guidelines will typically define the format for a title page or coversheet. Increasingly submissions are marked anonymously. It is important that you check designators and ID numbers carefully removing any direct references to your name if this is a requirement. Including the word count on the title page is very helpful to examiners. Better you measure this with your computer tools rather than the examiner making perhaps an incorrect estimate.

Saving Your Evidence

You are almost ready to hand in, but before you do make a back-up of your final version as securely as you can. Use your own memory device as well as a university system that is separate from the submission process. This might be in your allocated memory area, via a checking system such as Turnitin® or failing this send it to yourself as an attachment to an email. These actions create a reference copy that is complete and date stamped that could be later used to confirm that you had indeed finished. Make sure the file name is explicitly clear. If you need to find the file quickly you do not want the stress of trying to find the right version from several choices.

You should also back-up all your working files. Likewise gather up all your written notes, logs and activity diaries. Do not delete or discard any of this material until after your report has been graded and marks officially notified. You will need this material if there are any questions about the integrity of your work or if you have to present to a viva panel.

Printing and Binding

Typically hand in is by electronic means through a designated university system. In some programmes a written and bound copy is also required. In this case you will be one of many students who all want printing and binding services at the same time. A one or two day turn round can stretch to over a week when demand is high. Do not get caught up in this last minute panic.

Advise the printer/binding service providers that you will be part of a cohort with similar demands so that realistic response times are quoted. Verify their requirements for the master material identifying any special needs that you or they require. For example will diagrams need to be in a particular format? Will you require colour printing? Do they have the necessary originals and permission to create the university logo if this is a requirement? Will the printing and binding be done at the same place? If not think about how you will transport the printouts to the binders without damaging the paper edges. How many copies will you need? It is a good idea to get one for yourself for future use at interviews as evidence of your capability. Doing this preparation well ahead of actual requirements will identify the process to follow and give you a practical deadline.

Submission Requirements

Up to now you will have concentrated on the formatting and presentation of the written report. You must now shift focus to consider how this is to be physically or virtually presented for hand in. The university has to deal with many, possibly hundreds, of submissions at the same time. They have very specific rules about the process so that their systems and staff can cope. Sometimes there are requirements to complete hand in forms, provide separate files for archive and to submit material to plagiarism checking systems. Do not expect special treatment. You must be in step with their requirements to be sure that your work is logged in correctly.

Imagine there are fifty people in a queue in front of you and only half an hour till the deadline. Your work will not make it. Anticipate the last minute rush and allow some contingency. Online hand in can be just as problematic. The university system may be very slow when receiving hundreds of large data files. Make sure you have some time margin and that you are sending from a high quality connection. A café Wi-Fi hotspot may not be so hot when it matters most.

Interviews

Although they were once the norm few universities now conduct interviews where you will be asked about your work. When they are required make sure that you understand the format, the time and place and the general requirements. Make the necessary preparations so that you can give a professional account that reflects well on your hard work.

Viva Reviews

A viva is a panel interview that explores the detail of your work and how it was accomplished. The focus is on your report and what it says. You are not expected to know more than what you have written, but you should be able to explain and justify what you have said. This is not a memory test. Make sure you have a copy of your report and supporting notes organised for quick access.

Instead of trying to remember where everything is, arrange your material; your print outs, notes and diaries, into folders with numbered sections or separately identified files. Create an index sheet based on your report structure that lists topics of interest that relate to the content and activity including in and out of scope material. Answer any questions as best you can but be confident about using this index in front of the panel to find relevant material when asked specific questions.

Be open with your answers. In particular be prepared to justify a particular approach. Acknowledge that there is more that could be done and often better ways to do things. Remember that you had limited resources and did what you could with them. Hindsight gives you perspectives that were not available at the outset. The important thing is that you demonstrate the skills outlined in the learning objectives for your course. Identify key examples from your work that show each of the main points in the grading criteria and learning outcomes documents. Do not assume that everything has been covered satisfactorily in the viva. Before you finish, ask if you have shown them everything they need and be prepared with these examples if they express any reservations.

Academic Integrity Reviews

When there are doubts about the academic integrity of your work you may be called for interview to explain and justify what you have done. If you have cheated you deserve to be caught out and must face the consequences. However through misunderstandings, lack of experience or other factors your work may not be as academically robust as it should be. There can be cases when your work appears very similar to that of someone else.

Prepare for the interview as described for a viva above. Pay particular attention to evidence that shows that the work is your own. Dated material is useful in establishing a timeline of activities. Diaries, notes from supervisor meetings, emails and computer draft file listings have this information. Confirm that you will be able to use your own PC to show details and that access to the university system will be available if you need it.

Make sure you know how the interview will be conducted. The university will have detailed guidelines for the academic integrity interview process and these should be made clear to you. In the heat of this pressured situation you can easily get flustered. If possible have a responsible person with you to act as an independent observer. Their role is to see fair play and to make sure you are given adequate opportunity to address any stated concerns. Unless specifically directed their role is not to be there to give evidence or act as a character witness. If you are not able or not allowed to take a supporter ask your supervisor or tutor for a written statement outlining the formal procedure. This will avoid any misunderstandings, allowing you to respond professionally.

Do not assume that you know what the problems are. Do not rush to apologise. Wait to be questioned and then answer honestly. If it becomes clear that you have made a mistake or fallen short of requirements do not make rambling excuses. If there is a genuine reason then give it. Otherwise indicate that you have tried to meet the set requirements using your notes as evidence. It may be that the issue lies elsewhere and that someone else has copied your work. Help the panel get to the truth of the matter so that you can be treated fairly.

Dealing with Disaster

During the course of your dissertation things will get off track and go wrong. This is normal. Dealing with issues is part of the learning experience. Some disasters are outside your control. Health issues, personal and family problems can interrupt your studies. Speak with your supervisor or a tutor you feel comfortable with as soon as you can about your situation. It may be possible to get an extension or deferral but only if the case is strong. You must provide documentation to support your claims and seek help before rather than after the submission deadline.

Some students realise in the course of the project that things are going badly and do speak to their supervisor, but for some reason do not then follow the suggested course of action. By this stage you must realise that a dissertation requires sustained hard work. There are no prizes for procrastination or wishful thinking. The ownership of your project is with you and you must take responsibility for it or face the consequences.

A much more common situation is where the dissertation has gone off track and you only realise this near the end. You may think that all is lost, but this need not be the case. The dissertation grading criteria typically require you to demonstrate knowledge, understanding and a range of skills. There is no requirement for the project to be a success although this is nice. Good outcomes seem to make this easier, but if you have made some effort, gathered some data and examined your subject you can at least put together a working report.

It is unlikely that you will have time to find more or new data. If you do have time to gather some new material it should be merged into the appropriate sections. On no account should you introduce new material into the Conclusion. This will seem like an afterthought and indicates poor thinking.

Realistically you will have to make the best of what you have. The first thing is to review the Discussion section. Be honest and reflective about your information and the process of obtaining it set against your original intentions. There is no shame in admitting that you were naïve, too ambitious or unrealistic. The project process has shown you this and you can consider the outcomes in this light. Avoid excuses or apologies, but instead adopt a professional tone to review and conclude based on what actually happened. Be honest with your reflections to demonstrate learning and developing skills. You have nothing to lose by this approach and a lot to gain.

Pressed for Time: Key Actions / Final Check List

Even if you are not happy with your report you must hand something in for it to be marked. You need time to complete the submission process. Hence your working deadline should be at least a day before the submission deadline; much longer if printing and binding are needed.

Work through the following checklist concentrating only on the things that you can do and must do. Getting all available material into sequence as a single document and completing the hand in formalities are the bare minimum. It is better to include notes or draft material in the correct sequence than to submit a report with elements missing. The marker will not be happy dealing with unpolished material, but at least your intentions will be understood and marks can be awarded.

- **Format requirements:** Confirm that you have met all the set requirements for the layout of your report. Verify that the word count is within limits. Are all the required sections present and in the correct sequence? Is the Table of Contents accurate?

- **Appendices:** Have you included all of the necessary appendices and lists: references, image sources, acknowledgements, permissions and any other set requirements? If you have other appendices have you justified their inclusion?

- **Back-up:** Save a master copy of your final report and working files. Keep all your draft files, notes and diaries until after marking has been completed and officially advised.

- **Hard copy versions:** Arrange for printing and binding in good time if hard copy submission is required. Get a copy printed for your own use.

- **Hand in arrangements:** Check and confirm the submission requirements allowing time for the process. Chose a reliable connection for electronic submissions. Failure to follow the required hand in procedures is a sure path to failure.

And Finally

Celebrate and reflect on your achievement.

The dissertation submission is a major milestone at the end of a long journey. Regardless of how well it is received you should be proud of your sustained effort. Only you know how hard you worked and whether you were efficient and effective in your approach. Take a little time to reflect on the process and what it has taught you about yourself.

Hopefully your dissertation will receive positive comments and a good mark, but you will not know this for some time after hand in. A detailed review of the outcome can be done then. Meanwhile allow yourself a small celebration. It was a long and at times a lonely journey, but you did it. Well done.

Index

Items in bold refer to chapters that provide detailed cover of the identified topic.